SURPRISED
BY THE POWER
OF DANIEL

THE MIRACLES THAT BROUGHT
A SKEPTIC TO FAITH

C. S. MORRISON

QUALIAFISH

First published as a Special Iona Edition in the United States in 2018
by *CreateSpace Independent Publishing Platform* on behalf of *QualiaFish*, UK

This edition was published in the UK in 2018 by *QualiaFish* Publications

Copyright © Colin S. Morrison 2018

C. S. Morrison has asserted his moral right to be identified as the author of this
work in accordance with the 1988 Copyright Designs and Patents Act (UK).

All rights reserved. No part of this publication may be reproduced, stored in a
retrieval system or transmitted in any form or by any means, electronic, mechanical,
photocopying, recording or otherwise, without the publisher's prior permission.
This book is sold subject to the condition that it shall not, by way of trade or
otherwise, be lent, resold, hired out, or otherwise circulated without the publisher's
prior consent in any form of binding or cover other than that in which it is
published and without a similar condition including this condition being imposed
on the subsequent purchaser.

This book is a work of nonfiction.
Whilst every effort has been made to ensure the accuracy of the information in this
book, neither the author nor the publisher accept liability for any loss arising from
reliance on information that turns out to be inaccurate.
All quotations in this book are fair use as defined by the 1988 Copyright Designs
and Patents Act (UK) as they are all strictly for criticism or review
All Bible quotations are derived from the WEB Bible
(A Public Domain translation).

Cover illustration *Leaving Iona* © Colin S. Morrison 2018 All rights reserved.

Illustration on page 64 – *Daniel's Vision of the Four Beasts* – Engraving by Matthäus
Merian (1630) © Public Domain

Illustration on page 134 – 'First coin issued by the mint of Aelia Capitolina about
130/132 CE', *A Dictionary of Roman Coins, Republican and Imperial* (1889)
http://www.forumancientcoins.com/numiswiki/view.asp?key=Dictionary%20Of
%20Roman%20Coins © Public Domain

ISBN: 978-1-9993393-0-2

In loving memory of

Rev. William (Bill) McDonald

(1933 - 2018)

A brilliant father-in-law and a very dear friend.

FOREWORD

By the Author

Iona has played a large and beautiful part in my life. My mother-in-law and father-in-law met each other on the Island and fell in love there. Before she met me, my wife spent a very happy summer as a student working in Bishop's House, and has returned for short breaks every year afterwards. My daughter sprinted round the fountain in the Abbey on each summer holiday since she was a toddler, growing a little bit taller every year. And my son learned to ride his scooter really fast on his own for the first time on the slope into the village, squealing with excited exhilaration.

We have all enjoyed many a sunny day on the beautiful beach at the north end, and many happy evenings lighting fires on the sands around the Martyr's Bay restaurant. We have cowered through thunderstorms, woken up to corncrakes, clambered to the top of Dùn I, and enjoyed the peacefulness of the Abbey. We can see why St Columba chose this place for his church. It is indeed magical.

But let us remember why St Columba chose to plant his church here in the first place. It was not – or at least not solely – to enjoy the corncrakes and the beautiful beaches. He was on a mission. Iona was the base from which he set out to persuade the Picts that the Christian gospel really was God's message to humanity. I believe that those of us who hold that view today need to be doing something similar.

Of course, convincing others of the divine authorship of the Gospel was perhaps somewhat easier in St Columba's day than it is now. At that time, there were not nearly as many reasons to doubt that claim as there are in the modern era. St Columba lived long before the madness of the crusades, the terrors of the reformation, and the evils of the subsequent sectarian wars that ravaged Europe. He also preceded the development of empirical science, systematic archaeology, and biblical criticism, each of which has cast its own shadow of doubt upon the truth of that Gospel. It is hardly surprising that far fewer nowadays are as willing to embrace that Gospel message as they were in St Columba's day.

But don't despair. Just as God is claimed to have performed miraculous signs for St Columba to persuade the Pictish kings of the divine authenticity of the message he was bringing them, I believe he will do something similar for modern listeners as we also attempt to pass this message on to others. I think I have some very good reasons for that confidence. This book will tell you what they are.

CONTENTS

INTRODUCTION

Prayers Answered

The five-year-old quickly scribbled his name onto the scrap of paper, folded it up and threw it into the red bucket along with the rest of the class. He then trotted back to his seat, and, thinking no-one was looking, ducked beneath his desk and pretended to be getting something out of his schoolbag. Clasping his hands tightly and closing his eyes as he had been taught, he said silently, "Please God, let it be me! I ask this prayer in Jesus name. Amen".

"What are you doing down there Colin?", the stern voice of his teacher took him by surprise. Panic swelled momentarily. His hand rummaged hopefully in his schoolbag as he pulled himself up quickly onto his seat.

"Nothing", he lied.

He breathed a silent sigh of relief as the teacher did not press her interrogation further.

"Has everyone put their name in?", she asked the class. When everyone nodded, she continued, "Who wants to pick out the winner?"

"No looking in the bucket!", she said, as she went over to the girl at the front whose hand had shot up first. Now let's see who it is.

She unfolded the scrap of paper the girl had handed her.

"It's Colin!", she said.

Overjoyed, the five-year-old jumped to his feet and strode out to collect the large tissue-paper rainbow the class had made. As he did so, the thought "It worked!" was bouncing around excitedly in his head. He needed to tell somebody. He looked up at the teacher before going back to his seat, and while the class were busy commiserating amongst themselves, he said to her, "When I was under the table, I was praying!"

He didn't wait for his teacher's reaction. He didn't care. He hurried back to his seat before he had to answer any more embarrassing questions. The thought "It worked!" was still bouncing around inside his little head. He felt like somebody who'd just discovered he had a supernatural power.

It did cross his mind at the time that it could have been just chance. But that only made him more determined to try it out as often as possible. Over the next few years whenever he was put forward for an art or writing competition he worked hard at his entry. But once it had been handed in or sent off to the external judges, he said the same little prayer. He was astonished to find that he almost always won something. Usually not the top prize. But he felt that to win anything at all against such odds so many times was remarkable.

It seemed that his efforts were rewarded far more often than probability suggested they should be.

Nevertheless, there were occasions when he did not feel so lucky. His football career had never kicked off. Nor had he achieved fame as the successful artist and chess grandmaster he had expected to become. By the time he left high school to study astronomy and physics at university he had all but concluded that his luck was largely self-made. He'd worked hard for the prizes he'd won, and everything else was probably just plain old good fortune mixed with his fair share of hard times. Certainly, his premium bond numbers had never come up, and the few lottery tickets he'd purchased had earned him nothing. By then, he had pretty much abandoned his childish faith entirely. He still thought there was probably a God. But he was sure any claims about that God somehow coming to earth and playing a part in human history were misguided. As far as he could see, we humans were just too insignificant a part of the universe for God to care about what we believed. Such claims seemed far more likely to be delusions resulting from attention-seeking individuals or the desire of powerful elites to control the masses. His belief in God was now based upon certain things he felt he had discovered about human nature, though bizarrely his inspiration still came from out of this world.

Intrigued by the invented languages of Tolkien's Middle Earth, he had thought much about how meanings were represented by speech sounds in languages. His resultant forays into semantics and linguistics – his first curious steps into the chaotic jungle of incompatible theories that modern philosophy of mind consists of – had led him to the rather strange conclusion that the human voice was unnecessarily well-designed for representing meanings. If so, such design could not be accounted for as a product of natural selection. It could only be explained as the work of a designer.

His faith thus rested on an argument from design. But it was not a faith in Jesus. He was convinced that a far more sophisticated understanding of God would emerge from science – and from physics in particular. That was why he'd chosen to study the subject. At the beginning of his second year, though, he changed his mind.

He suddenly realised that it was probably arrogance to simply dismiss the claims to a revelation from God that were found in the world's religions. What right had he to expect to be the first to discover God's true nature? If humanity were not too insignificant to be worthy of a God's revelatory efforts, then that God could reveal his nature to whomever he wished. And the possibility that a God might have chosen to do so did not seem quite as improbable as it had before. That is because he had begun to question whether humans were really as insignificant as he had previously assumed. The more he studied, the more he became aware of the astonishing complexity and ingenuity evident in the human organism. There was nothing else in the known universe that had the incredible sophistication of humanity. Nothing else that could converse freely and think about things and create extraordinary art and technology. Nothing else that could conceive of communicating with a creator of the universe. If we really were designed, he concluded, then it is perfectly reasonable to expect that our designer might take an interest in what we do, and even attempt to make contact with us in a non-invasive manner. The world's religions seemed by far the most likely place we might expect to find evidence of such contact, and the one that was easiest for him to investigate was the one he'd been brought up with: Christianity.

It was then that he made a conscious effort to mix with Christian students. He had begun his second year of undergraduate study at the university of St Andrews – an attractive Scottish seaside town fifty miles north of Edinburgh which was famous for being the "Home of Golf" and a mediaeval religious and political centre that once hosted the pre-1707 Scottish Parliament. It was the third-oldest university in the UK and boasted a large and prestigious theology department in its ancient St Mary's College building. Consequently, it attracted a lot of Christians of all denominations seeking a career within the established churches, and the religious societies and institutions of the town and gown were full of them. As a result, he had little difficulty meeting people who professed to be followers of that faith and were prepared to debate its merits.

Despite the annoyingly indefensible views some of them claimed to believe about the Bible, he generally found them a friendly and welcoming community, and he realised that this was very probably because of the goodness and healthiness of Christ's commands and social teachings. He soon found himself professing to be a Christian, though with the disclaimer that he would never accept claims by Christians that the evidence seemed to strongly refute. Unlike many of the Christians he knew, his decision was not based on the Bible or Church history, or even personal experience, all of which he felt to be of very little relevance. He felt attracted to Christianity purely by the goodness of Christ's social teachings. His decision to abide by those teachings was based more on a feeling that if enough people were to unilaterally and seriously adopt those teachings a utopian society would follow – a society lacking both in greed and idleness, where no-one felt left out, and where suffering was minimised – and he did not see such a society in the established churches or the institutions of Biblical times.

On a trip home around this time, he mentioned his newfound religion to his Dad. He was fortunate enough to come from a very loving and supportive family, and his Dad was an elder in the Church of Scotland with a deep and justifiably sceptical interest in the Bible and Christianity. However, he had still encouraged his children to pray. With the best of intentions, his Dad dug out all his Bible commentaries and church history books for his son to read, and placed them on his bedside table. Being not at all interested in the Bible at the time, and feeling quite misunderstood, the thoughtful nineteen-year-old lay quietly beside the pile of books and mulled things over in his head.

He hadn't spoken seriously to God before. The prayers of his childhood had really just been a game. They were a means of ensuring that if divine help were available, he'd done his best to obtain it. They were never an appeal for evidence of God's existence, and he never saw the beneficial circumstances that transpired as any such evidence. But now he asked God silently and with all the seriousness he could muster, "If you really are there, give me a sign that I will have no reason to doubt!"

Nothing happened.

He waited.

Still nothing happened.

Wearily, he sifted through the collection of books. There was only one he could be bothered reading. It was the testimony of a soldier from World War II who'd come to faith in a Japanese prisoner-of-war camp. It was called *The Miracle on the River Kwai* – a title no doubt modelled on the much more famous *Bridge on the River Kwai* which is set in similar circumstances.

He turned to chapter 1 and began to read about the Death House – clearly the lowest point in the writer's wartime experience. The book then took the reader back in time to the author's carefree summer before the war began. This was the start of the author's journey to that Death House and beyond. But it found him yachting round the Firth of Clyde on the west coast of Scotland making the most of the beautiful weather in a carefree state brought on by the uncertainty of the impending war. The carefree feeling was caused by the fact that there was no longer any point in worrying about doing anything relevant to one's career prospects, etcetera, because it was likely not going to make any difference. But it was the Firth of Clyde that grabbed the nineteen-year-old's attention.

This was a welcome surprise to that reluctant reader because it happened to be the very part of the British Isles where he was at that moment situated. His parents lived in the unremarkable small Argyllshire town of Lochgilphead on the shores of Loch Fyne, a sea-loch that opens into the Firth of Clyde. He'd grown up there. He felt a connection to his own life in that chapter. So he read on.

The author – a company commander in the Argyll and Sutherland Highlanders called Ernest Gordon who, many years later, became dean of the chapel at Princeton University in the United States – then described how following the declaration of war he headed over to St Andrews to get some things… This gave the nineteen-year-old another jolt. Prior to the war the author had studied at St Andrews university, which was where he was studying now. And like him, he spent his summers on the west coast of Scotland. He read on, intrigued to find out what would come next.

The author quickly described his march to war in the far east, how he narrowly escaped capture at the fall of Singapore by sailing out to sea, and how he was soon picked up by a Japanese warship and marched to Burma. He then described life as a Japanese POW, building the Burma railway. He told how he and his fellow POWs were so hungry and badly treated that they were reduced to a state worse than animals – stealing from each other and ignoring the plight of those too weak to help themselves in the desperate struggle to stay alive for another day. He related how he himself became so seriously ill with life-threatening conditions that very few thought he would survive, and how he was nursed back to health by two fellow prisoners who were Christians. The Death House turned out to be the morgue of the camp hospital where he lay at death's door prior to his recovery, being regularly cleaned and fed by those two Christian companions, who risked their own health and fitness in an effort to restore his.

It was there that he learned of other sacrificial acts of kindness that had started to take place in the camp all around him. One in particular stood out as the one that had started it all. A highly respected Scotsman had given all his rations to his dear friend who was similarly close to death. The patient got better but his saviour suddenly dropped dead from exhaustion as a result. This was being widely hailed as an instance of the most noble and honourable of acts that anyone had ever seen. As a result, people began to follow his example.

The mood in the camp was so changed by those heroic acts that people started to look out for each other again and share their gifts and abilities. Those who were craftsmen began making things to improve the lives of the injured. Those who were artists, musicians or scholars of any discipline began to freely offer their knowledge and talents. And despite the continuing harshness of their captivity, this desire to share grew. It even blossomed into a camp university, art gallery and orchestra. Recognising the Christianity of the heroes who had begun this movement through their self-sacrificial acts, the prisoners whose lives had been saved by those kindnesses – including Ernest Gordon – set up a 'church without walls' and began to discuss the Bible and Christianity and share testimonies.

This was all incredibly interesting to that idealistic second-year undergraduate because it demonstrated the transforming social power and goodness of Christ's teaching – which was precisely the features that had attracted him to Christianity at that time. But that was not all that piqued his interest. When the tale of the man who had turned everything round by giving his life to save his friend was told, some biographical details of this hero were shared. One in particular immediately leapt out at the reader: 'He came from Lochgilphead at the top of Loch Fyne.' the book said, 'Fine stock in his family.'

Suddenly, the reader felt an overwhelming sense of certainty. Lochgilphead had a population of two or three thousand at most. The probability that this hero would hail from his own home town was almost negligible. And that this detail would be remembered and remarked upon in the text was even more unlikely. To find this in a book he had already decided was uncannily representative of his own life and spiritual state made the hairs rise on the back of his neck. Tears of joy and gratitude suddenly welled up. He knew now that God was real and that he cared about his life. He also knew that God heard his prayers. He thanked and praised God for this answer and promised never again to doubt his presence. However, he did also ask his Dad about the book – just to be sure! His Dad was as surprised as he was to see that reference to Lochgilphead. He had added that book to his son's holiday reading pile merely because he knew it was a Christian story written by a man who later became a Presbyterian minister. It was for these same reasons that he'd bought the book many years before. This link with his home town was not the reason that extraordinary testimony had found its way into his bookcase. Until that time, he never even knew that reference to Lochgilphead was in it.

This book tells the story of that child's spiritual life after this remarkable experience (or coincidence – call it what you may). It is about his scepticism over evangelical claims that the Bible was inspired by God, and his journey to a firm and sure understanding of why and how this can be so. But it also answers the doubts of anyone sceptical about the claim that the Christian gospel is God's intended message to human beings. It presents fully objective evidence of God's endorsement of that gospel that the author believes has not yet been fully presented anywhere else.

As a middle-aged man, that boy became somewhat uncertain about just how much of the coincidences and experiences that had shaped his faith in the past ought to be attributed to God. Hopefully most of them. But they could just have been really weird coincidences. It was the objective evidence of Christ's reality that this book will tell you about that saved him from dismissing it all, as many have done in the past. Having discovered that evidence he could no longer kid himself that Christ might not have been from God. Nor could he ever doubt that God involves himself in the lives of individual human beings. That objective scientific evidence, which this book will reveal, would always be there as an immovable anchor that secures his faith against anything life can throw at him. It is the hope of this author that it will also be of such tremendous future benefit to all who read this book, and especially to those who find the Christian revelation hard to accept for scientific or scholarly reasons.

CHAPTER ONE

Vanishing Metal

"Lazarus is dead," Jesus told his disciples plainly. "He's not just asleep. He's dead. And I'm glad for your sakes that I was not there, so that you may believe. Now, let us go to him in Judea."

"Rabbi," Thomas protested, "last time you went to Judea the Judeans tried to stone you! Are you sure you want to go there again?"

"Aren't there twelve hours of daylight?" Jesus asked as though avoiding Thomas' question.

Thomas groaned inwardly. When Jesus had told him Lazarus was asleep, he'd taken his master literally and had pointed out the obvious: 'If he's asleep he'll wake up.' Still feeling rather foolish, his newly sensitised mind detected the onset of another of his master's notorious parables, and he determined not to say anything at all this time round. His companions clearly felt the same.

"If a man walks in the day," Jesus continued, "he doesn't stumble because he *sees* the light of this world. But if a man walks in the night, he stumbles, because the light is not *within him.*"

"Our friend, Lazarus, has fallen asleep. But I am going so that I may wake him out of sleep."

"Why don't we go too," Thomas muttered unnecessarily as Jesus went off to gather his things, "so that we may die with him!" he added out of earshot.

When Jesus arrived at Bethany in Judea he found that Lazarus had been in the tomb for four days. Women from the village had gathered to console Mary and Martha over the death of their brother, and many people had come out from nearby Jerusalem to join them. When Martha heard that Jesus had arrived she left the house and hurried out to meet him.

"Lord, if you had been here my brother wouldn't have died," she sobbed as she clung to him, "But even now I know that whatever you ask of God, God will give you." She raised her head and gazed imploringly into his kind eyes and immediately felt a peacefulness descend over her.

"Your brother will rise again." Jesus whispered gently. Suddenly she felt a warm ray of hope stirring in her heart. She remembered how Jesus had once made a blind man able to see for the first time.

"I know he will rise again at the resurrection on the last day," Martha persisted, not yet daring to believe what she thought Jesus was promising.

Jesus smiled, "*I* am the resurrection and the life." he assured her, "He who believes in me will still live, even if he dies. Whoever lives and believes in me will never die. Do you believe this?"

"Yes Lord. I believe that you are the Christ, God's Son, He who comes into the world!"

"Then you will see God's glory." Jesus told her. With the hope now burning brightly inside her, she hugged Jesus tightly and then rushed off to fetch her sister.

"Where have you laid him?", Jesus asked Mary and her companions after Mary, weeping profusely, identified his lateness as the reason for her brother's death, just as Martha had shortly before. There was none of her sister's quiet confidence in Mary's words, however. They expressed four days of sheer pain and despair together with no small hint of anger and disappointment, which Jesus knew he was responsible for. Jesus groaned in his spirit, troubled by the suffering he knew he had had to allow in order to secure the faith and consequent salvation of his disciples.

"Come and see!" they beckoned sadly. Tears of pity welled up in Jesus' eyes as he thought of what they'd all gone through over the previous four days – the discomfort Lazarus must have felt as his internal organs shut down, the helplessness suffered by his carers in these last harrowing hours, and the terrible sense of permanent loss they'd all had to endure afterwards. As he let the tears flow he could hear some of them openly voice the thought that had no doubt been the source of Mary and Martha's grief-stricken rebukes: "Couldn't he who had opened the eyes of a blind man have stopped this man from dying?"

The thought of how much faith in him they had lost by this moment troubled Jesus deeply.

"Take away the stone!" he instructed his disciples as they reached the tomb.

"Lord, he has been in there for four days! There will be a terrible smell by now." Martha warned instinctively.

Jesus looked at her quizzically. "Didn't I tell you that if you believed, you would see God's glory?"

After the stone was rolled away and Martha had satisfied herself that the smell was not nearly as bad as she had been expecting, Jesus raised his eyes to heaven and said, "Father, I thank you that you listened to me. I know you always listen to me but I am saying this for the people who are standing here so that they may believe that you sent me!"

Turning to the tomb he shouted, "Lazarus, come out!"

Bound head-to-toe in grave wrappings Lazarus walked out into the open air. Mary, Martha and the erstwhile mourners, together with Thomas and the other eleven disciples, all stared wide-eyed in sheer astonishment. Through his bandages Lazarus stared back at them, his disorientated mind trying desperately to understand where he was. Last thing he remembered he was lying in his bed trying desperately to breathe, and now here he was in a crowd of people outside the village. Then he suddenly realised he was *still* struggling to breathe.

"Untie him," Jesus instructed, "and let him go."

None of them heard the last instruction. As their shock suddenly gave way to joy and curiosity, they all rushed to be the first to remove Lazarus' grave wraps and explain to him that he was now a national celebrity. They would not be letting him go for quite some time. Seeing the look of amazement and admiration in the eyes of his disciples as they occasionally glanced in his direction while fussing over Lazarus, Jesus breathed a sigh of relief. His painful gamble had paid off. Even Thomas would think twice about doubting him now.

What would it take to convince you that the gospel of Jesus really is a message from God? And if you are already convinced of this, what was it that persuaded you? How confident are you that a being who made the whole universe was responsible for the Christian gospel?

I don't know about you, but it took a miracle to convince me.

Before I describe that miracle, I must first tell you how and why I became a Christian. I was a nineteen-year-old student of astronomy and physics. I had come to believe that the astonishing intellectual capabilities of humanity, and the surprisingly life-friendly nature of the universe's laws, made the existence of a God (a universe-wide consciousness that could steer the process of evolution) *more likely than not*. For me, the key to appreciating this was when I stopped and really thought about what my *experiences* might be made of. What is it in my brain that forms my visual experience of what my eyes are looking at? What are the colours that it consists of? What forms the sound of the quiet voice in my head that privately pronounces the words that I read to myself? What is the feeling of touch that I get when my finger touches the keys of my laptop; and why does it feel like it happened on the end of my finger when scientists tell us that all our feelings must be arising from events that take place in our brain?

I had long been aware of the fact that something about our experiences was not explained by science. It wasn't the data they contained. I was quite sure all that data could be accounted for (at least in principle) by identifying its origin in our sensory stimuli and stored memories, and by working out how the brain was using it to guide our actions. But the data we are talking about here is just the way one thing changes in response to changes in another thing. The way the image of this page increases in size as you move it closer to your eyes, for example. Or the way the colours that form that image change abruptly to other colours as your gaze reaches the edge of the page. What's unexplained about our experiences is not those changes – which can be put down to the changing sensory data gathered by the eye – but the *things* that change: the *colours themselves*, and the *sounds* and *feelings*, etc.

We have no idea, for example, what in our brain a colour is. Nor do we know what a sound is, or a smell, or a taste, or a feeling of touch or pain or confusion. And we don't know what it is in our brain that *has* all these experiences – the thing we often refer to as a 'mind'. Our different types of experience (the things we call colours, sounds, feelings, flavours, scents, meanings, etc., which have to be located in our brain in view of the brain-based sensory data they encode) are totally inexplicable in terms of the particles and forces with which science currently explains our brain and everything else. We do not know what they are, what they do, or what conditions (if any) are required for their existence.

This realisation led me to the view that there was nothing in principle that stops simpler instances of these things – experiences that don't contain brain-based information – occurring outside a brain, or indeed anywhere in the universe. If experiences were not made of the particles and forces that make up the brain and its activity, what was to stop them occurring elsewhere? And even if they *were* made of those same particles and forces as everything else, they could easily constitute very *simple* combinations of them – combinations that are perfectly capable of arising by chance outside the confines of a skull.

Of course, outside a brain, experiences could not be organised to specifically represent such things as patterns of incoming light stimulating a retina at the back of an eye, or the presence and concentration of a chemical released by a type of food that's good for a human being to eat. Such arrangements of experience obviously are brought about by the human brain, and it is the ability of the human brain to represent the world with patterns of experience that makes the human mind intelligent. However, it is possible that a human mind only needs such organised experiences to make it intelligent because the things it needs to understand are *outside that mind*, and therefore need to be represented by the organising of its experiences. With a universe-wide mind everything that exists in the universe would be *instantly* represented in its experiences (by definition!). Everything would occur *inside that mind*. It would not be a universe-wide mind if that were not the case. Hence it would not need to have its experiences arranged by a brain in order to know what things are. Provided it continued to experience the past of the universe as well as its present moment, it would *automatically* know the history of everything. It would 'see at a glance' how one thing relates to another. So it *could* be intelligent. It *could* understand and interact with created things in a creative way. But could it care about *us*?

As an astronomy student, I was well aware of the incredible vastness of the visible universe. I had examined photographic plates from large telescopes showing hundreds of distant galaxies packed into tiny regions of the night sky. I knew that in each of these there were billions of stars like our sun, and that there were estimated to be billions of such galaxies. The sheer vastness of the universe did give me some doubts about whether there could possibly be a mind that experiences everything, and if there were, whether such a mind would even notice what was happening in the minuscule part of its experience representing the surface of planet earth. But I realised that those doubts were probably due to the fact that I was trying to imagine the experience of that mind with only my tiny brain-based version to compare it to. As it says in Isaiah 55:8-9, '*My thoughts are not your thoughts, and your ways are not my ways, declares Yahweh. For, as the heavens are higher than the earth, so are my ways higher than your ways and my thoughts than your thoughts*'.

The fact that my mind had a relatively broad and rich experience within it, despite being such a small entity, gave me reasonable grounds to expect that a larger version could quite easily have a broader and richer experience, and may well be able to zoom in at will on local regions. Moreover, the fact that my experiences were so highly organised seemed impossible to account for scientifically unless whatever they were had some effect upon the brain. I was thus pretty confident that minds (whatever they are) must affect matter – even non-biologically-organised minds such as the universe-wide consciousness I had inferred to be possible. So, my early intuitions about the nature of mind gave me no insurmountable problem with the possibility of their being some kind of monotheistic God.

Having researched philosophy of mind for twenty years and written a book on the matter that was described in the *Journal of Consciousness Studies* as 'very refreshing' and 'a scientific agenda that a lot of scientists would do well to emulate', I am still very much of the opinion that this is true. But those early views on the possibility of a God didn't give me grounds to believe the gospel accounts. Even if such a God existed, why would such a being bother trying to communicate with humankind? And how could we possibly know whether any particular religious view was part of such a communication?

The reason I had chosen to go along with Christianity, rather than adopt some other religion, or continue with my previous intellectual opposition to revelatory claims of any kind, was simply an assumption. It was my belief that any real God would be strongly inclined to reveal his or her existence to any intelligent, learned and enquiring species (us – or at least some of us!) that happened to come into being in his or her universe; and it was also my feeling that the social teachings of Jesus were so ethically sound that their attributes were consistent with what I would expect such a being to say.

But remember, a God, by definition, has free will and therefore need *not* do or say what one would expect or hope he or she would do or say. And even if a God *would* choose to fulfil those expectations, how was I to be sure he or she had done so by now? Perhaps humans weren't ready yet, and the followers of Jesus had just jumped the gun, so to speak, in assuming that he was It! Of course, they did claim that Jesus performed powerful acts of healing and weather control (which needless to say could not have been accomplished by humans with the technology available in his day). But how was I to know whether these were honest and accurate memories of real events? His followers could easily have exaggerated these stories, or misinterpreted unusual coincidences as being somehow caused by Christ's presence. I needed evidence to really believe this gospel, and that evidence had to be more than just the frequent little coincidences that had constantly nudged me towards that intellectual adoption of Christianity. Even the strong sense of God's presence that I received from finding the mention of my small home town of Lochgilphead in a powerful wartime testimony immediately after asking God for a sign of his reality did not convince me that this God would or could bring about the incredible feats accredited to him by the gospel writers.

That was where I found myself when I attended an evening celebration at Dundee's Gate Christian Fellowship in 1993. I had never attended such an event before, so I didn't really know what to expect. Afterwards, I sort of assumed that what I witnessed that evening was typical in the Charismatic/Pentecostal movement. After a quarter of a century of involvement in that type of Christian worship, I can assure you that it is not. I have heard many second-hand reports of such a thing but never witnessed anything like it since. And a couple of years later, at a meeting of the Bute Medical Society of St Andrews University, I even heard the pastor who had led the worship that evening refer to this particular event as something truly extraordinary. What he said about it left me with the impression that this was his only example of a medical miracle he had witnessed first-hand and found absolutely convincing. Twenty-five years later I can honestly say the same.

The evening celebration had begun with some lively worship. A keyboard, electric guitar and drums struck up a familiar melody. Words flashed onto a screen where the old pulpit used to be, and, after an extended build-up that caught more than a few eager worshippers off-guard, a singer's amplified voice finally joined the swell, only to be drowned out by the response from the packed pews of the beautiful nineteenth-century gothic-style church building – the former St Mark's perched high up on Perth Road where branching cobbled alleyways wind steeply down towards the railway and the silvery Tay beyond. Dundee's attractive and very student-friendly West End was soon reverberating to such lively new numbers as *The River of God*, *Praise God from whom all Blessings Flow* and *There is Power in the Name of Jesus*.

I had by then become accustomed to this type of worship. As a regular at the Gate's daughter church, the Eden Fellowship in St Andrews, for the previous few months, I was quite used to the rock-band-and-worship-leader combo. But the band at the Gate that evening happened to be especially good, and the worship was extremely uplifting. It was very much what the so-called 'Evening Celebration' was all about – an event that the Gate only held occasionally during the year. This was what myself and the group of Christian students and Fifers who had crossed the Tay that evening had come here to experience.

All of a sudden, though, the music quieted down to the level typically used in Charismatic services to provide what I have often felt to be a rather unnecessary emotional background to a prayer or reading. An oldish man with a mop of grey hair, a goatee beard, and a youthful demeanour that belied his years, had stepped up onto the green carpeted platform at the front of the church guiding a younger man, an arm wrapped firmly about his shoulders.

Both had an ecstatic look upon their faces. The younger seemed quite disorientated. The older man whom I later learned was the then pastor of the Gate, Stewart Brunton, took the microphone from the speaker's stand and, in a voice quivering with barely contained excitement hurriedly welcomed everyone and thanked the band. Respectfully, the musicians ceased their playing, and the pastor went on to announce that his friend here had something important to tell us.

The old pastor's face was beaming, and the packed congregation hushed immediately to hear what his companion had to say. In a question-answer type interview the man explained how several years ago he'd had a metal plate affixed to his spine due to serious injuries sustained in a road accident. That evening he'd been experiencing extreme stiffness in his neck as a result of this condition, and the pastor had offered to pray for some relief from that excruciating stiffness. During the prayer he'd felt the stiffness subsiding. As the worship was ongoing at the time, the pastor had insisted on praying for more, and all of a sudden the man had started to feel a lightness all over. He'd found for the first time since his accident that he was able to bend down and move around freely. He began to demonstrate by skipping and jumping about on the platform. The congregation roared praise to God and erupted into spontaneous applause as the pastor tried to get the man to stop overdoing it, saying he was somewhat concerned about what had happened to the metal plate and thought he should probably get it checked out by a doctor first.

The band burst into song again, and my mind began to seriously doubt what I'd just been told. I had of course heard of charlatans and people who had faked miracles before. I was also well aware of the placebo effect and the ability of emotion to switch off pain and allow people previously disabled by pain to move for a short time in ways they once could not. I had also never attended this church before and did not know this pastor. I later found out that he had an unblemished reputation as a very honest, thoughtful and decent person – a pastor whom some have said to be one of the most genuine, honest and caring people they have ever known. For all I knew at that time, though, he or this man may merely have been eager for a bit of attention, and either made the whole thing up or were making a great deal of some very small improvement that could have happened naturally.

That was what I was thinking when the pastor grabbed the mic again and asked the happy man's two young children who had just arrived at the church door to come up front. They ran forward, and the happy man scooped them up in his arms and hugged them while the congregation again erupted with applause and delight. He then approached the mic himself, his youngest still in his arms, and explained that since his accident he had never been able to lift his kids up. The kids were crying in amazement and joy. Tears were trickling down their cheeks. If this was acting, it was extremely good – Perfect in fact. The kids subsequently spoke of their experience of their Dad's condition, and what they now thought about it. Real tears of joy and surprise were clearly visible on their faces, and it was this that definitely convinced me something utterly astonishing really had taken place that night.

Unfortunately, I do not remember the happy man's name and did not follow up on the story. At the time I was so convinced I saw no need of further evidence. I know nothing of what his doctor discovered when he later examined his spine. What I do know is that this man was well-known to the pastor of the church, and two years later, at a talk organised by the Bute Medical Society in

St Andrews, that same pastor was still convinced he had witnessed a genuine medical miracle that day. Had the doctors found out otherwise, I suspect he would have known by then. And as I said before, I now have every reason to believe this pastor was a genuine, upright and very honest man who would not have hung onto a belief that later evidence refuted.

On the other hand, as one grows older one grows more wary of one's youthful assumptions. There are, I don't doubt, other ways of explaining what I witnessed that night. Perhaps the plate had rusted away inside the man's body. Perhaps the pastor's prayer did just create links in his brain that stopped the pain via a purely natural process, allowing his muscles to move freely. Perhaps I was wrong to attribute his apparent healing to the Holy Spirit of Christ.

Over the two decades that followed I have come to strongly distrust the mainstream interpretations thrust upon us by our news media of the strange fatality-rich and virtually footage-free random attacks that are becoming more and more frequent all over the modern world (usually involving supposedly religious people behaving in a way that runs quite contrary to our human nature). I once accepted those interpretations without question. I trusted the institutions from which they came. But that was largely because almost everyone else trusted them. It was only when I began to look into alternative explanations for those events, and examine the objections that have been raised to the popular accounts, that my confidence in the reports I once trusted began to rapidly disintegrate. But that is another story – one that will be familiar to those inquisitive enough to look into what people have said about such events, but not one the rest of us will want to touch. Suffice to say, though, that for the many like me who nowadays, rightly or wrongly, have little trust in what we hear or see, even an apparent miracle of the sort I remember witnessing that night at the Gate Christian Fellowship in Dundee will no longer be enough to convince us of the power and reality of the God that Christ spoke about. Even the tears and testimony of young children will no longer be sufficient. We need *objective proof* of that reality. We need a miracle that we have no plausible alternative explanation for, other than the direct involvement of the God of Jesus Christ. It was therefore with great astonishment that a decade or so later I discovered that such a miracle really does exist.

It is found in a very specific part of the Bible, and it is there for all to see – all, that is, of the inquisitive sort who are willing to question what we hear and see, and examine the alternative explanations. Those are the very people I believe God is catering for by providing this astonishing piece of objective evidence of his existence and his deliberate authorship of the Gospel message. That is because to see it a person must be willing to look for the most plausible explanation for the content of that part of the Bible. One needs to examine all the proposed explanations and decide which is most likely, and not be frightened away when that explanation appears to conflict with traditional views.

In the five chapters that follow, I am going to show you that evidence, the context in which it is found, and the key to understanding its significance. I shall not at this stage demonstrate why it is objective proof of the Gospel's authenticity. I shall leave that until chapter 7. My reason for this is mainly the fact that at this early stage I wish to avoid straying into territory where the uninquisitive among us do not want nor need to tread. However, knowing why it is objective proof of the Gospel's authenticity is not necessary to give you a glimpse of the truly extraordinary nature of this evidence. Once you have witnessed that, you may well be filled with a desire to know what more this part of the Bible has to offer. If so; if you want to discover its full significance, and you don't mind treading the difficult territory I mentioned earlier, you can read on through chapters 7, 8, 9 and 10 where the true significance of this part of the Bible will be made wonderfully explicit, providing objective evidence of Christ's involvement in history that even the most sceptical of minds will never find any good reason to dismiss. Alternatively, you can put this book away after reading its sixth chapter with your confidence in the divine inspiration of scripture renewed, leaving the difficult climb ahead for the adventurous and those who feel they need a more solid foundation for their faith.

If you do not mind your preconceptions being tested and perhaps abandoned in favour of a far more defensible perspective on scripture, one that is equally honouring of God and Christ, and which appears to give this passage of scripture a unique purpose perfectly in line with the loving reality, minimal unsolicited interference, and bounteous provision typical of the God that Jesus Christ made known to us, then you will probably find chapters 7-10 a blessing of a sort you will rarely encounter in evangelical works. In my view, the fear of questioning established tradition in the search for a more defensible understanding of a particular passage of scripture has largely prevented seekers from receiving the gift that these chapters describe – a gift that could provide an amazingly secure foundation for their faith, and one of the most powerful tools for evangelism that the Bible offers.

CHAPTER TWO

A Magic Mountain

It was my experience at the Gate Christian Fellowship in 1993 that persuaded me to read the Bible. Convinced that the Christian God really did move in such powerful ways, I wanted to know more about him. I had previously dismissed the Bible – or at least the Old Testament – as largely irrelevant to this day and age. It seemed a mix of myths and legends, histories with a decidedly Semitic bias, a legal system suited to a nomadic or semi-nomadic nation, and the songs and rants and famous sayings of that nation's long-dead celebrities. What possible relevance could these things have to the modern world?

The New Testament taught about Christ, and so retained some relevance in my estimation. However, I had been brought up attending a Church of Scotland, and up until that time I had felt that this regular exposure to the Gospel message had taught me enough of the New Testament to get by. The discovery that God really did occasionally act in dramatic and exciting ways changed all that. It made me want to examine the accounts of those who claimed to have witnessed such things in the past, or at least to become familiar with the text that so many people regarded as God's word.

I read the whole Bible from beginning to end three times. The first time I read it as you would a book. The second time I sought out and highlighted passages that I found particularly meaningful. But the third time I went through it highlighting all the passages that appeared to be prophecies of Christ. I had heard that there were many, and I wanted to find out whether that was in fact true. At first, I was disappointed. By the time I finished reading Ezekiel, the fourth of the so-called 'major prophets', I had indeed come across several prophecies one might consider to be predictions that Christ had fulfilled. However, none of these seemed detailed enough to specify the time of the predicted events or the specific historical context in which they were to arise. Hence although they could easily be applied to Christianity, one could never know for certain whether they had really been intended as predictions of Christ, or whether they had originally been intended to predict or even celebrate someone who did similar things many years before.

There were, of course, many more-specific predictions in the Old Testament. The fulfilment of these might once have been powerful evidence of the reality of the Jewish God. However, I had no way to tell. For all I knew they could simply have been written *after* the events they predicted as a sort of explanation or justification for those events, or as propaganda to convince the Jewish faithful that their God had not deserted them but was merely disciplining his beloved nation. Hence, I read through the Pentateuch, the books of Joshua, Judges, Ruth and Samuel, Kings and Chronicles, Ezra,

Nehemiah, Esther and Job, the Psalms and Proverbs, Ecclesiastes, Song of songs, Isaiah, Jeremiah, Lamentations and Ezekiel, and I delighted in these wonderfully meaningful passages, passages that Christ himself apparently said 'spoke of him', but all the while I was acutely aware that they were relatively useless as a means of persuading a nonbeliever of the reality of God and the relevance of the Christian gospel. Then I reached the second chapter of the book of Daniel.

There at last, in verses 31 to 45, I found a prophecy that was different. Like the others, it seemed to be about Christianity. But this time the rise of the religion it predicted was set in a specific historical context. It was predicted to come about during

a second phase of the fourth distinct world-dominant empire in a sequence beginning with the empire of Chaldean-ruled Babylon whose greatest king Nebuchadnezzar was the one who received the prophecy.

This seemed to make it possible to check whether the prophecy really had been specifically fulfilled by Christianity, a religion I knew very well to have arisen during the world-dominance of the *Roman* Empire.

A quick glance at the footnotes of the NIV Bible I had received from an evangelist a year or so before filled me with delight and excitement. It simply said that the second empire in the dream was *Persia*, the third was *Greece*, and the fourth *Rome*. Since I was pretty sure the book of Daniel, being in the Old Testament, was written long before the rise of Christianity, which followed Rome's great transition from Republic to Empire, I was confident that here was a genuine prediction of Christianity that *had indeed come true*.

Eagerly I immersed myself in the rest of the book of Daniel to see what else it had to offer. I was not disappointed. Its seventh chapter (Daniel 7) revealed what appeared to be a more specific version of that earlier prophecy of Christianity. In this one the fourth empire was predicted to have at least *eleven kings*; and there even seemed to be an image of Christ himself! Then, in the very next chapter (Daniel 8), I encountered an instantly recognisable portrayal of Alexander the Great and his conquest of the Persian Empire. I had read about that event in a children's book long before, and I can still recall the frighteningly impenetrable wall of Macedonian spears piercing through the lightly-clad Persian infantry by which the modern illustrator depicted that event. Its depiction in Daniel 8, which we will look at in chapter 9 of this book, is no less dramatic.

Since the book of Daniel placed this vision of Alexander the Great during the reign of another Chaldean king of *Babylon* (the very first empire in the sequence of four empires I'd found in Daniel 2 and Daniel 7), the fact that the two empires it portrayed were Persia and Greece seemed perfect confirmation that my NIV was right! The second and third empires in that sequence *must indeed* be Persia and Greece. And since the Greek kingdoms that the Romans conquered (the Kingdom of Macedon and the Seleucid Empire) are very clearly portrayed in Daniel 8 as *parts* of the Greek Empire of Alexander the Great – they are represented by horns on the head of a beast called 'Greece' in that vision – it seemed obvious that Rome was indeed the fourth.

This intrigued me so much that I made a mental note to check out what other people had said about the more-detailed version of Daniel 2's prediction that I'd found in Daniel 7. Nowadays one can do this at the click of a mouse, or the tap of a smartphone screen. The worldwide web and the broadband internet are such wonderful tools for the inquisitive (We should all be lobbying out politicians to keep them completely free and uncensored!). However, in the early nineties the worldwide web was only just getting started, the wonder of Wikipedia did not exist, and no home had broadband. I would have to look for a suitable book, and I had little opportunity during term time to go browsing the university library.

When the holidays arrived, though, and I found myself back at my parents' house with some time to spare, I pulled a copy of *Peake's Commentary on the Bible* out of my Dad's bookcase. As the head teacher of the local primary school, my Dad had been involved in the religious education of young people for much of his career. He had also run a Bible class in his local parish church, and Peake's Commentary on the Bible had been one of the books he consulted. This was due mainly to the fact that it was highly acclaimed by mainstream academics. Due to that same fact, what I read in its chapter on the book of Daniel put me off that section of the Bible for the best part of a decade.

I didn't read very much of it. The author of the chapter on Daniel was a distinguished university professor called James Barr; and it was clear from his comments on the prophecy I was interested in that he thought the second empire wasn't Persia at all. He said it was in fact intended to be a nation called *Media* and that the *third* empire is Persia, and the fourth Greece. This would of course mean that the religion the passage portrayed was predicted to arise during a second phase of the *Greek* Empire. If Barr's assessment was correct, that religion wasn't predicted for Roman times at all, and therefore wasn't fulfilled by Christianity.

Even at that time I did have my doubts about this assessment. The third empire in Daniel 7 was represented by a *four-headed, four-winged leopard,* and it was clear from Daniel 8 that the Greek empire had *split into four independent kingdoms,* each ruled by a separate head of state. Nothing like that had happened to Persia (the empire that Barr identified as the third in the sequence). Barr's suggestion that the heads might just represent four famous Persian kings, and the wings perhaps the four corners of the earth into which the Persian empire extended, seemed by comparison weak and *ad hoc.* Barr also seemed to be unable to come up with any interpretation of the features of the animal (a lopsided bear) representing the *second* empire in the sequence – saying merely that they were 'obscure' and that their meaning was now lost to us.

However, he was adamant that it stood for Media. Not being familiar with the relevant history, and having no quick way to check it out, I assumed there must be reasonable grounds for this assertion. I was somewhat puzzled that the writer of the footnotes in my NIV Bible had reached an entirely different conclusion, but I realised that this writer may have been trying to make the prophecy predict the rise of Christianity. It never once crossed my mind at the time that James Barr may have been trying to make the prophecy *not* predict the rise of Christianity! In any case, it seemed to me that there must be ambiguity in the way the prophecy could be interpreted, and in view of this I thought it not worth spending any more time on.

Instead, I devoted myself to my studies in physics and my growing philosophical interests. I was fascinated at the time with the nature of meanings. What were meanings in our brain? And how did they combine to give us the wonderful understanding of our circumstances that we manipulate so effortlessly with language? This soon led me to the mind-body problem. It was not just meanings that were mysterious. Our whole experience of the world was completely inexplicable in terms of the models scientists were using to understand their particular fields of expertise. Everything other than our experiences seemed to be entirely composed of the properties and interactions of a handful of tiny particles that modern physics described extremely well. Moreover, the ways in which everything behaved seemed to be governed by laws that suggested it was entirely the result of the *interactions* of those constituent particles. Only our experiences seemed different. But I soon realised that these did not merely consist of thoughts and meanings.

Familiar concrete entities like colours, sounds, pains, feelings of hardness, softness and all kinds of texture, were all equally unexplained. They did not arise from contact between a sense organ and the stimulus it was designed to detect, as I had sort-of unthinkingly assumed. They were all generated sometime *after* that event somewhere deep within our *brain*. Yet the fact that they are so highly organised into patterns that perfectly represent those sensory stimuli means that whatever these things ultimately constitute, they must be able to be carefully manipulated by the brain. And for the brain to have evolved to manipulate them so appropriately and effortlessly, they would also have to *do* something that the brain is now using to control some part of our behaviour. They would have to have some effect upon other brain processes, an effect that physicists would expect to be the result of the interactions of tiny particles. In other words, the existence of our different types of experience really ought to be explicable in terms of the known laws of physics – which is why I found this mysterious phenomenon so fascinating.

My thoughts were thus diverted for many years to the problem of explaining this mysterious yet law-like consciousness. This was not entirely unconnected with my faith. For reasons I hinted at in chapter 1 of this book, I was convinced that a proper scientific understanding of consciousness may well entail the existence of a God – much as Einstein's theory of gravity entailed the existence of black holes. And I remain confident of this today. It was while writing about the theological implications of a science-respecting theory of consciousness in the mid-noughties that I got thinking about the book of Daniel again.

I realised that philosophical inferences of the sort I was considering could only lead one to faith in a general theistic God. They could not give one grounds to believe any *particular revelation* about such a being. Only a fulfilled prophecy could really do this. And it could only do this if it predicted the revelation in question, and if its accuracy could not be accounted for by any means other than the direct involvement of a powerful nonhuman intelligence.

I remembered that the book of Daniel was the only book I knew about that appeared to contain such a prophecy. Perhaps I had dismissed it prematurely ten years before. This time, I had the benefit of the internet to check things out, and what I found there immediately renewed my interest in this book.

Firstly, I discovered that pre-Christian copies of the book of Daniel were found among the *Dead Sea Scrolls!* The Dead Sea Scrolls are our oldest surviving texts of the Hebrew scriptures (and other writings). They were hidden away in caves at Qumran near the shores of Israel's Dead Sea *around 68 AD*, never to be retrieved by their owners (who were almost certainly slaughtered by invading Romans as you will find out in chapter 3). However, most of the fragments of the book of Daniel they contain are much older than this. Some of them have even been dated to the second century BC – more than a hundred years before Christianity – and scholars are fairly sure that even these came from complete copies of the book of Daniel as we have it today.

Secondly, I found out that the interpretation of Daniel's "Four Kingdoms" prophecy proposed by the writer of the chapter on Daniel in Peake's Commentary (James Barr) *totally disagreed with accepted history*. I learned that accepted history offered far greater support for the view that the prophecy was a prediction about the *Roman Empire* as I had first thought (rather than the Greek or Seleucid Empire in the second century BC as Barr was claiming). The main reason for this is that it provides zero grounds for Barr's view that the second empire in the sequence – the one to follow Babylon – is Media. Every ancient historian knew that Babylon had fallen to the *Persian* Empire of Cyrus the Great who had already ruled over the Medes and Persians for ten years prior to that time. As you will see shortly, this Medo-Persian Empire is precisely how the book of Daniel *portrays* the empire that conquered Babylon. And if Medo-Persia is the *second* distinct empire in the sequence, Greece has to be the *third* (the four-headed, four-winged leopard), and Rome is definitely the fourth.

But that was nowhere near the most serious weakness that my newly acquired knowledge of established history exposed in Barr's hypothesis. As well as not supporting Barr's claim that the second empire was Media, established history also confirmed the view I had picked up from Daniel 8 and Daniel 11 that the *Greek Empire* had split into *four kingdoms* ruled by *four distinct dynasties*. This means that any reader in the second century BC was bound to identify the *four-headed four-winged leopard* in Daniel 7 as that empire – Greece – and not Persia as Barr was proposing.

This realisation suddenly made the mainstream position seem highly illogical. Why would a writer who supposedly needed his readers to recognise the third empire as Persia portray it in such a way that every single one of them was bound to identify it as Greece? And it was not just the four heads and four wings of that leopard that would have led them to this view.

I also discovered that the leopard itself was a common symbol of the Greek god Dionysus throughout the period of Greek dominance (what scholars call the *Hellenistic* Period). This further supported the view that the third empire – the leopard – was indeed Greece as I had first thought. Looking at the symbolism of the *second* empire in the prophecy (a bear raised up on one side with three ribs in its mouth between its teeth), it suddenly occurred to me that one aspect of that symbolism (the fact that the bear had *one side higher than the other*) was directly analogous to the main symbolism used in Daniel 8 to represent *Persia*, the empire I'd assumed the bear to be, which in Daniel 8 is a ram with *one horn higher than the other*. Moreover, far from being obscure, the rest of that bear's symbolism could be very easily explained under the assumption that it was Persia, whereas it could *not* be accounted for under Barr's view that it was Media, as Barr readily admits.

Since it requires some knowledge of the relevant history to establish this, I shall leave this task until chapter 10. It is worth remembering, though, that under the historically accurate view that the second empire in the sequence is Persia, *all* the symbolic features of the animal representing it can be convincingly explained. Whereas with his unhistorical assumption that the bear is an erroneous portrayal of Media (the empire of the Medes), James Barr was unable to come up with *any* convincing explanation for its raised side and the three ribs between its teeth.

This made me wonder if there was any justification at all for proposing his theory. He seemed to be going out of his way to make the prophecy predict the events he wanted it to predict. But if Jewish readers at the time he believed the book of Daniel was written (the mid-160s BC) would never have interpreted the prophecy his way, surely its writer could not have *intended* it to be interpreted in that way. The slight possibility that this writer didn't *realise* that they might interpret it as a prediction of their future seemed to me to be ruled out by the rest of the book of Daniel.

As you will see throughout this book, the content of the book of Daniel strongly supports that obvious and straightforward historically-accurate interpretation of this prophecy, and it shows that the book's writer was no ignoramus. Barr even accepted that the writer of the book of Daniel had good reason to include a genuine prediction of the future in his book. He uses this to account for the content of a later prophecy the book contains (Daniel 11:40-45). Consequently, it seemed to me he was unjustifiably excluding this possibility in the case of Daniel 7.

I thus realised that on this particular prophecy (Daniel 7) the position of James Barr and other mainstream scholars was not just weak. It simply *could not be defended*. There were absolutely no grounds to believe it. Jewish readers in the 160s BC were bound to see this prophecy as a prediction of their future, so if it was included in the book of Daniel at that time as Barr made out, that simply *must* have been its purpose.

Having the freedom to easily compare this prediction with established history that the internet enabled, I was soon convinced that not only was this prophecy a *prediction* at the time it was included in the book of Daniel (the second century BC according to Barr), but that it had also turned out to be one hundred percent accurate. Amazingly, the events that fulfilled it – including an extremely specific part of it that we will examine in chapter 3 – took place in the correct historical context more than two centuries *after* the date that critical scholars like Barr say it was included in the book of Daniel. As you will see in the rest of this chapter, one of those events was definitely the rise of Christianity.

Before I can explain why this is definitely the case, I will need to give you a very brief introduction to the book of Daniel and an even briefer account of the history of the world between the time of its hero Daniel and the rise of Christianity. As I mentioned earlier, I think the book of Daniel provides strong objective reasons to believe that the rise of Christianity was indeed the work of the Christian God. But these reasons are concerned with the fulfilment of prophecies, and in order to be able to decide whether or not a prophecy has come true, you need to be familiar with the times and nations that it appears to be referring to. We have so far been discussing the four empires predicted by Daniel 2 and Daniel 7. Although we will touch upon Daniel 7 again in this chapter, the really surprising details of that passage will each require a full chapter to make its significance clear, and will therefore be postponed until chapters 3 and 4. But don't worry. The rest of this chapter will focus on the prophecy that is found in Daniel 2, which is every bit as fascinating as Daniel 7, and perhaps even more significant. So let us now open our history books.

Firstly, who was this Daniel that the book of Daniel is about? If, like me, you attended a Sunday school or Christian youth group as a child, you will probably have heard the story of *Daniel in the Lion's Den*. It is found in the sixth chapter of that book, and it tells a tale of uncompromising faith and divine salvation against the odds in which a Jewish prophet Daniel refuses to follow a royal decree that requires him to disobey his God. As a result, he ends up spending a night in a den of hungry lions. His God duly saves him from the lions, which so impresses the king that he gets put in charge of the whole province, and all his enemies – together with their wives and children – are cast to their deaths in the lions' den.

It is set around 538 BC in the ancient city of Babylon (located fifty miles south of modern Baghdad). By this time the hero it talks about is an old man in a position of immense power in a vast, newly-conquered region of the largest empire the world had ever known – the *Persian (Achaemenid)* Empire founded over the previous ten years by a king called Cyrus the Great. Cyrus was a Persian who had risen to rule the Median and Persian tribes of Iran (already united at the time) in place of his unpopular Median grandfather Astyages. As a result, his empire is often referred to as the *Medo*-Persian Empire. Some months previously the armies of Cyrus (the Medes and Persians) had defeated the native Babylonian people – the Chaldeans – and installed their own government in the city of Babylon, and Daniel quickly became one of its highest ministers.

But Daniel, surprisingly enough, is a Jew – and a devout Jew of uncompromising faith. The presence of Jews in Babylon (Iraq) at that time is not surprising at all. They were deported there in large numbers by a Chaldean King of Babylon called Nebuchadnezzar half a century previously, after that king destroyed the city of Jerusalem and demolished the first Jewish Temple (the famous Temple of Solomon). That was in 587 BC, and the deportation of Jews to Babylon may even have begun as much as two decades prior to Jerusalem's destruction (as a date given in Daniel 2 suggests) when the Babylonians defeated the Egyptian Pharaoh and exerted their imperial authority over Judea and all the surrounding nation-states. It was a deliberate ploy to extinguish the nationalism of that people as a punishment for their rebellion against Babylon or their traditional allegiance to Egypt, and they were never meant to return. The surprising thing is that one of their number should attain a position of power within the empire (Chaldean Babylon) that had conquered them. And yet, if the book of Daniel is to be believed, that did indeed come to pass.

Of course, by 538 BC that Babylonian empire was itself history. Daniel was a governor in high position in the regime set up by *Cyrus of Persia*, Babylon's conqueror. Persia now ruled the world. But Daniel had risen to fame and power long before this according to the book. Its second chapter relates how this had happened.

Around 603 BC, the Chaldean-Babylonian King Nebuchadnezzar (the builder of Babylon's famous 'Hanging Gardens' – one of the so-called 'seven wonders of the ancient world') had suffered a nightmare that was so vivid he believed it to be a message from the gods he worshipped. He called in all his wise men to interpret the dream. But, fearing they would just tell him what they thought would make him happy, he insisted that they tell him what the dream *was* as well! As they all complained that this was impossible and unreasonable, he ordered that they be executed unless they could find someone who was up to the task.

At that time Daniel was one of several youths from noble Jewish families selected to serve at the Babylonian court. He was being trained there in Babylonian customs (no doubt to spread them amongst his people), and he was proving a very promising student. Tired of excuses, the king orders that all the wise men including Daniel be killed. Daniel, however, begs for time to do what the king wishes in exchange for all the wise men's lives. The king agrees, and after much prayer Daniel returns with his answer.

To the king's astonishment, he accurately recounts what the king had dreamt. A massive gleaming statue of a man had appeared to the king. It was made of four different metals – Gold head, Silver chest and arms, Bronze belly and thighs, Iron legs, and feet that were a mixture of iron and clay (or pottery). Those feet were struck by a stone, which had been cut magically from a mountain, and they broke into pieces. Then the rest of the statue broke up also, turning to dust that blew away in the wind. And in its place the stone that struck it became a mountain that filled the entire world. The text is as follows:

> **DAN 2**: [31] "You, O king, looked, and behold, a great image. This image, which was mighty, and whose brightness was excellent, stood before you; and its appearance was terrifying. [32] As for this image, its head was of fine gold, its breast and its arms of silver, its belly and its thighs of bronze, [33] its legs of iron, its feet part of iron, and part of clay. [34] You watched until a stone was cut out [of a mountain – see verse 45 on page 42] without hands, which struck the image on its feet that were of iron and clay, and broke them in pieces. [35] Then the iron, the clay, the bronze, the silver, and the gold were broken in pieces together, and became like the chaff of the summer threshing floors. The wind carried them away, so that no place was found for them. But the stone that struck the image became a great mountain, and filled the whole earth."

The king, no doubt struck dumb by this telepathic-like power, listened intently as this young Daniel gave what he claimed was

God's interpretation of the dream: The four parts of the statue, distinguished by different metals, were four kingdoms that would rule on earth. The first (the gold head) was King Nebuchadnezzar himself (and thus his empire of Babylon). An inferior kingdom (the silver chest and arms) would come after his, and then a third kingdom (the bronze belly and thighs) would rise that will 'rule over the whole earth'. After that there would be a fourth kingdom, 'strong as iron', that will break all the others into pieces. But later this kingdom would be weakened by mixed marriages and divided loyalties (the feet of mixed iron and clay). The amazing thing is that Daniel then says that in the time of those kings the God of heaven will set up a kingdom (the world-filling mountain) that will reign over all peoples and last forever. That, he tells the king, is the meaning of the stone cut magically from a mountain, which struck the statue on its feet of iron and clay, pulverised it to dust, and became a mountain filling the whole world. The full text is below:

> **DAN 2**: **36** "This is the dream; and we will tell its interpretation before the king. **37** You, O king, are king of kings, to whom the God of heaven has given the kingdom, the power, the strength, and the glory. **38** Wherever the children of men dwell, he has given the animals of the field and the birds of the sky into your hand, and has made you rule over them all. You are the head of gold. **39** After you, another kingdom will arise that is inferior to you; and then another – a third – a kingdom of bronze, which will rule over all the earth. **40** The fourth kingdom will be strong as iron, because iron breaks in pieces and subdues all things; and as iron that crushes all these, it will break in pieces and crush. **41** Whereas you saw the feet and toes, part of potters' clay, and part of iron, it will be a divided kingdom; but there will

be in it of the strength of the iron, because you saw the iron mixed with miry clay. [42] As the toes of the feet were part of iron, and part of clay, so this kingdom will be partly strong, and partly broken. [43] Whereas you saw the iron mixed with miry clay, they will mingle themselves with the seed of men; but they won't cling to one another, even as iron does not mix with clay. [44] **In the days of those kings the God of heaven will set up a kingdom which will never be destroyed, nor will its sovereignty be left to another people; but it will break in pieces and consume all these kingdoms, and it will stand forever**. [45] Because you saw that a stone was cut out of the mountain without hands, and that it broke in pieces the iron, the bronze, the clay, the silver, and the gold; the great God has made known to the king what will happen hereafter. The dream is certain, and its interpretation sure."

This made a lasting impression upon that king of Babylon because, many years later in his reign (according to Daniel 4), the same king called upon Daniel to interpret another dream he had experienced. On this occasion, though, the dream was about his royal self. It predicted the duration and outcome of a major illness he was to undergo. When that illness did indeed take place, and the king survived as Daniel said he would, this Babylonian king was all but converted to the Jewish faith, and Daniel's fame grew.

In fact, it grew so much that when Cyrus' Persian army was at the gates of Babylon around 539 BC, Daniel was again called upon to interpret a Babylonian king's dream. This time it was the dream of the last Babylonian to be made king over that city, the coregent Belshazzar (son of the reigning Babylonian emperor Nabonidus). According to Daniel, it predicted the imminent conquest of that king's empire by *the Medes and Persians*. Surprisingly Belshazzar honours Daniel for this undesirable reading by making him 'the third highest ruler in the land' (the second being presumably king Belshazzar himself and the first his father Nabonidus). However, in my view this was probably a cynical gesture brought on by recent word of the defeat of his father's army and the inevitable capitulation he would have known lay ahead, where being any ruler of that nation was not likely to be good for one's health.

But the new regime, portraying themselves as liberators rather than conquerors, were relatively merciful to every Babylonian except Belshazzar, and Daniel's power only grew. He was recognised early on as a talented governor, and his survival of the Lion's Den (Daniel 6) merely served to consolidate his high position. The final chapters of the book of Daniel even claim that he lived on in such high esteem for several more years, well into the period when the high king of the whole Persian Empire (Cyrus the Great) made Babylon his seat of power. Perhaps he was even instrumental in persuading that king to let the Jewish people return to their homeland and rebuild their Temple at Jerusalem, an act (recorded in the book of Ezra) for which King Cyrus of Persia is fondly remembered in Jewish literature.

So much for Daniel. He had lived and served the kings of two world-dominant empires and probably even survived to see his people receive their famous royal mandate to return and rebuild their centre of worship. But remember, the Babylonian king's statue dream predicted a succession of, not *two* empires, but *four* – the first being his own. It was the fourth of these that would be shattered by the stone that was magically cut from a mountain, and which became a mountain that 'filled the whole earth'. In view of this, it is quite astonishing that two centuries after Daniel's death the Persian Empire that had conquered Babylon in his lifetime was totally overrun by the armies of Alexander the Great, king of *Macedon and Greece* (who would definitely have been regarded immediately after this event as a world-ruling king). And a century and a half of Macedonian world dominance was terminated by Rome in 189 BC. It was Rome that eventually made the remaining Macedonian kingdoms mere provinces of her empire. As a result, only Rome can be considered the *fourth distinct empire* from the time of Daniel to rise to dominance over the Middle-Eastern world. This is astonishing because, as you know, Rome was conquered by a religion fashioned from Moses-based Judaism during the time of her emperors. As you will now see, that is precisely what Daniel's interpretation of his king's Statue Dream predicted.

Recall the stone cut magically out of a mountain which struck the statue on its feet of mixed iron and clay, and shattered them, followed by the rest of the statue, to dust that blew away in the wind, and which then became a mountain that filled the whole earth? It was interpreted by Daniel as representing an 'everlasting kingdom' that God would set up during a second phase of that fourth empire – a phase that would be characterised by weakness caused by mixed marriages as represented by the mixed iron and clay of the statue's feet compared to the pure iron of its legs. But if an 'everlasting kingdom of God' is to constitute something substantial that we can recognise from history, it can only refer to a *religion*. And due to the context of this prophecy, that religion must be one venerating the *Jewish God* – the God of Daniel. The significance of this is that if the world-filling mountain into which the stone grew represents a religion, then it stands to reason that the mountain from which the stone was magically hewn *also* represents a religion. The fact that this religion is portrayed as a pre-existent mountain that needs no introduction, and from which God is happy to fashion his everlasting kingdom, means that it can only be *Moses-based Judaism – Daniel's* religion. It is not often noted that this entails that the world-filling mountain into which that stone grows *cannot* be Judaism. It must stand for a *distinct* religion that *came from* Judaism, and *not* Judaism itself.

The dream in Daniel 2 thus predicts that a new religion would be formed from Judaism during a second phase of the Roman empire (the iron-and-clay feet) when Rome would be ruled by kings, and that it will take over that empire and spread out to fill the whole world. The exact meaning of the statue's pulverisation will be discovered in chapter 3 when we look at the more-detailed version of this prophecy in Daniel 7, but the fact that the stone lands on the statue's feet and shatters them first does indeed suggest that this empire (Rome) will be the first one conquered by that religion.

And that is exactly what happened. In the third and fourth decade of the first century AD, in Rome-occupied Palestine during the reign of the Roman emperor Tiberius, the Jewish carpenter Jesus of Nazareth founded the sect of the Jewish faith that became known as Christianity. Over the next three centuries the number subscribing to that faith grew steadily, despite sporadic episodes of cruel and prolonged persecution, until in 312 AD the Roman Tetrarch Constantine I chose to support rather than suppress that faith as his ticket to absolute power in the West. Under a Christian banner, with a Christian symbol painted on his soldiers' shields, he crushed his main rival to that position at the battle of the Milvian Bridge outside Rome – later establishing himself as sole emperor of the whole Roman world by similar means. All of a sudden the worm had turned. Christians, the object of state-sponsored persecution barely a year or two before, suddenly held positions of tremendous political power and influence. And whilst the political Roman Empire was finally conquered by the Ottomans over a thousand years later, its faith, Christianity, has spread throughout the world, and continues to grow in strength even to this day.

Hence, a cursory glance at established history shows that the most obvious interpretation of the statue dream in Daniel 2 (a prophecy supposedly received at the end of the seventh century BC) has come absolutely and perfectly true! It even correctly locates the rise of Christianity within a *second phase* of the Roman empire.

It is worth noting that no scholar actually denies this fact. No critical scholar of Daniel says that the *historical* sequence of four distinct world-dominant empires beginning with Babylon was not *Babylon, Persia, Greece* (Macedon) then *Rome*. Nor do they deny that Rome, as a world-dominant empire, had two phases of government (republic then autocracy); or that the second phase (the iron-and-clay feet of the statue) involved greater participation of non-Romans in her armed forces, and resulted in the intermarrying of her people with those of other nations. They may quibble about whether this was really a *weakening* influence. But as the loyalties of those non-Romans would usually be first and foremost to their own nation, I can't see why it would not be. And none of these scholars will dispute the claim that during this phase of Rome's empire a religion fashioned from Moses-based Judaism completely took over that empire, before spreading out across the world. The obvious meaning of this prophecy *definitely did come true*. No serious scholar disputes this. And if it was written in the sixth or late seventh century BC, that accuracy really would be astonishing.

Although many have quite reasonably argued that it may not have been written at that time, no-one argues that it was written any later than the *second century BC*. By the end of that century several independent versions of the book of Daniel were in relatively wide circulation. Fragments of one of them, dating to the end of that century, are even found among the Dead Sea Scrolls. Hence, the perfect fulfilment of this prophecy is *still* an absolutely astonishing fact. Its accuracy simply cannot be accounted for as the result of hindsight by later writers in the Christian era.

Of course, other attempts have been made to explain the content of this passage. The hope of the sceptics is that its accuracy can be put down to chance. This would be the case if its content can be plausibly explained as the work of a Jewish writer predicting an imminent future conquest of the world by his own religion for propaganda purposes. The problem is that the second mountain imagery, and its rise during a second phase of the *fourth* empire from the time of the dream, is not at all consistent with such a theory. Even ignoring the number of empires, if the hypothetical writer was a Jew, he would surely have had the *first* mountain – the one representing *traditional (Moses-based) Judaism* – grow to fill the world. There would have been no second mountain.

One could of course argue that he was imagining the rise to prominence of what he regarded as a *purer version* of the Jewish faith – and perhaps, like James Barr, he had a different view of the succession of distinct empires from the historical one I have presented here. Fascinatingly, however, the book of Daniel does not leave that option open to a rational investigator.

The reason the book of Daniel does not leave a rational investigator with the option that the second mountain represents a purer version of traditional Judaism is because of the content of the more-detailed version of this same prophecy that is found later in the book (Daniel 7). There the religion of each empire is depicted. A winged lion stands for the Babylonian guardian deity Lamassu, a leopard the Greek god Dionysus, a bear the angel of Persia, and a slain monster that of Rome. But the new religion is portrayed as *a man enthroned next to God and worshipped by all peoples*. It says,

> **DAN 7:** [9] I watched until thrones were placed, and one who was ancient of days sat. His clothing was white as snow, and the hair of his head like pure wool. His throne was fiery flames, and its wheels burning fire…
>
> [13] I looked in the night visions, and behold, there came with the clouds of the sky one like a son of man, and he came even to the ancient of days, and they brought him near before him. [14] Dominion was given to him, and glory, and a kingdom, that all the peoples, nations, and languages should serve him. His dominion is an everlasting dominion …and his kingdom that which will not be destroyed.

Such imagery implies a religion quite distinct from traditional Judaism. In Judaism, God alone is worthy of human worship. And God is *one*. The idea of someone else being enthroned next to God and served by all peoples forever would have been considered blasphemous to traditional Jews in the second century BC or earlier. It is therefore not something one would expect someone predicting a Jewish conquest of the world at that time to include.

But as you will see in chapter 3, Daniel 7 poses even *greater* problems for those who deny that Daniel 2 predicted Christianity. That is because the imagery it uses to symbolise the four empires makes it *absolutely impossible* for an educated Jewish reader in the Rome-dominated world of the second century BC and afterwards to interpret those empires as anything other than the historical sequence of Babylon, Persia, Macedon (i.e. Greece) then Rome. As a result, the rise of the world-filling religion out of Moses-based Judaism cannot be something that was to happen to the dwindling Macedonian world in the 160s BC, as the sceptical explanation for this prophecy – the so-called 'critical consensus' of James Barr and most other scholars – requires. It can only be understood as a prediction about a second phase of the newly-risen *Roman* empire.

In fact, Daniel 7 makes that event even *less* imminent to the mind of a Jewish reader in the second century BC because it postpones the takeover of that empire by this new religion until sometime after that empire's *eleventh king*. Although Rome became the world-dominant nation very early in the second century BC (January 189 BC to be precise), she was at that time a *republic* – a nation presided over by annually elected leaders, not lifelong rulers. Hence the rise of eleven kings of that empire would certainly have seemed a long way off.

Now, the sceptic could still argue that this was just the strategy of a predictor who didn't want to make a prediction of the sort that could fail to come true within his lifetime. But again, the book of Daniel – as if anticipating this objection – provides us with extremely strong grounds to dismiss this hypothesis. That is because Daniel 7 not only predicts the rise of this new religion. It also makes at least one far-more-specific prediction. I will be arguing in chapter 4 that it actually makes *two completely independent* predictions of similar specificity. But this first prediction is of a major world event which it sets in an extremely narrow window of time, and yet any rational scholar inquisitive enough to examine the history of the late Roman Republic and early Roman Empire over the first centuries BC and AD can see at a glance that this event definitely took place.

In chapter 3 you will learn that this *exceptionally specific* prediction, which involves *the toppling of three kings by the eleventh king of the same empire*, is not something that had happened prior to the writing of the book of Daniel, and it is therefore not something that anybody at that time had any reason to put forward as a guess at the future. You will also learn that there is indisputable evidence in Daniel 7 that this was a prediction about a phase of the Roman empire that had not yet come to pass in the second century BC when critical scholars believe the book of Daniel was completed. Consequently, there are no reasonable grounds to argue that this very specific prophecy was not a genuine prediction of the future that came true in an absolutely astonishing and historically salient manner. Although the 'everlasting kingdom' prediction in Daniel 2 and Daniel 7 could have been guesswork, the fact that it features in the same passage of scripture as that *exceptionally specific* prediction (whose fulfilment we have no grounds to attribute to chance) makes it far more reasonable to expect that whoever brought about the fulfilment of that really astonishing part of Daniel 7 was also responsible for ensuring the fulfilment of the 'everlasting kingdom' prediction as well.

In the next two chapters, I will take you through the amazing prophecy in Daniel 7. I will show you why it cannot be reasonably explained as anything other than a genuine and specific prediction about the distant future. And I will prove to you that it was perfectly fulfilled, right on time, by the eleventh king of the Roman empire and by the sudden rise of Christianity to a position of political power and influence over that empire. But we shall not be leaving Daniel 2 for good. We shall be returning to that fascinating Statue dream in this book's tenth chapter. There we will examine its purpose in the light of Daniel 7, and deal with some of the various – in my view futile – attempts that have been made to portray this prophecy as something other than an accurate prediction of the rise of Christianity. As such, it is strong affirmation that true Christianity (adherence to Christ's teaching) is indeed God's kingdom on earth as Jesus claimed.

Remember, no serious scholar denies that the everlasting kingdom prophecy in Daniel 2 and 7 was fulfilled by the rise of Christianity. The fulfilment of that prophecy is a well-established historical fact. No-one can argue that there was not a sequence of exactly four distinct world-dominant empires from the time of those visions until the time of Christ: Babylon-Persia-Greece-Rome. That is why critical scholars – who don't want it to predict Christianity – have had to resort to the quite unconvincing claim that the author of this prophecy had a totally different idea of his nation's history from everyone else in his day. That is why they have had to assert that he believed there was an *extra empire* in that sequence – a completely unhistorical conquest of Babylon by an independent *Median* empire. That claim is unconvincing because it is not supported by the rest of the book of Daniel. Although the conqueror of Babylon in Daniel 5 is a Mede, it is very clear from Daniel 6 that this Mede follows Medo-*Persian* laws, which he is afraid to break. He is therefore a Medo-*Persian* ruler. There is no way the silver chest and arms in Daniel 2 or the huge leaning bear in Daniel 7 were ever meant to represent a couple of years where the world was falsely thought to have been ruled by Media. But even if that strange assertion of critical scholars really did happen to be the origin of this prophecy, that would take nothing away from the fact that this prophecy came true. In fact, if its accuracy were the result of such extremely unlikely errors (as I very much doubt), it ought to be considered even *more* astonishing.

HOW THE ETERNAL KINGDOM PROPHECY CAME TRUE!

Daniel 2	Daniel 7	Established History
First Empire = *GOLD* head = Nebuchadnezzar = **Babylon**	First Empire = *LION* with eagle's wings (*Lamassu**) = **Babylon**	Chaldean **BABYLON** ruled Judea and Syria from fall of Assyria in 609 BC until 539 BC.
Second Empire = *SILVER* chest and two arms (tactfully described as *inferior* to Babylon to make this prediction less negative to the king of Babylon who receives it).	Second Empire = *BEAR* '**raised up** **on one side**' with *three ribs in its mouth* *between its teeth.* It is told to arise and **eat its fill of flesh!** (The bear symbolises the religion/guardian deity* of that empire)	Cyrus' Medo-***PERSIAN*** empire (**Persia**) conquered Babylon in 539 BC. Cyrus spared the life of Babylon's king *Nabonidus* (just as he oddly spared king *Croesus* of Lydia and king *Astyages* of Media). **Persia expanded greatly** but got halted by Greece.
Third Empire = *BRONZE* belly and two thighs. = a kingdom that will 'rule over the whole earth.'	Third Empire = *LEOPARD* with **four birdlike wings** and **four heads** 'given power to rule'. (The leopard stands for that empire's *religion**)	In 331 BC Alexander the Great of ***MACEDON,*** Greece, conquered Persia. His empire split into **four Greek kingdoms,** each with **its own king** (crowned like *Dionysus*).
Fourth Empire = *IRON* legs with *IRON & CLAY* feet = strong kingdom that crushes and breaks all others, later weakened by mixing of peoples.	Fourth Empire = highly distinct and terrible *BEAST* with iron teeth, bronze claws and ten (plus one) horns. = empire like no other: Exceedingly powerful.	**ROME** conquered the Greek kingdoms of Syria (189 BC) and Macedon (168 BC). Egypt and Pergamon also submitted. *REPUBLIC* till 27 BC, she became an *AUTOCRACY*.
	*Beast slain, others live! Animal types = *Religions*	
Stone cut by God from mountain (Judaism) hits statue feet, *pulverising it.* It then becomes a **world-** **filling mountain**: an eternal *kingdom of God.*	Sometime after her eleventh king, the holy people will *receive the* *kingdom* so that the ***Son*** ***of Man*** will be served by all peoples forever.	In 312 AD, her fifty-ninth emperor Constantine I *won Rome for* <u>***Christ***</u> – the *stone* the builders rejected. **Rome's pagan religion** **was *completely replaced.***

As you can see, there is no doubt that this prophecy perfectly portrays established history from the time of Daniel's dream onwards. Since there is also no doubt about the fact that it was in circulation from at least the second half of the second century BC, its perfect portrayal of Constantine's conversion of the Roman Empire to a religion that was formed out of Judaism by a man (Christ) who described himself as 'the son of man' and 'the stone the builders rejected' (Matthew 21:42 and 9:6) is truly amazing.

Emperor Constantine I was of course long after the eleventh emperor of Rome. So you might be thinking that, since the version of this prophecy in Daniel 7 portrays only eleven kings of the Roman empire, perhaps it did get something wrong after all.

Then again, perhaps not. The replacement of Rome's religion is very clearly portrayed in Daniel 7 as the work of *God*. It is not in any way suggested to be the work of any particular Roman emperor. Moreover, the eleventh king that the prophecy mentions is predicted to be an *oppressor*, not a saviour, of the holy people. Hence, the uprooting of three previous kings by that predicted eleventh king of Rome need not be anything to do with the replacement of Rome's religion by a son-of-man-worshipping sect of Judaism that the prophecy so amazingly predicted.

But if that is the case, and the prophecy really was inspired by God as its accurate prediction of Christianity suggests to a believer, why does it refer to an eleventh king at all? Why does it single out that king so specifically if he were not meant to be a major player in the rise of Christianity? In the next chapter you will discover the astonishing significance of this obscure reference. And as you will see, it is a discovery that I think proves beyond all reasonable doubt that the fulfilment of this prophecy was no accident.

CHAPTER THREE

The Most Astonishing Text Ever Written

Shocked, and trembling with growing excitement, I looked again at the web page in front of me. My attention focussed on the portraits of three stern and worried-looking men. Each showed only the subject's profile, looking to the right, as though he were gazing in horror at the back of the laurel-wreathed head of the next-in-line. Converging arrows linked each of these portraits to a single narrow interval on a timeline running above them. I couldn't believe it.....and yet, it was exactly what I had *expected* to find! The implications of what I was seeing, however, were so immense that some part of me must have seriously doubted it would be there – or at least suspected it would be a lot less obvious.

The screen on my computer showed the names, dates and portraits of a long list of Roman emperors. I had typed "early roman emperors" into Google, and the site before me had been one of the first to come up on the results page. Clicking on each emperor's name brought up a separate web page describing the background and significant events in the reign of that emperor. But on this occasion it was the dates on that homepage that I was really interested in. And one in particular immediately leapt out at me: *"69 AD: The Year of the Four Emperors"*.

The timeline along which all those emperors were placed began at 27 BC with the accession of the first Roman emperor, Caesar Augustus (also known as Octavian). His portrait and dates were then followed by those of Tiberius, Caligula, Claudius, Nero, Galba, Otho, Vitellius, Vespasian, Titus and Domitian (to name only the ones that were of interest to me at that time). But it was the fact that three of them (Galba, Otho and Vitellius) were violently deposed in the same year – 69 AD – that nearly knocked me off my seat.

It was exactly what I had expected to find – though prior to that moment in the mid-noughties I'd known virtually nothing about those emperors. I knew only the names Augustus and Tiberius that were familiar to me from the New Testament, and the names Claudius and Nero that I vaguely remembered from films I'd seen long before. I also had a vague recollection that Nero was an excessively vain and paranoid character who liked feeding lions with Christians, and I had the apparently mistaken belief that Julius Caesar had been the first Roman emperor. But I knew nothing else about those early emperors or their dates and careers.

The reason I had expected to see that "Year of the Four Emperors" was because I had read about it earlier that day in the seventh chapter of the *book of Daniel* – and because by then I had become convinced that another momentous event which that chapter said would happen sometime after the reign of those early Roman emperors had indeed taken place just as Daniel 7 said it would. The fascinating thing is that the book of Daniel is in the *Old Testament* of the Bible; and as we shall see in chapter 7 of this book, there is very strong evidence that it was written in its current form long before Caesar Augustus and those other Roman emperors were even born!

Before I go on, I should mention that the book of Daniel does not actually use the phrase "The Year of the Four Emperors", or even the word 'emperors', and it doesn't explicitly specify that the event referred to was going to occur in a single year. However, it did clearly tell me that

> **three kings of the Roman empire were going to be violently deposed during the rise to power of the eleventh king of the Roman empire,**

and since one can hardly not consider an emperor to be a king of the empire he ruled, it also indicated that

> **these kings would probably be among the first *eleven* *emperors* of Rome, and could not be later emperors.**

Their actual position in that list of emperors is also clearly deducible from the book of Daniel and our knowledge of the history of the Roman empire and it turns out to be the four emperors that came after Nero, just as I discovered that day. The key, as we shall find out later in this chapter, is the realisation that 'kings' are not necessarily rulers who get called 'kings' or 'emperors' by their subjects or by later historians. They are in fact generally understood to be 'rulers of a nation who have *no legal time limit* on their reign'. Wouldn't you agree with that definition?

This is an important point because if we want to decide whether a prophecy has been fulfilled in a really *surprising* way we cannot simply interpret the prophecy any way we like. And we are also not at liberty to compare its predictions with just any perception of history. We must identify only the *most obvious* meanings of the words and symbols it uses (the ones that are most justified by the text of the book in which the prophecy is found), and thereby work out the most obvious (i.e. most *justifiable*) meaning of the prophecy as a whole. We must then look at established history to see if that most justifiable meaning has indeed been fulfilled. If it hasn't, the prophecy should be dismissed as inaccurate unless future discoveries happen to prove otherwise. Hence, if there were other rulers of the Roman empire who were granted an unlimited reign length prior to the first emperor, those people *must* be counted as 'kings' for our purposes regardless of whether they were labelled as such by the people they governed or by future historians. And every one of those rulers must be counted even if doing that turns out to render the prophecy *un*fulfilled. That is why I couldn't simply identify the first of the eleven kings the prophecy predicted with the person modern scholars consider to be the first emperor of Rome (Caesar Augustus). I had to be certain there were no rulers of the Roman empire prior to Augustus that were granted an unlimited reign length.

From the fact that it would be difficult to regard three kings of the same kingdom as being 'subdued' by another king of that kingdom during that king's rise to power (as the text in my NIV Bible clearly indicated) unless the reigns of those kings were very short and in rapid succession, I figured that I was looking for three consecutive emperors who reigned during a year or so of civil war, which is exactly what I found. Moreover, I was of the opinion that if that prediction in the book of Daniel was to be considered fulfilled, it would have to refer to a very *unusual* and *remarkable* event that would be well known in the history books, which is why seeing "The Year of the Four Emperors" on that homepage made such an impression on me.

Even more amazing, though, was the fact that when I examined the career of the *last* of those four emperors – the survivor of that civil war – I immediately found that he had led a war against the Jews and defeated them. This was a key feature of the king who would subdue three kings before him that the book of Daniel predicted! And intriguingly, it is not a feature that applied to any of the previous Roman emperors. That Roman emperor was also known for his omen-rich propaganda and his extremely unusual claim to be the fulfilment of a Jewish scripture, both of which also apply to the king in the prophecy. And like that king, he was even seen as unlike all the earlier ones. The only puzzling feature was the fact that according to this website he was the *ninth* Roman Emperor. If that meant he was the ninth ruler of the Roman empire to be given an unlimited reign length, it would mean that despite these other amazing features he could not be claimed to have fulfilled that prophecy. That prophecy definitely referred to the *eleventh* king of the fourth empire from Daniel's time. It was the eleventh king of the Roman empire who was to subdue three kings before him, speak against the Jewish God, and make war upon the Jews.

Clicking on a link that said *'The Late Republic'*, it did not take me long to find the last piece of the puzzle (an easy puzzle by any standards). And there it was: In 82 BC, by decree of the Roman Senate, Sulla was pronounced 'Dictator', *and no time limit was placed on his time in office.* The granting of such power to an individual had not happened in Rome since the days of its monarchy, and would not be repeated until Julius Caesar was made *'Dictator for life'* in 44 BC.

I once watched a documentary on the book of Daniel that claimed its seventh chapter predicted the whole of the remaining history of nations from Daniel's day all the way up until the second coming of Christ, which it claimed lay sometime in our future. Since Daniel 7 didn't suggest anything like that to me, I was interested to know how the makers of that documentary could possibly have come up with such a view. What I learned is that this view (which is very popular in evangelical churches) is based upon a "last resort" interpretation arrived at by the early church fathers to explain away the fact that the most obvious reading of this prophecy (Daniel 7) appeared to them to have failed to come true.

Daniel 7 predicts the same four empires as Daniel 2, but it adds the very specific prediction about the first eleven kings of the fourth of those empires that we have just been discussing. By the time those church fathers wrote their commentaries, *more* than eleven kings had risen to rule that fourth empire, and the eleventh, as far as they could see, had not achieved what this prophecy said he would achieve. Rather than conclude that this astonishing prophetic book had failed, they chose instead to reinterpret the prophecy in a way that pretty much guaranteed it would come true (which is just as well, since otherwise the book may not have survived to come down to us). How did they achieve this feat? They simply said that the word 'kings' in the prophecy need not actually refer to individual human beings but could instead stand for *whole nations*

– ones that would emerge from that fourth empire in their future (the future from the perspective of those early church fathers).

This is not actually as dubious as it sounds because the word translated 'kings' is used to refer to the *empires* (ruling kingdoms) that the vision portrays. That is presumably because empires are kingdoms that *rule over other kingdoms* and the word translated 'kings' probably meant 'those that rule'. Since a nation usually survives far longer than a king, though, there is a whole lot more time available for the event that the new interpretation of the prophecy predicted to take place. This of course makes it far more likely to come about purely by chance. But its occurrence by chance becomes even more likely when you consider that the term 'nation' is a loose one. It is applied not only to specific tribes of related individuals but also to broad people-groups like 'the Jews' or 'the British Empire'. By interpreting those kings as 'nations', the church fathers made it almost certain that the problematic part of the prophecy would be fulfilled sooner or later. But in so doing they obscured what is probably the most remarkable feature of the book of Daniel, and caused this book to be dismissed – unduly as you will see – by reasonable sceptics who have no problem seeing how totally unimpressive any claims to the fulfilment of that early Christian interpretation of this prophecy actually are.

In this chapter, I adopt the view that only if the most *justifiable* interpretation of a prophecy comes true can we regard that fulfilment as surprising – and then only if the events that fulfilled it were predicted to occur within a window of time narrow enough to ensure that their occurrence there would be extremely unlikely to happen by chance. As you will see, such a narrow window of time is in fact ensured by the most obvious reading of Daniel 7 – the one the church fathers rejected because they thought it hadn't come true. We, however, have an advantage over those church fathers because we have a broader – and somewhat less biased – view of history than they had: A view for which we are deeply indebted to the dedicated work of many expert researchers examining and comparing the ancient sources. As you will discover, when one compares our modern perception of history with the most justifiable interpretation of that prophecy, one suddenly realises that those church fathers were wrong. The most obvious interpretation of that prophecy *has indeed* come true! And it has done so in such a visible and dramatic way that it is a real wonder those church fathers didn't spot it.

In the archaeological remains of the ancient Greek city of Pella, the birthplace of Alexander the Great, king of Macedon and Greece and conqueror of the Persian Empire, there's a large pebble mosaic dating to Alexander's lifetime. It depicts the youthful warrior-god Dionysus who was lovingly worshipped by the Macedonians as the God of the harvest, the "Good Deity" responsible for wine and merriment, and as a heavenly protector in battle. His trademark 'Mitra' headband may even have inspired the diadem crowns that the Greek kings wore. He was also revered as a god who, while on earth in an age of myth and legend, had successfully invaded the mysterious far-off land of India. As a result, when Alexander achieved the same incredible feat in 326 BC, after crushing the Persian Empire, it was natural for the Macedonians to believe that this undefeated hero-king who loved wine and merriment, and whose mother was a priestess of Dionysus, was really another incarnation of their favourite god (or perhaps that is just what his spin-doctors wanted them to believe). Either way, Alexander the Great in the eyes of many Macedonians was equated with the Greek god Dionysus who was probably their most popular deity.

The relevance of this to Daniel 7 is the fact that on Hellenistic pottery and artwork (the pottery and artwork of Alexander's empire) this god is widely depicted in the company of leopards. He is also usually depicted wearing leopard skins – his traditional battle-dress – and leopard-skin patterns that appear on Greek coins of the period are widely understood to be symbolic of that same deity. Although he is pictured naked on the pebble mosaic at Pella, he is nevertheless sitting side-saddle on the back of a magnificent spotted feline creature, which the museum identifies as a panther, but which could just as easily be a leopard. What matters is that it is definitely '*like* a leopard'. But why is this relevant to Daniel 7?

Like the Statue vision in Daniel 2 that we examined in the previous chapter, Daniel 7 is a prophecy of four great empires that would follow each other in sequence and lead up to the establishment of an everlasting, world-wide kingdom of God. In other words, it is quite clearly meant to be recognised as predicting the same four kingdoms as Daniel 2. But in this vision, those four kingdoms are not portrayed as parts of a statue made of distinct types of metal. They are portrayed as totally distinct *animals* – or rather, *monsters* (beasts) made of wild-animal-like parts. And one of them – the one that a straightforward comparison with history indicates to be representing the Greco-Macedonian Empire of Alexander the Great (referred to in the Bible as 'Greece') – is 'like a leopard'.

The first six verses of this astonishing vision of future history read as follows (look out for the leopard in verse 6):

> **DAN 7:** [2] Daniel spoke and said, "I looked in my vision by night, and, behold, the four winds of the sky broke out on the great sea. [3] Four great animals came up from the sea, different from one another.

[4] The first was like a lion, and had eagle's wings. I watched until its wings were plucked, and it was lifted up from the earth, and made to stand on two feet as a man. A man's heart was given to it.

Daniel's Vision of the Four Beasts – Engraving by Matthäus Merian (1630)

[5] Behold, there was another animal, a second, like a bear. It was raised up on one side, and three ribs were in its mouth between its teeth. They said this to it: 'Arise! Devour much flesh!'

[6] After this I looked, and behold, another, **like a leopard**, which had on its back **four wings of a bird**. The animal also had **four heads**; and dominion was given to it.

> [7] After this I looked in the night visions, and, behold, there was a fourth animal, awesome and powerful, and exceedingly strong. It had great iron teeth. It devoured and broke in pieces, and stamped the residue with its feet. It was different from all the animals that were before it. It had ten horns."

Recall from chapter 2 that the straightforward historically-consistent identification of those empires is *Babylon, Persia, Greece* (Alexander's Macedonian empire), then *Rome* (the nation that conquered the Macedonians). So, the leopard-like *third* beast in the vision has to stand for Alexander's empire. Remember also that Alexander's empire became split into **four Macedonian kingdoms each ruled by a separate head of state** for most of the third century BC. I will be discussing this in more detail later, but you will probably agree that this four-way-splitting is most likely to be what the **four wings and four heads** of that leopard are meant to represent. None of the other empires split in such a way.

In view of the fact that the leopard was such a popular symbol of Dionysus – the Greek god most closely associated with Alexander and the Macedonians – it looks almost certain that the leopard-likeness of this third beast has been deliberately chosen to symbolise the *religion* of the empire that it stands for. It seems therefore quite reasonable to interpret the animal-likeness of each of the other beasts as also being representative of a *religion*. The interesting thing is that when you do this the meaning of several puzzling features of this dream's imagery becomes crystal clear.

One is the fact that the fourth beast gets killed prior to the establishment of God's kingdom, while the other beasts *remain alive for a time but without power*. Daniel 7:8-12 reads as follows:

DAN 7: [8] "I considered the horns, and behold, there came up among them another horn, a little one, before which three of the first horns were plucked up by the roots: and behold, in this horn were eyes like the eyes of a man, and a mouth speaking great things. [9] I watched until thrones were placed, and one who was ancient of days sat. His clothing was white as snow, and the hair of his head like pure wool. His throne was fiery flames, and its wheels burning fire. [10] A fiery stream issued and came out from before him. Thousands of thousands ministered to him. Ten thousand times ten thousand stood before him. The judgment was set. The books were opened. [11] I watched at that time because of the voice of the great words which the horn spoke. I watched even until the animal was slain, and its body destroyed, and it was given to be burned with fire. [12] As for the rest of the animals, their power was removed; **yet their lives were prolonged for a season and a time**."

Since the next two verses, below, describe *the establishment of God's kingdom*, it is natural to conclude that whatever the killing and burning of the fourth beast symbolizes it either precedes or coincides with this event. Hence whatever the other beasts symbolize, they must therefore (verse 12) *go on beyond the event most obviously alluded to by those verses*. As you will see, the only justifiable possibility is *national religions*. Those verses say,

DAN 7: [13] "I looked in the night visions, and behold, there came with the clouds of the sky one like a son of man, and he came even to the ancient of days, and they brought him near before him. [14] Dominion was given him, and glory, and a kingdom, that all the peoples, nations, and languages should serve him. His dominion is an everlasting dominion, which will not pass away, and his kingdom that which will not be destroyed."

It has been widely assumed that the killing and burning of that fourth beast is the conquest and destruction of the empire it represents. But since, after this, the other three beasts (representing already-conquered empires) *remain alive for a time*, that cannot be the case. In Daniel's interpretation of the vision (Daniel 7:15-26, below) the fourth empire is described as crushing and breaking up its victims, which naturally must include the previous empires.

> **DAN 7:** [15] "As for me, Daniel, my spirit was grieved within my body, and the visions of my head troubled me. [16] I came near to one of those who stood by, and asked him the truth concerning all this. So he told me, and made me know the interpretation of the things.
>
> [17] 'These great animals, which are four, are four kings [which all scholars agree means 'empires' – 'ruling nations' – rather than 'ruling persons', as is clear from verse 23], who will arise out of the earth. [18] But the holy people of the Most High will receive the kingdom, and possess the kingdom forever, even forever and ever.'
>
> [19] Then I desired to know the truth concerning the fourth animal, which was different from all of them, exceedingly terrible, whose teeth were of iron, and its nails of bronze; which devoured, broke in pieces, and stamped the residue with its feet; [20] and concerning the ten horns that were on its head, and the other horn which came up, and before which three fell, even that horn that had eyes, and a mouth that spoke great things, whose look was more stout than its

fellows. [21] I looked, and the same horn made war with the holy people, and prevailed against them, [22] until the ancient of days came, and judgment was given to the holy people of the Most High, and the time came that the holy people possessed the kingdom.

[23] Thus he said, 'The fourth animal will be a fourth kingdom on earth, which will be **different from all the kingdoms**, and will **devour the whole earth**, and will **tread it down**, and **break it in pieces**.'"

And we know for a fact that Rome turned all the Macedonian kingdoms into provinces of her empire, breaking them up into smaller regions of government as she saw fit. Moreover, each of the two previous empires was completely conquered by the empire that followed it (Persia under Cyrus completely conquered Babylon, and Macedon/Greece under Alexander the Great completely conquered Persia). Yet their beasts live on. Interpreting those beasts as religions offers a perfect solution to that dilemma. Religions, unlike political institutions, often do live on well beyond the demise of the nation that made them popular.

Not only does this obvious interpretation explain how the beasts representing the three previous empires happen to still be alive at the demise of the beast representing the fourth empire, it also makes this imagery a perfectly accurate representation of the rise of Christianity. Remember, the fourth beast has to stand for the *Roman* empire for the sequence of the former three to make sense historically (as well as for certain other reasons we shall consider shortly). Hence, if its destruction were the *destruction* of the Roman empire, which did not finally take place until the fall of Byzantium in 1453, then the religion described as an 'everlasting kingdom' and established by God in this dream could only be Islam. That is because it is after the destruction of this beast that all authority passes over to the followers of this religion, and the people who gained such authority and power with the conquest of the Roman Empire were the Ottoman Turks, who were Muslims. If, however, that fourth beast stands for the *religion* of Rome, as we have very reasonably inferred from the way the other beasts 'live on', its destruction cannot be interpreted as the destruction of the Roman Empire. It must be understood to mean the destruction of the Roman *religion*. And that can only be equated with the events of the fourth century AD (Constantine's conversion of Rome to Christianity). Provided the fourth beast stands for the Roman religion, then the fire that consumes it in the dream can only be Christianity, since it was state sponsorship of Christianity from Constantine I onwards that spelt the end of Rome's religion.

A question that now comes to mind is this: Did the religions associated with the other three beasts really live on beyond this time as the prophecy suggests?

The first beast in this dream – the lion with eagle's wings – must represent the religion of the *Babylonians*. This actually explains the chosen imagery quite well. Lions with eagle's wings (and human heads) were often used in Babylonian art to depict the *Lamassu*, which was the deity that protected the Babylonian kings. And the Babylonian religion definitely continued in Babylon throughout the Persian and Macedonian (Greek) periods of occupation. Moreover, although the city of Babylon was eventually abandoned, some of the gods her people believed in would no doubt have continued to be worshipped in the countryside well into the period when Rome was the dominant world power. Since Babylonia remained largely beyond Rome's sphere of influence, her people were not forcibly converted to Christianity following Rome's sudden Christianisation. So her religion did indeed live on for a time after this episode in history.

It was the same with the religion of the Persian empire. The conquering Greeks made no effort to destroy religions, and much of the territory where that religion was practiced also remained beyond the eastern boundary of the Roman Empire. The religion in question (Zoroastrianism) actually survives to this day in some regions of Asia. Why it would be represented by a *bear* (the second animal in the vision) is an interesting question. But the Jews definitely thought that this was what the bear stood for. We know this because the guardian angel of Persia in the Talmud (the Jewish rabbinical scriptures composed in the first half of the first millennium AD) was given the name 'Dobiel' which means 'Bear god'. My guess is that the author of the vision in Daniel 7 chose a bear because in the Old Persian language the name 'Persia' (originally pronounced 'paarsa') meant 'bear-protected' ('pa' definitely meant 'protected', and 'arsa' probably meant 'bear').

Although the Macedonian (Greek) kingdoms that emerged from Alexander's conquests were totally conquered by Rome, their Dionysian faith, in the Roman form of Bacchus, remained as strong as ever until Rome's Christianisation, and there is some archaeological evidence that after this moment it was still practiced in places for many years to come. Like the Babylonian and Persian faiths, it lived on for a time beyond the destruction of the traditional religion of Rome. But just as Daniel 7 predicts, it no longer had any political power.

So, the dream was right in these respects. However, the continuation of a religion is not a particularly unlikely event to predict. If the religion had sufficient followers, that was almost bound to happen. The really interesting fact about Daniel 7 is that it doesn't just contain predictions of this relatively likely sort. As I mentioned at the beginning of this chapter, it actually makes an extremely *specific* prediction. And within that prediction, not only are the events detailed and momentous enough to make them extremely rare occurrences, they are also predicted to happen within a very narrow window of time.

For me this is an essential criterion that an accurate prophecy must satisfy if one is to consider its fulfilment to be in any way surprising. A prophecy that doesn't limit the time-period in which the events it predicts are to happen is almost certain to get fulfilled at some point in the future. After all, given enough time anything possible is likely to happen. By not limiting the time-period in question, a prophecy in effect allows an indefinite time for its prediction to come true, which in my view renders any claim to its fulfilment quite uninteresting. The fascinating thing about Daniel 7 is that it not only contains a prediction that is highly *specific*, but that highly specific event is predicted to take place within a very limited window of time – a time-frame so short in fact that it would be an absolute miracle if that prediction came true. Yet, as we shall now see, that does indeed appear to be what's happened.

The prediction I'm referring to is Daniel 7: 24-27, and it reads as follows:

> **DAN 7:** [24] "As for the ten horns, ten kings will arise out of this kingdom. Another will arise after them; and he will be different from the former, and he will put down three kings. [25] He will speak words against the Most High, and will wear out the holy people of the Most High. He will plan to

change the times and the law; and they will be given into his hand until a time and times and half a time.

26 But the judgment will be set, and they will take away his dominion, to consume and to destroy it to the end. 27 The kingdom and the dominion, and the greatness of the kingdoms under the whole sky, will be given to the people of the holy people of the Most High. His kingdom is an everlasting kingdom, and all dominions will serve and obey him."

Recall that a simple comparison of the predicted sequence of world-dominant empires in this dream with the actual historical sequence of distinct world-dominant empires (where 'distinct' can be very simply understood as meaning that the empires were founded by different nations) indicates that the fourth empire – the one represented here by the ten-horned monster – is Rome (see page 53). Consequently, the ten horns, described here as ten *kings* of that empire, can only be reasonably interpreted as standing for the first ten kings to rule over the *Roman* empire. Technically they could stand for *any* ten kings of that empire. However, if one allows oneself to interpret a prophecy any way one wants, then any fulfilment one may find will be quite unsurprising. It could just be pure chance. It was for the same reason that we rejected the claim that these kings could be referring to emergent kingdoms or nations. For this to be considered an accurate prophecy, those ten horns must stand for the *first* ten kings to rise from that empire, they have to be ordinary human-being-type kings, and the eleventh such king must subdue three of those ten!

As you can see, this is indeed a highly specific and time-limited prophecy. If the eleventh king or his supporters didn't in some way overthrow three of the ten before him, then it will have failed. Thus, its window of opportunity for fulfilment was the lifetime of that eleventh king. In fact, it is even narrower than that. A king cannot be regarded as subduing another king if the other king's reign was ended by circumstances that the first king or his supporters could not have engineered. Hence the window of opportunity for a fulfilment of this prophecy was the time over which the lifetime of the eleventh king of the Roman empire was contemporaneous with the reigns of the ten before him. As soon as the reign of the last of these ten kings ended, the opportunity for a fulfilment of this prophecy was over.

Yet just look at how hard a task it would have been to achieve a *deliberate* fulfilment of this prophecy. The man who became the eleventh king of the Roman empire had to be (or have been) responsible for the demise of three of the most powerful people in the world at the time AND not lose his life in the process AND ensure that the subjects of those emperors accepted him as their king instead! If that doesn't seem like a tall order to you, don't worry, because there's more. The prophecy also requires that this eleventh king *makes war on the Jewish nation and defeats them*, that he is somehow *different from all ten of the previous rulers* of that empire, and that he is particularly well-known for his *religious boasts*. For the prophecy to be regarded as fulfilled, all these specific features would have to apply to the eleventh king to rule over the Roman empire.

There is also a less-specific feature: "He will plan to change times and laws and the holy people will be given into his hand for a time, times and half a time". Given that the prophet Daniel who received this vision is a devout Jew, it seems reasonable to interpret the words 'holy people' as a reference to the Jewish nation (or at least devout followers of the Jewish God), and 'times and laws' as a reference to the Jewish festivals or calendar, and to the Law of Moses. However, the time-phrase here seems intentionally difficult to make sense of. We know that this is not just because of our lack of knowledge of ancient Jewish idioms because, in Daniel 12:8, Daniel himself claims to not understand this time-phrase. It could mean *any* length of time, though the popular view is that it simply means three-and-a-half *years* (a year, two years and half a year).

In the next chapter, I will be arguing that this popular view is not the most justifiable one. Nevertheless, it is supported by some parts of the book of Daniel, so it is probably reasonable to add a three-and-a-half year 'giving of the Jewish nation into the hand of this king' to that list of requirements. The claim that he will 'think to change times and laws' is also rather general. All we can really say is that the context in which these words occur requires them to refer to *Jewish* times and laws. Since no specific laws or occasions are referred to, and since such an action would not be atypical of a conqueror, this for me does not add anything more restrictive to the list of criteria that must be satisfied for the prophecy's fulfilment. But that list of conditions is nevertheless still formidable: He must

1. Subdue three of the previous ten kings of the Roman empire.

2. Wage war on the Jewish Nation (or other devout followers of the Jewish God).

3. Defeat them and hold them in submission for at least three-and-a-half years (and plan to change their times and laws).

4. Be known for speaking against the Jewish God.

5. Be different from all ten of the previous kings of the Roman empire.

If the eleventh king of the Roman empire satisfies even the first of these criteria, we should definitely sit up and pay attention. That is because this prophecy was clearly in existence many years before the Roman empire had any kings. This fact is not in any kind of doubt, as you will see in chapter 7. Rome did once have a monarchy, but only when she was a small city-state, and it is quite clear from Daniel 8 that such kings don't count. That institution was removed and replaced with a republic long before she gained any form of empire; and by the second century BC when mainstream scholars think the book of Daniel was completed *no ruler of that republic had ever been granted lifelong power.* Since Daniel 8:21 describes Alexander III of Macedon (Alexander the Great) as 'the *first* king' of Greece (page 222), it is clear that those eleven kings cannot include Rome's early monarchs. They must rule during the time she possesses a large empire.

It is also important to realise that the deposing of three kings of the most powerful nation in the world is not something anyone who wanted to be king of that nation would strive to do unless he had to. Nor is it anything any religious zealot who wanted to make the prophecy come true could realistically hope to get away with. As a result, it is not really possible for this prophecy to be a *self-fulfilling* one (one that people succeeded in fulfilling by deliberate intention). And since the event it predicts is an incredibly rare one, which had to transpire within a very narrow window of time, we have very good reason to expect the occurrence of that predicted event to be the result of the deliberate intervention in human history of a powerful non-human intelligence. After all, if humans would neither have been capable nor willing to engineer such a fulfilment of prophecy, and if its specificity all but rules out chance, what other explanation is left?

So, who was that eleventh king of the Roman empire, and did he subdue three of the ten kings before him? Let us look at the history books.

Whenever I think of kings of the Roman empire, I immediately think of the Roman Emperors – the Caesars. If you consult any modern history of Rome you will read that the first Roman Emperor was a man called Gaius Octavius Thurinus (Octavian for short) who took the name *Caesar Augustus* in 27 BC, shortly after he became effectively the sole ruler of the Roman empire.

But things are not quite as simple as this – if only because the early Roman historians themselves did not consider Augustus to have been their first emperor. Instead they attributed that status to their famous general *Julius Caesar*, the conqueror of Gaul (France), and one of the few who had established himself as sole ruler and dictator over the whole Roman world. They had very good grounds for this view. Octavian took the name Caesar Augustus precisely to associate himself with this man. He was one of the generals who had avenged Julius Caesar's famous assassination. And he owed the political support that allowed him to establish his emperorship precisely to the fact that he was this hero's adopted son, and was widely seen to be merely taking up the powers and offices that had been rightfully awarded to his dead father.

The reason modern scholars do not see things this way is merely because it makes the history of Rome look messy. By 27 BC Rome had already dominated the world for over 160 years. For almost all of that time she had been ruled by the Senate – a parliament of representatives of Rome's nobility presided over by elected leaders who were granted only a limited period in office. Usually these consisted of two 'consuls' – heads of state who were elected each year in pairs in order to limit the amount of power the Senate invested in any individual. However, in times of crisis a single individual could be invested with dictatorial power over the whole Roman empire. This was intended to be only a temporary measure, and the office of Dictator usually came with a time limit of just six months. Centuries before (around the time of Daniel, in fact), Rome had been ruled by elected kings (a period known as the Roman Monarchy), and the Roman nobility had hated it. While still only a small Italian city-state they had rebelled and removed their king and set up the institutions that became known as the *Roman Republic*. It was the Republic under its annually elected leaders that had forged her empire, and most Romans in the first century BC wanted to keep it that way. During almost all of his life even the famous Julius Caesar only managed to persuade the Senate to grant him ten-year-long military commands, and he only managed to do that because he had agreed to share his control over Rome's armed forces with two other generals.

However, in 48 BC Julius Caesar had become the sole ruler of the empire having that year vanquished his remaining partner in power, Pompey the Great, in a bloody civil war. And although the office of Dictator was initially only granted to him for limited time-periods, extended to ten years in 46 BC, this arrangement changed in January or February of 44 BC. As is well-attested in the history books, at that time the Senate abandoned tradition and awarded Julius Caesar the office of *Dictator for Life*.

Did that not make him an emperor? In the eyes of Rome's early historians, it did. It presumably also did in the eyes of Brutus and Cassius and the other conspirators who stabbed him to death in the Senate chamber only a few weeks afterwards and announced the restoration of the Republic.

However, his assassination shows that Rome wasn't ready for an emperorship at that time. The transition from Republic to the continuous line of emperors was the work of Augustus two decades later, and modern scholars are of the opinion that one can't call a ruler of Rome an 'emperor' if he ruled during the *Republic phase* – even if the Senate did grant him lifelong dictatorial powers typical of those it later awarded Augustus and his successors.

The question for us is this: If this prophecy were the work of a God, is it reasonable for us to interpret 'king' as 'emperor' in the sense in which modern scholars apply the word, or should we consider those leaders of the Republic who had the powers of the later emperors to also be 'kings' of the Roman empire? I definitely think we need to adopt the latter position.

On the other hand, we cannot allow ourselves to arbitrarily decide who constitutes a king and who doesn't. That would allow us to shift the time of the predicted events in this prophecy any way we want, which would mean any fulfilment could not be considered surprising. Instead, we must stick rigidly to the most basic and unambiguous definition of 'king' we can think of.

The definition of 'king' that I think is most basic is this: **'A ruler of a nation who has been given no limit on his time in office'**.

Such a definition fits all usages of the Aramaic word for 'king' elsewhere in the book of Daniel, and does not make demands that would rule out historical characters who are widely regarded as kings. The question is, besides Julius Caesar, whose Dictatorship for Life, despite its violent curtailment, clearly qualifies him to be called a 'king' by this straightforward definition, are there any other leaders of the Republic to whom this definition applies?

Well in actual fact there is only one. By imposing time limits on all the dictatorships and highest offices in the Republic, the Roman Senate managed to prevent this happening right up until the first century BC. However, in 82 BC, a Roman general called *Sulla* marched his legions on the capital in a move that would be echoed with equal success by Julius Caesar thirty-three years later. After defeating his enemies, he had himself made 'Dictator' by the Senate, and crucially, for the first time since the founding of the Republic, the Senate did not impose any limit on his time in office.

In his classic textbook *From the Gracchi to Nero* (1970), University of London professor of ancient history H. H. Scullard tells us,

> 'Sulla received full powers from the hands of the People to reorganize the constitution as dictator, an office which had lapsed since the Hannibalic War. But apart from the name, Sulla's office had little in common with the emergency magistrates whom the consuls used to name for periods of six months: Sulla held supreme authority as long as he wished...' (H. H. Scullard, *From the Gracchi to Nero*, 1970, p.82)

By our straightforward definition of 'king' this makes Sulla the *first king* to rule over the Roman empire. Julius Caesar (whose life Sulla is reputed to have reluctantly spared during his dictatorship) became its *second* king in 44 BC when the Senate awarded him a Dictatorship for Life. Nobody else was invested with life-long powers over the whole nation until Julius Caesar's adopted son and heir, Octavian (Caesar Augustus), the man whom modern scholars see as the founder of Rome's continuous emperorship. Consequently, that so-called 'first emperor' should in fact be regarded as the *third king* to rise out of the Roman empire.

So, who was the eleventh king? If you agree with me that 'a ruler of a nation who has no limit on his time in office' is the most straightforward and reasonable definition of 'king' – the definition that a God who sees the whole of history would most probably have in mind – then Augustus was definitely the *third king* of the Roman empire (where 'empire' stands for a nation that has conquered other nations, rather than one ruled by a continuous emperorship). The fourth king was therefore his successor Tiberius. The fifth was the mad Caligula. Claudius, whose armies began the conquest of Britain (first invaded by Julius Caesar a century before), was the sixth; and the seventh was Nero, famous for setting fire to Rome and blaming it on the Christians. He was the last of the so-called 'Julio-Claudian' dynasty, and it was during his reign that the Jews in Judea rose up in revolt against Rome. He dispatched a very capable general called Vespasian to deal with this revolt, keeping Vespasian's brother Sabinus back in Rome to serve as Prefect of the City. Not long after that, Nero's excesses sparked leading senators to rebel, and in 68 AD, seeing he no longer had any loyal friends, he committed suicide.

His place was taken by an army general called Galba. Some months later, however, in January 69 AD, Galba was slain in a coup d'état. The new emperor, Otho, rewarded his fellow conspirators generously with prefect posts. And the one to receive the highest of those offices was Sabinus, the brother of the general Vespasian whose legions had withdrawn from their siege of Jerusalem while their leader watched events unfold in Rome. Sabinus had evidently not retained his post of Prefect of the City under Galba (suggesting he probably had not backed that general) because as soon as Otho became emperor he was re-awarded that influential office. The first-century historian Tacitus tells us that this was because he had held it under Nero (see *Histories* I, 46). However, he makes it clear that the other prefect posts Otho dished out went to people who were consequently suspected of being his co-conspirators. For this reason, I think it is safe to assume that Sabinus played an even greater role than them in Galba's downfall.

Not everyone was happy with Otho's takeover though. Vitellius, the commander of several legions in Germany had been declared emperor by those legions shortly before Galba's assassination, and he now prepared to march on Rome. Taking council from his friend Sabinus (Vespasian's brother) and from other nobles whose eyes, according to Tacitus, were very probably on Vespasian, Otho set out to meet Vitellius in battle. At the end of his first largescale engagement, however, he lost heart, and to avoid further destruction of the flower of Rome's youth he committed suicide, leaving the emperorship to Vitellius.

In April 69 AD, Vitellius thus became the tenth *king* of the Roman empire (the last of the ten horns in Daniel 7). However, his reign would not last long. Vespasian in the east had been gathering support all this time whilst his friends and family in Rome had been making life difficult for each of the powerful senators who had attempted to establish themselves as emperor. In July he made his move. Having been declared emperor by his loyal legions, he seized control of the grain shipments from Egypt that Rome relied upon, and sent an army of his supporters sweeping towards Rome. The effectiveness of Vespasian's preparations in Rome became clear when all support for Vitellius evaporated, and the man himself was captured and executed while attempting to slip away unnoticed. Sabinus who had surprisingly retained his Prefect post under Vitellius also perished in Vespasian's battle for Rome. In December, 69 AD, the Senate recognised Vespasian as emperor

– their fourth emperor that year! – and he eventually headed to Italy, leaving his son Titus to finish the reconquest of Judea.

Vespasian was thus the *eleventh* ruler of the Roman empire to be granted a life-long tenure. This, of course, makes him the *eleventh king* of that empire – the king represented by the eleventh horn in the vision of Daniel 7 (page 71). Since this king's rise to power was the culmination of the so-called 'Year of the Four Emperors', it is astonishingly appropriate that three of the ten horns on the beast standing for the Roman empire get 'plucked up by the roots' as this eleventh horn emerges. That imagery alone is amazing!

The fact that these horns get plucked up by the roots is remarkably symbolic of the fact that neither Galba, Otho nor Vitellius were in the job long enough to lay down any roots – any achievements for which they might be remembered, or any dynastic successors. The small size of the eleventh horn is also remarkably symbolic of the fact that, in the eyes of many Romans at that time, Vespasian would have been regarded as quite illegitimate. Unlike all ten of the previous unlimited dictators, his father was never a senator, and his family had no distinguished history. The wealthy families from which Rome's previous rulers had come would have frowned at the appointment of this mere knight – nicknamed *the mule-breeder* – to the highest post in the land. He owed his generalship in the Roman army to merit alone (which is probably why Nero felt safe enough to assign the legions needed for the reconquest of Judea to him rather than to some high-ranking member of Rome's nobility).

So how did Vespasian persuade those powerful senators that he was worthy of this title? The answer is, he used lots of propaganda. He published divine omens that supposedly foretold his reign, built vast monuments to honour his own achievements, and even claimed he was the coming world-ruling king predicted in Jewish scripture! Yes. Remarkable as it may seem, he did indeed speak boastfully against the Jewish God, just like Daniel's eleventh horn.

Thus, just as Daniel 7 predicted, the eleventh king of the Roman empire was indeed 'different from his ten predecessors' (a very *little* horn). He subdued three of them. He was notably boastful and even equated himself with the Jewish Messiah ('Christ' in Greek) – thereby speaking against the Jewish God. And amazingly, he also waged war in person on the Jewish nation and defeated them just as the most justifiable interpretation of Daniel 7 predicted. He was one of only four kings of the Roman empire who could be said to have made war on the Jews in any largescale, reasonably-obvious way – and the first of only three to vanquish them.

I find that very remarkable.

It is also worth noting that from the moment his son Titus captured Jerusalem until the end of hostilities with the fall of the fortress of Masada was very probably just over three-and-a-half years (late August 70 AD to mid-April 74). That is the interpretation of the 'time, times and half a time' handing-over period that a literal reading of the text of Daniel best supports (Even the extra month-and-a-half can be justified since a reinterpretation of that phrase in Daniel 12:12 is *two* months over). I will be arguing in the next chapter that one can obtain a *more* justifiable meaning of that time-phrase when one takes the rest of the Old Testament into account, but that takes nothing away from the fact that the long-drawn-out conclusion of Vespasian's war does seem to fulfil that most straightforward interpretation. Judging from a reference (page 124) in St Jerome's *Commentary on Daniel* to a 'three-and-a-half year treaty' between Vespasian and the Jews, this may well have been what the Jewish historian Josephus who lived through these events believed (though I cannot find the comment Jerome was citing anywhere in the works of Josephus as they have come down to us).

Jerusalem fell during Vespasian's first full year as emperor, and his soldiers burned down the Jewish Temple making it very difficult for the Jews to hold their festivals. He is also reported to have spared the life of a famous rabbi responsible for reinterpreting the Jewish law in a way that did not require the Temple, which suggests to me that he really did 'think to change times and laws' as the most straightforward reading of the prophecy also predicted.

But the most amazing fact about Vespasian is that he almost certainly did subdue three of the previous ten kings of the Roman empire. Although it could be argued that Vespasian was only really responsible for subduing Vitellius in the Year of the Four Emperors, there is that strong evidence (page 81) from the Roman historian Tacitus that his brother was involved in the plot that resulted in Galba's death, and that he and his supporters were very probably acting with a view to Vespasian becoming emperor. And although Vespasian pledged his support for Otho against Vitellius, it is quite likely that he was just playing one powerful contender off against the other, thereby ensuring that one of them fell and the other was weakened in the process. The plot worked since many of Otho's disgruntled supporters fled to Vespasian's banners.

I find these facts absolutely astonishing. They fulfil what was definitely predicted in a very straightforward manner in the book of Daniel hundreds of years before it came to pass. With any other prophecy, its very existence would have been sure to lead to attempts being made to deliberately fulfil it. However, with this one, the nature of the predicted events pretty much rules this out.

No human being would have been in a position powerful enough, or with sufficient motivation, to ensure that exactly three emperors were accepted by the Senate and then toppled by Vespasian's supporters prior to Vespasian's own attempted takeover. And no human being could have guaranteed that Vespasian himself would not have suffered the same fate as his three immediate predecessors. The fact that all this came to pass just as the prophecy predicted – and in such a dramatic time-frame – is therefore robust evidence for the deliberate involvement of a powerful non-human intelligence in human history.

Unsurprisingly, people who do not want this to be widely recognised have tried to hide this fact with the claim that the idea that this was a prediction about the Roman empire is mistaken. They claim that the person who wrote the vision was really writing about the Macedonian (Greek) empire in the first half of the second century BC. They explain away the fact that *four* distinct empires are predicted in the dream by presupposing that the writer had an entirely different view of history from that which has come down to us (and from every ancient source we know of) in that he supposedly believed Babylon had fallen to an independent *Median* empire which was then conquered by Cyrus and the Persians.

Even if this were true, it would take nothing away from the miraculous fact that *true history* (or at least the history we currently *believe* to be true) was perfectly represented by this dream. However, those scholars neglect to mention that there is no evidence in the book of Daniel itself for such a view. By the time of Babylon's fall, the Persians and Medes were *a single empire under a single legal system*, 'the law of the Medes and Persians', and this is exactly what the book of Daniel indicates. King Darius the Mede, the conqueror of Babylon in Daniel 5 and its ruler in

Daniel 6, is clearly afraid to break these laws (by cancelling a decree he'd issued) despite knowing he'd been tricked into issuing that decree, and despite the fact that his most trusted and beloved servant (Daniel) was likely to be torn to pieces by hungry lions as a result. This does not sound like the king of an independent Median empire. The suggestions to that effect by critical scholars seem to me to gain zero support from the text of Daniel or from anywhere else. In the very next chapter of the book of Daniel (Daniel 8) the empires to come are named and clearly identified, and in that chapter it is the so-called *Medo-Persian* empire – the empire of Cyrus the Persian (who had usurped the Median throne as much as ten years previously) – that conquers Babylon.

We will leave that evidence from other parts of Daniel till later in this book because it is not in fact needed to establish beyond reasonable doubt that the writer of this prophecy was predicting a sequence of empires that extended *well beyond the Macedonian empire of Alexander the Great and his successors*. We can see this immediately from the imagery of Daniel 7 itself. Although we have already identified the leopardlikeness of the third beast in the sequence as symbolising the Dionysian religious beliefs that characterised the religion of the Macedonians, this was only because Alexander's Macedonian Empire (Greece) was the *third distinct nation* to dominate the world from the time of the vision, and the leopard is the *third distinct beast* in the dream. But a sceptic will say, how do we know that the writer of this prophecy didn't have a different understanding of history from that which has come down to us? Perhaps he believed Babylon had fallen to a different nation, which had then succumbed to the Persian onslaught, and that this other nation is the second beast in the dream, making Alexander's empire the fourth.

The reason we can know *for sure* from Daniel 7 that this is not the case is because the third beast – the leopard – is *split in four*. It has *four heads* and *four wings* (page 64). As any classical historian worth his salt will know, this is exactly what happened to the Macedonian (Greek) empire of Alexander the Great. By the middle of the third century BC that empire had split into four great kingdoms ruled by four separate Macedonian dynasties: the Ptolemies in Egypt, the Seleucids in Syria and Asia, the Antigonids in Macedon, and the Attalids in Pergamon (now Bergama in Turkey).

Not only is this four-way-split apparent from the history books, but it also clearly features in Daniel 8 and Daniel 11 (pages 222 and 224) where a four-part-divided nation is *named* as 'Greece'. Although Alexander's empire was ruled by kings descending from the aristocracy of the northern Greek nation-state of Macedon, the ancients clearly regarded it as the dominion of Greece. As we saw earlier, Macedon's capital Pella falls within the border of modern Greece, and the Macedonians regarded themselves as Greeks, and adopted Greek language, customs and religion. This is why scholars call the period of Macedonian dominance the 'Hellenistic Period' (the word 'Greece' comes from the more ancient pronunciation 'Hellas'). Hence the fact that Greece is specifically portrayed as a four-part-divided empire in both Daniel 8 and Daniel 11 is surely very strong grounds to conclude that a four-part-divided beast representing a world-dominant empire anywhere else in Daniel is also a portrayal of Greece. Wouldn't you agree?

In the light of this compelling evidence, to not accept that the leopard with four heads and four wings in Daniel 7 was meant to represent the four-part-divided Greek empire of Alexander the Great, when this is clearly what a straightforward comparison with history suggests, strikes me as being irrational. I suspect that the only reason many scholars of Daniel maintain such a position is because if one accepts the obvious conclusion, that the third beast – that four-headed leopard – *was* meant to be the Macedonian (Greek) empire, one is forced to acknowledge that the fourth beast in the sequence has to stand for the *Roman* empire. It simply cannot be argued to constitute one of the successor kingdoms of that Macedonian empire as those scholars would desperately like. That is because it is described as representing a kingdom that is 'different from all the former ones' and 'far more powerful'. Why would any writer emphasise the distinctness of this empire if he were referring to an empire that had emerged from the previous one and whose kings saw themselves as the successors of the founder of that previous empire, spoke the same language, worshipped the same gods and so on? And why would he emphasise the power of that fourth empire when both Daniel 8 and Daniel 11 portray the Macedonian successor kingdoms as being relatively *weak* in comparison to the united phase of the Macedonian empire under Alexander the Great?

Since those scholars believe the writer was writing in the second century BC, when Rome was *already* the most powerful nation in the world, if they were to acknowledge that the four-headed, four-winged leopard has to constitute the Macedonian empire (Greece), they would thereby make it impossible for themselves to coherently argue that the fourth empire is anything other than Rome. Yet they cannot deny that this is what careful readers of this prophecy in the second century BC were bound to conclude. If it was added to the book of Daniel with these readers in mind, as those scholars all claim, there is therefore an extremely high probability that this is precisely the conclusion they were *meant* to reach (a point I will cover in much more detail in chapters 7-9).

As we have seen, with that historically accurate and well-supported conclusion, the whole dream becomes an astonishingly specific prediction of the future that – incredibly – all came true, right on time, in the form of the Year of the Four Emperors (69 AD), one of the most historically salient political events of the first century. I personally believe that this accuracy can only be satisfactorily explained as the result of the deliberate intervention of a powerful nonhuman intelligence in human history. As the vision refers to just such an intelligence in the form of Daniel's God, I therefore have every reason to suspect that this is indeed a reference to the true author of this vision.

Fascinatingly, though, the events predicted in this dream are not just those that were fulfilled by the Year of the Four Emperors. The dream also includes the *destruction* of the fourth monster (like the pulverisation of the statue in Daniel 2). As we saw earlier, the animal imagery (the fact that the leopard was a popular symbol of the Greek god *Dionysus*, and the winged lion the Babylonian deity *Lamassu*) allows us to quite confidently interpret this event as the destruction of the *pagan Roman religion*, and its replacement by *Christianity* – the worship of a Son of Man honoured by the Jewish God predicted in Daniel 7:13 – which began in 312 AD.

In the next chapter I am going to show you why this may be a clue as to the true meaning of the strange time-phrase that the prophecy contains. As I said earlier, the claim that it means 'three-and-a-half years' is supported elsewhere in the book of Daniel. However, for reasons that will become clear in chapter 8, I think this was a diversionary tactic on the part of the prophecy's author – a deliberate ambiguity designed to save lives and reduce suffering. As you will see shortly, there is a very obvious and far more justifiable interpretation of that time-phrase, and that interpretation just happens to make it span precisely the time over which the devout followers of Daniel's God were given into the hand of the ruler (or rulers, as it turns out) that the eleventh horn in the dream represents. Surprisingly, this interpretation was even backed up, long *before* then, by Christ himself in Mark 13 and Matthew 24.

But before we look at that interpretation of Christ's, let me remind you of what we have discovered here and the effect it had on my faith. All serious scholars agree that the book of Daniel was complete with this prophecy in it by the mid-second century *BC*. The early church fathers didn't recognise its fulfilment, so it cannot have been later doctored to match history. It is the most justifiable interpretation of the prophecy that came true. And the predicted events are so specific that their fulfilment cannot be reasonably put down to chance. Yet they are also so momentous that they couldn't have been deliberately brought about by humans.

When I realised this, and read the evidence in Tacitus' *Histories* (see page 81) that Vespasian's supporters were probably responsible for the deaths of Galba and Otho as well as Vitellius, it suddenly dawned on me that here was objective evidence that Christ was from God. One cannot explain away the accuracy of this prediction. From that moment on, I have never had any more doubts about the reality of the God of Jesus Christ and the truth of the Gospel. Hence, if you agree with me that the most justifiable definition of king is 'a ruler of a nation who has no limit on his time in office', then you too can be absolutely confident that the gospel of Jesus Christ is from God. You need no longer have any doubts. The fulfilment of that 'eleventh king' prediction is the perfect divine signature on the Four Kingdoms prophecy that all but proves it was fulfilled by God, and a part of that astonishing fulfilment we've not yet fully explored was the rise of Christianity.

CHAPTER FOUR

A Century and Three Quarters on the Dot

Having carefully and sensitively explained where he stood on the subject of whether or not it was wrong to have an abortion, the male pastor put the slip of paper containing that tricky question onto the "done" pile and looked at the next one up.

"What is meant by the phrase 'a time, times and half a time' in Daniel 7?".

He chuckled as he read out my anonymous question to the assembly of inquisitive churchgoers. The majority responded sympathetically, before settling down to see what his answer would be.

It was a fantastic new way of doing church. A new initiative I had never seen before in evangelical or mainstream churches, and one that is, in my view, extremely important in modern times for encouraging new people to take an interest in the gospel of Jesus.

Experienced Christians can often ask the questions that trouble them at home-groups or one-to-one discussions. But those who are new to the church rarely have that opportunity or feel able to advance such questions. The brilliant stroke of genius of this pastor was to hold an evening meeting where anyone could write their question for him anonymously on a piece of paper and place it in a box. He then went through them one-by-one trying to answer them as best he could.

It was a brilliant idea. The brevity ensured by written questions permitted an excellent range of points to be covered, and I learned a lot from those questions and answers. They especially illustrated the sea of doubt that heaved not far beneath the cold, blindingly-white surface of the church's doctrines on scripture. The warmth of the summer of scientific knowledge was clearly melting that surface in places, and people were finding it hard to stay on their feet. Worse still, cracks were beginning to appear. The freezing abyss beneath threatened to engulf those who stumbled, as it had done to many a devout Christian in the past whose increasing knowledge about science or church history, the origin of scripture, or merely the unfairness of life's tragedies and unanswered prayers, had caused them to lose confidence in the Gospel's claim to divine endorsement. Even I knew of one or two who had become enthusiastic believers at university, and who now, looking back, saw that phase of their lives as merely an embarrassing adherence to claims they had not fully thought through and now considered unjustified – the exuberance of youth now checked by the wisdom and knowledge they had since acquired.

Of course, many believers will no doubt manage to simply walk on that water as Peter did on lake Galilee, their faith buoyed up by their certainty of Christ's presence and power. However, even

Peter did not manage that strength of faith for long, and the more inquisitive among us may well need the security of a vessel to keep them afloat as they explore this new and perilous terrain. I believe that just as God encouraged Noah to build his Ark to ensure the survival of himself and his family (together with numerous species of animal who went in two-by-two), God is encouraging us to seek a proper understanding of the book of Daniel, and the extent of its fulfilment in history. He wants us to do this to ensure *our* survival – the continuation of the faith that, according to the Gospel, guarantees us eternal life. Only that ancient text provides the robust evidence of the Gospel's authenticity that many of us will need in order to stay afloat as that sea of knowledge begins to wash over us. Only an appreciation of the true accuracy of Daniel's prophecies of Christ, will prevent some of us being swept away when those waves of information dislodge us from the security of the temporary scaffolding of overly simplistic assumptions on which our faith was built.

Even if we are lucky enough to possess a sufficiently buoyant faith already, we may still need this life-boat to rescue *others* from the waves. Remember, Christ called us to be fishers of men. I suspect the book of Daniel is the boat from which we can safely cast our nets. After all, it must be important or God would not have gone to the considerable trouble of creating it, and ensuring the fulfilment of certain prophecies that it contains. These prophecies were by no means easy to fulfil, and as we shall see in chapters 7-10, he has also included within it a datable seal and a key to unlock its mysteries. He has not gone to this much trouble so that we can just ignore it or blindly rely on the opinions of others.

"Well," the pastor answered with a shrug, "I have no idea what it means. And if anyone tells you that they do, don't believe them!".

The congregation laughed appreciatively at this good-humoured and honest admission. How many of them were aware of that strange phrase in the book of Daniel, I do not know. But for me, the pastor's advice seemed overly pessimistic.

It is true that the mysterious features of the prophecies in the book of Daniel have prompted a large number of different interpretations, some of which have even been claimed to predict events in modern times. People have done this frequently throughout the two millennia since those prophecies were first widely circulated (and perhaps even before), reinterpreting them to suit the times in which they lived, or their political or religious ideology. So, I can totally understand where the pastor was coming from.

Nevertheless, if scripture is God's word – as that pastor claimed to believe – God presumably had some good reason for including that prophecy in the book of Daniel and using that strange time-phrase within it. And if that reason was not just to confuse his followers and lead them astray into all sorts of false hopes, which is not the nature of the Christian God, there had to be a correct interpretation of that time-phrase which people were not seeing simply because they were not interpreting the prophecy in the most justifiable way – the way God's word was telling them to interpret it.

That of course would not apply if this prophecy did *not* come from God. However, by the time I attended that "grill the pastor" church meeting, I was absolutely convinced that the rest of the prophecy where that time-phrase first appears in the book of Daniel had come true in a totally astonishing and inexplicable way. The prophecy in question is Daniel 7, the one we looked at in the previous chapter. As we discovered in that chapter, the most justifiable interpretation of its prediction about the eleventh king of the Roman empire subduing three before him and making war upon the Jews was dramatically fulfilled by the Year of the Four Emperors (69 AD). Moreover, the arrival of the 'everlasting worldwide kingdom' predicted by both Daniel 7 and Daniel 2, which is most justifiably interpreted as the conquest of the *religion* of Rome by a new religion formed out of Judaism, was also completely fulfilled. It was fulfilled by the rise of Christianity to political dominance in the fourth century AD. I therefore felt very confident that the 'time, times and half a time', which appeared to denote a time of persecution somewhere in between these events, must refer to something specific and historical whose fulfilment ought now to be evident from history.

In this chapter I will tell you what I think that is; and more importantly, I will show you why I think my proposal is fully justified by the rest of the Bible. Something I find quite surprising is that I first arrived at this view from my initial interpretation of Daniel 12:7, the *other* instance where this time-phrase occurs in the book of Daniel. The irony is that, in the case of that passage, I no longer consider that initial interpretation to be justifiable.

Daniel 12:7 is situated near the end of the detailed vision of Daniel 10-12. As the Appendix of this book demonstrates, this vision portrays, relatively accurately, the history of the first six *Syrian wars* between the Seleucid and Ptolemaic kingdoms, which were two of the four Greek kingdoms that emerged from Alexander the Great's Macedonian empire. These kingdoms were respectively centred to the north (Syria) and south (Egypt) of the Jewish homeland of Judea (Israel), and they frequently fought each other over that territory and its neighbouring lands. The prophecy in Daniel 10-12 portrays these conflicts up until the Seleucid persecution of the Jews which began with an attack on Jerusalem in 168 BC, and which resulted in the revolt of the Jewish freedom fighter Judas Maccabeus. After describing that persecution, a linen-clad messenger-angel with metallic limbs and torch-like eyes who has just narrated the prophecy whilst hovering above the river Tigris gets asked by another angel, "How long will it be to the end of **these wonders?**" (Daniel 12:6). Daniel then tells the reader,

> **DAN 12:** [7] I heard the man clothed in linen, who was above the waters of the river, when he held up his right hand and his left hand to heaven, and swore by him who lives forever that "it will be for a time, times, and a half; and when they have finished breaking in pieces **the power of the holy people**, all these things will be finished."

At the time, I assumed that 'these wonders' in verse 6 referred to the whole of the 'great war' that the prophecy claimed to be about (i.e. the Greek conquest of Persia and all the Syrian wars put together), the most obvious beginning of which was the moment Alexander the Great became 'king of all Greece' in 335 BC. That is undoubtedly the most justifiable interpretation of Daniel 11:3, where it says, 'A mighty king will arise who will rule with great dominion and do according to his will'. Since the prophecy then says, 'After he has arisen, his kingdom will be…divided toward the four winds of the sky', we know that his kingdom is *Greece* (i.e. the Macedonian Empire which split into four kingdoms), as indeed the rest of the prophecy clearly confirms. So it has to be Alexander the Great.

Led – or perhaps *mis*led – by my initial interpretation of the phrase 'these wonders', I therefore looked for the first major event after the Seleucid attack on Jerusalem that happened to fit the description 'they have finished breaking in pieces the power of the holy people' (where the holy people were obviously the Jewish faithful). It seemed immediately apparent to me that this was the defeat and death of that very successful Jewish freedom fighter, Judas Maccabeus, which took place in 160 BC, 175 years after the rise of Alexander the Great. 'Maccabeus' meant 'the hammer', and most Jews would probably agree that he would at that time have been quite fittingly described as 'the power of the holy people'.

For reasons I will leave until chapter 8, I now think this argument is misguided. I think the phrase 'these wonders' was intended to refer to a much more limited part of the prophecy, and I think the phrase 'a time, times and a half' was being used by the writer of that prophecy to refer to the time for that very limited set of events, which lasted just over three-and-a-half years. Nevertheless, rather bizarrely, I have come to the conclusion that 'three-and-a-half years' is *not* what the same time-phrase in Daniel 7 is most justifiably interpreted to mean. Surprisingly, I *still* think that God meant us to interpret that time-phrase as 175 years, *but not for the reasons I have given here!* I think that this meaning is justified by *other* scriptures that the Old Testament contains, and it is justified to a far greater extent by those scriptures than the 'three-and-a-half year' interpretation is justified by the text of the book of Daniel.

The rest of this chapter will explain why. If you are at present confused by this claim and wondering why I appear to be deviating from what is seemingly the most justifiable view (that the time-phrase means the same thing in both passages), don't worry. There are very good reasons for expecting that time-phrase to have *different* meanings in these two passages, though unfortunately I must leave these reasons until chapter 8. This chapter will, however, explain why the meaning of this phrase in Daniel 7 is most probably '175 years'. And it will also show that God had an extremely good reason to make this fact not immediately obvious to the readers of this book. As you will see, God's motive for doing this was not to deceive but to protect. It was forward planning of the thoughtful and loving sort typical of the teaching of Jesus Christ. And that same protective thinking also perfectly explains why the dominant nations in this prophecy are unnamed.

For some time after I recognised the significance of Daniel 2 and Daniel 7 I was troubled by the fact that the empires in these visions aren't specified by name. If God can really see into the future, or – more probably in my opinion – *bring about* events in the future that *fulfilled* the predictions of his chosen prophets, surely he would know the names of those empires. So why has he not removed all possibility of disagreement about the identity of the fourth empire in this dream by telling Daniel that the second is Persia, the third is Greece, and the fourth is Rome?

The answer, however, had been lying under my nose in the book of Daniel all this time. It is found in Daniel 11:14 which says simply,

> **DAN 11:** [14] "In those times many will rise up against the king of the south. Also the children of the violent among your people will rise up to establish the vision; but they will fall."

The events being alluded to in this prophecy took place at the end of the third century BC. This is obvious from the rest of the prophecy detailed in the Appendix to this book. But what is interesting is the mention of the Jews 'rising up to establish the vision'. It is not clear what vision this refers to, but what we can deduce from this is that, in those days at least, people did act violently to try to fulfil visions (or to prevent them being fulfilled as the case may be). This fact almost certainly explains why a loving God might choose not to identify people or nations by name in such visions. If people or nations were named, they would very quickly become the target of those who did not want the prophecy to be fulfilled, and could suffer intense hardship, persecution, and perhaps even death, as a result.

The amazing thing about Daniel 2 and Daniel 7 is that they allow the nations they speak of to be unambiguously identified, but only *after* they have risen to power and dominance. This would prevent those nations being crushed out of existence by the reigning superpower before they got their chance on the world stage, and it would not have been possible had those empires been named.

As you will see in this chapter, the same reluctance to cause unnecessary suffering and distress may also account for why the time-period in Daniel 7 is somewhat ambiguous. It is given as 'a time, times and half a time', and as I mentioned before, we know that this phrase was ambiguous or obscure to its early readers because it occurs again in Daniel 12:7-8 and there the prophet Daniel himself claims not to understand its meaning.

On the other hand, there is a very obvious meaning for that time-period – the 'three-and-a-half years' view mentioned earlier – which can be fully justified from the text of Daniel, and fits perfectly the duration of the historical event alluded to in Daniel 12. Yet from the perspective of Jewish history, the length of time thereby obtained seems far too short for what it is meant to measure in Daniel 7. Fascinatingly, the only other length for that time-period that can be justified from the text of Daniel turns out to be *exactly the right length*. And intriguingly, it seems to cover precisely the time-period indicated by Christ's reference to Daniel in Mark 13:14-30. About that time-period Christ says, 'Unless the Lord had shortened the days, no flesh would have been saved; but for the sake of the chosen ones, whom he picked out, he shortened the days.' I believe the rest of this chapter will show you what that time-phrase *really* signified – what it signified *before* its most justifiable meaning was 'shortened' by God as Jesus informs us.

Out of all the Old Testament prophets, Daniel is unique. The prophecies in the book of Daniel are the only ones that are specific enough and time-limited enough for their fulfilment by chance to be unlikely. And it is the only book where some of the prophecies predict events that, at face value, lie beyond the latest date at which scholars believe the book we now have was completed. This was what first got me interested in this prophet, and it was recognised as long ago as St Jerome in the early fifth century AD, and even by Josephus as far back as the first century AD. In no uncertain terms, Jerome tells us,

> 'None of the prophets has so clearly spoken concerning Christ as has this prophet Daniel. For not only did he assert that He would come, a prediction common to the other prophets as well, but also he set forth the very time at which He would come. Moreover he went through the various kings in order, stated the actual number of years involved, and announced beforehand the clearest signs of events to come.'

(St Jerome's *Commentary on Daniel*, translated by Gleason L. Archer, 1958, p.15)

Little did Jerome know just how right this statement would prove to be. As we saw in the previous chapter, the early church fathers, which included St Jerome, thought that the most obvious interpretation of Daniel 7 hadn't come to pass, and, rather than admit this, they proposed an alternative interpretation – in fact *several* alternative interpretations. Since those didn't limit the predicted events to any narrow window of time, they weren't unlikely to come true, and they are therefore, in my view, of little interest. What those church fathers didn't realise was that the really obvious and straightforward interpretation of that prophecy had in fact come true exactly as it was written. There had in fact been exactly ten kings of the Roman empire prior to Vespasian, and he almost certainly had subdued the three kings before him (if only by the fact that his presence as a powerful rival candidate prompted people to act against those other emperors on his behalf, though he probably did play a far more active role than this).

One possible reason those church fathers didn't see this was the fact that classical historians did not count the dictator Sulla as a king of Rome, even though he was granted similar lifelong powers to Augustus. Another, though, may have been the fact that Vespasian's war was against the Jews of Judea, rather than a specific oppression of Christians.

Since Daniel himself was a Jew, the term 'holy people' in the prophecy should almost certainly be interpreted as either 'the Jewish nation' or 'devout worshippers of the Jewish God'. Christians do come under the latter category, but it is clearly not limited to that sect of the Jewish faith, so Vespasian's conquest of Judea *definitely does* count as a fulfilment. By the time of Jerome, though, Jews and Christians were rival religions, and other church leaders would have been highly critical of any interpretation of Daniel 7 that allowed the term 'holy people' to embrace Jews as well as Christians. After all, it was clearly not the Jews who had inherited the Roman empire as the holy people were predicted to in Daniel 7:27. For Jerome, the holy people could only be Christians.

As you will see in this chapter, such a restricted view of the holy people makes it impossible to recognise the moment when those holy people were 'given into the hand' of the king represented by the eleventh horn. Only by recognising that moment in history can one discover the astonishing *second* match between prediction and history that Daniel 7 contains.

Let us begin our search for that handing over point by reminding ourselves that the eleventh horn, which started small and uprooted three of the ten, has to be identified as the actual eleventh king to rule over the Roman empire (i.e. Vespasian). If one allowed it to be just any king, the subduing of those three kings would not be a specific prophecy (and any fulfilment couldn't therefore be considered surprising). Nevertheless, within this prophecy no further horns are mentioned prior to the destruction of the beast. Are we to conclude from this that the prophet simply got the timing of the rise of Christianity wrong, locating it at the end of the reign of Vespasian rather than at the beginning of the reign of Constantine I (230 years and fifty emperors later)?

You may be interested to know that there is another possibility. Puzzlingly, Daniel sees (or remembers) this horn a second time in the vision, saying it was 'more imposing [stout] than its fellows' (verse 20) – which seems to conflict with its earlier description as 'a little one' (verse 8). Could it be that the continuous line of pagan Roman emperors after Vespasian are in fact represented by this later imposing appearance of that same eleventh horn? (After all, there'd have been little head-space for fifty more horns – a problem perhaps solved by introducing more-compact symbolism).

Well, there is one other clue that suggests this is indeed what the divine author of this prophecy intended, and that is the fact that this eleventh horn, while still small, gains both a mouth and a pair of eyes.

> **DAN 7:** [8] "I considered the horns, and behold, there came up among them another horn, a little one, before which three of the first horns were plucked up by the roots: and behold, in this horn were eyes like the eyes of a man, and a mouth speaking great things."

Commentators generally conflate the mouth and eyes as a single symbolic feature suggesting the humanness of the horn's referent or illustrating the boastfulness of the eleventh king. But it seems to me that these are two distinct symbolic features standing for different referents. The mouth clearly suggests the boastfulness mentioned in the interpretation, and in view of this I think it has to be interpreted as representing the boastful king that the interpretation describes. But why represent that king with the mouth if he is already represented by the horn itself? Well one reason could be that the horn at this point no longer stands for that single eleventh king, and this view seems to be supported by the appearance of the eyes. Those eyes do not seem to stand for *any* feature of that king in the given interpretation. As an uninterpreted aspect of the imagery with the same horn-embedded status as the mouth representing the eleventh king, they suggest to me a later notable king whose most characteristic feature involved seeing rather than boasting.

In view of the number of those pagan emperors that succeeded Vespasian, it is probably not all that surprising that this description does apply most prominently to one of them (though it is rather intriguing that it singles out *only* one). That emperor was Hadrian, the ruler after whom Hadrian's Wall in the north of England is named. He became famous for spending most of his long reign touring all over his vast empire to see it with his own eyes. Thus, eyes are an extremely suitable symbol for that particular emperor – but as I said, that by itself isn't all that surprising. What *is* really surprising is that this emperor, like Vespasian, *fought against and conquered the Jews of Judea*, and he also passed laws specifically banning the Jewish calendar and law (Note the reference to times and laws in the prophecy, page 72). In fact, his plans to rebuild Jerusalem as a Roman colony under Roman law, and presumably not hosting Jewish festivals, are probably what caused that war.

In 132 AD, the Jews of Judea declared themselves independent from Rome for the second time since the Romans first occupied their land. Over the next three years Hadrian (only the sixth emperor from Vespasian) fought a bloody campaign against them which, despite severe initial setbacks, ended in total victory for the Romans. Other than Vespasian (with his son Titus), Hadrian is *the only emperor to have done this*, and it was his victory that resulted in the Jewish nation being expelled from their homeland in the spring of 136 AD and thereby becoming a stateless people.

As a historically salient event (an event like "The Year of the Four Emperors", the destructions of Jerusalem by Titus and Nebuchad-nezzar, the famous fall of Babylon, or Alexander's conquest of Persia) this seems to me to be the event that best fits the first part of the description **The holy people 'will be given into his hand** until a time, times and half a time' (Daniel 7:25, page 72). As I pointed out earlier, the words 'holy people' in this context refer either to devout followers of Daniel's God (Daniel himself, for example) or to the Jewish Nation or both. Although there are several events from Titus' capture of Jerusalem until the last Roman persecution of Christians that could fit such a description, only this one resulted in the holy people having a powerless status with respect to the Roman emperors that they did not previously have. They had indeed been 'given into their hands'. After the fall of Jerusalem in 70 AD, the Jews who had not opposed Vespasian were treated relatively well. They did not have to hide their holy books, or break their sacred laws. And although they no longer had a religious centre, they were not kicked out of their homeland or prevented from worshipping in Jerusalem's ruins. They lived alongside their Roman occupiers much as they had done before.

That was not the case after Hadrian's conquests. His losses had been so high, he sought revenge. As well as massacring the Jews in large numbers, he expelled many from their homeland, and forbade them entry to Jerusalem on pain of death. He then rebuilt that city as a Roman colony named *Aelia Capitolina* after himself and the Roman God Jupiter Capitolinus. Their land he renamed *Palestine* in honour of their historical enemies (the Philistines), and he prohibited the Jewish Law and calendar – all to ensure that the 'holy people' would never again pose a military threat to Rome. From that time until Constantine I, the followers of Daniel's God – both Jews and Christians – had no military or political power and were frequently the target of state-sponsored persecution.

That all changed with the victory of the first Christian emperor Constantine over Maxentius in 312 AD. From then on, devout followers of Daniel's God had the protection and blessing of the Roman emperors. If the eleventh horn stands for the pagan Roman emperors from Vespasian to Maxentius, the dominion of that horn did indeed get taken away by the holy people in 312 AD (Daniel 7:26, page 72). Those people did 'consume and destroy it to the end'. And the people of those holy people – their supporters – really did receive that kingdom at that moment in history.

In fact, in the spring of the previous year the emperor Galerius had issued a decree forbidding the persecution of Christians, and thereby officially bringing to an end the longest and most severe period of persecution. That decree is known as 'The Edict of Toleration' and it officially ended The Great Persecution – a time of immense and prolonged suffering for Christians begun eight years earlier by the emperor Diocletian. In view of this, the time of hardship indicated by the 'handing over' of the holy people to the kings represented by the imposing phase of the eleventh horn in Daniel 7, which lasted for 'a time, times and half a time', whatever that may mean, is most obviously fulfilled by the period of statelessness, persecution and lack of legal protection that the Jews and Christians endured from the moment Hadrian expelled them from Judea until Galerius Edict of Toleration officially ended the last period of state-sponsored persecution of Christianity.

So, if this vision was from God as the accuracy of its prediction of the Year of the Four Emperors clearly suggests, what was the point in calling that time-period 'a time, times and half a time'? In view of the fact that the Aramaic word translated 'time', here, is similar to the Aramaic word for 'year', many people have argued that it just means 'three-and-a-half years'. And indeed, several three-and-a-half year periods have been put forward as candidates for this time of hardship. From Vespasian's invasion of Galilee until the fall of Jerusalem in 70 AD was about three-and-a-half years. From the fall of Jerusalem to the capture of the last enclave of Jewish resistance at Masada was probably just over three-and-a-half years. The rebellion against Hadrian lasted exactly three-and-a-half years. Even the persecution of the Jews by the Macedonian king of Syria at the time many scholars think the book of Daniel was completed lasted exactly three-and-a-half years (at least according to Josephus

– it is hard to know if this last claim was based upon accurate records or merely an attempt by Josephus to fit history to his interpretation of a time frame obtained from the twelfth chapter of the book of Daniel where this strange phrase recurs).

Nevertheless, I think there are several very good reasons to doubt that 'three-and-a-half years' was the intended meaning of this phrase in Daniel 7. For a start, when this phrase appears (in its Hebrew translation) in Daniel 12:7-8, it is in a very different context, and in that passage the prophet Daniel claims that he 'did not understand' its meaning. If that phrase really had the straightforward translation suggested by replacing the 'times' with 'years', its meaning is hardly difficult to understand, and Daniel's confusion here doesn't make much sense. In fact, if the aim of the author of the prophecy was to make the time-period a puzzle (perhaps to reduce the potential for the holy people to suffer even further at the hands of a nation who did not want its religion to be wiped out), if that time-period was meant to be three-and-a-half years, that author hasn't done a particularly good job! Almost everyone thinks that this is what that time-phrase means.

A second and more compelling reason to dismiss this interpretation is that three-and-a-half years is hardly a respectable time of hardship in Jewish history. It doesn't even come close to the top three. The Israelites under Moses wandered the desert for *forty* years, they spent an even longer period as slaves of the Pharaohs of Egypt, and they lived as exiles in Babylon for at least *forty-six* years (possibly as much as the magic *seventy* for some Jewish families). In comparison, three-and-a-half years at the mercy of the kings of the Roman empire is hardly a very frightening prediction. And yet, that time of hardship is most probably what is described by Jesus Christ in Mark 13:19 as 'oppression, such as there has not been the like from the beginning of the creation which God created until now, and never will be'. Mark 13:14-20 says the following (Matthew 24:15-22 is almost identical to this):

> **MARK 13**: [14] "But when you see the abomination of desolation, spoken of by Daniel the prophet, standing where it ought not (let the reader understand), then let those who are in Judea flee to the mountains, [15] and let him who is on the housetop not go down, nor enter in, to take anything out of his house. [16] Let him who is in the field not return back to take his cloak. [17] But woe to those who are with child and to those who nurse babies in those days! [18] Pray that your flight won't be in the winter. [19] For in those days there will be oppression, such as there has not been the like from the beginning of the creation which God created until now, and never will be. [20] Unless the Lord had shortened the days, no flesh would have been saved; but for the sake of the chosen ones, whom he picked out, he shortened the days."

We know Christ is referring to Daniel 7 here, because he later says that after this the son of man will come on a cloud as Daniel 7:13 predicts (page 66). Yet it suggests a time of hardship much longer than three-and-a-half years. And interestingly, as you will discover in chapter 5, the events leading up to it recall the time of Hadrian rather than Vespasian. The 'abomination of desolation' can only refer to Daniel 9:27, where it predicts the raising of a foreign idol by the Roman ruler who 'puts an end to Jewish sacrifice and offering'. That ruler St Jerome tells us was Hadrian, not Vespasian.

So, let us forget about replacing the word 'time' with the word 'year' and look instead in the Jewish Law for a more respectable possibility. There are in fact *two* options for longish time periods that the Jews had to observe: A seven-year "week" required by Leviticus 25:1-7, and a fifty-year 'Jubilee' period that Leviticus 25:8-10 demands. Of course, using the first of these will only make the 'time, times and half a time' amount to twenty-four-and-a-half years, only around half the time the Jews spent as exiles in Babylon. Moreover, those seven-year weeks seem to be denoted in Daniel 9 by the word 'sevens', not 'times'. So let us try the second.

Fifty, plus two fifties, plus half of fifty, is 175. Hence, under the straightforward assumption that the times are actually the fifty-year Jubilee periods of Leviticus 25:8-10, we get an interval of 175 years for the meaning of 'a time, times and half a time'. This is somewhat longer than all previous periods of hardship in Jewish history. It also emerges from the same passage in Leviticus that yields the 'seven-year weeks' – a unit of time that is clearly used in Daniel 9:24-27 (as you will see in chapter 5). As a result, 175 years is by far the most *justifiable* meaning for that time-phrase in Daniel 7:25, and it is thus the predicted length of the terrible persecution.

In view of this, I find it quite astonishing that from the time Hadrian exiled the Jews from Judea in the spring of 136 AD until Galerius Edict of Toleration in the spring of 311 AD which ended the last Roman persecution of Christians, the Jews and Christians suffered exactly 175 years of hardship and sporadic state-sponsored persecution, with no effective means of resistance to their oppressors. It was exactly 'a time, times and half a time'.

Although not as incredible a fulfilment of prophecy as the Year of the Four Emperors, I still find this match between the most probable meaning of that time-period and the history of the holy people quite stunning. It is yet further evidence that the predictions in this passage have been deliberately fulfilled by a powerful nonhuman intelligence. Although our decision to interpret the imposing phase of the eleventh horn as a succession of pagan emperors whose mouth is Vespasian and whose eyes symbolise Hadrian may seem somewhat contrary to our commitment to interpret the prophecy in the most obvious way, the uninterpreted features of the imagery (the eyes and imposing nature of that horn) do in my view allow such an extension of the given interpretation. And as you will discover to your astonishment in chapter 5, there is an equally specific prophecy two chapters later in the book of Daniel, and it accurately predicts not only the expulsion of the Jews by Hadrian but the very time of Hadrian's death.

One last question that may have occurred to you is why would a God capable of ensuring the fulfilment of such a prophecy not just make the time-period explicit? Why didn't the author of this prophecy just say that the holy people will be given into the hand of the kings represented by the eleventh horn for one hundred and seventy-five years? Moreover, why did the angel interpreting the imagery for Daniel not mention the eyes on the eleventh horn? Why did he or she forget to mention that the imposing phase of the eleventh horn stands for a *line* of kings rather than just one?

Just imagine what would have happened if the prophecy had said these things explicitly. This fact would almost certainly have come to the attention of the Romans. Vespasian's reconquest of Judea would probably have ensured this. But if not, the locals persecuted by the Jewish forces rebelling against Hadrian, sixty years later, would surely have brought such a damning prophecy to Hadrian's ears. It would then have been publicised throughout the Roman Empire as another reason for Romans to rid themselves of this troublesome threat to their religion, and perhaps to the empire itself – a people who had rebelled three times already. As well as the two revolts in Judea that I've mentioned, they had also led a widespread rebellion out-with Judea in 115-117 AD – a major insurrection that became known as the *Kitos war* after the Roman general aptly named Quietus who suppressed it. An explicit 175-year prophecy of the holy people taking over the Roman Empire would thus have played into the hand of their oppressors. As the countdown got closer and closer to the finishing point, the persecution of the holy people would have intensified, and it is very likely that a campaign of brutal ethnic cleansing would have led to the complete eradication of both Jews and Christians from the lands that constituted the Roman Empire. Moreover, nations beyond its boundaries would probably have followed suit as a means of ingratiating themselves with the Romans and denying them any reason to invade. The Jews and Christians would thus have been totally wiped out. None would have survived. By writing this vision in a way that made everyone think the time-period for the conquest of Rome was just three-and-a-half years from the victory of Vespasian, the author of this vision ensured that if this prophecy did become widely known to the Romans, they would all think that it had simply failed to come true.

It is thus interesting that, in speaking about this predicted time of hardship, as we saw on page 108, Jesus Christ tells his followers:

> "Unless the Lord had shortened the days, no flesh would have been saved; but for the sake of the chosen ones, whom he picked out, he shortened the days." (Mark 13:20)

I suspect that this shortening that Christ is referring to is not actually God deciding to reduce the time of trouble to a mere 175 years. I think Christ is hinting at how the writing (or editing) of this prediction in the book of Daniel has let everyone *think* that this time is much shorter. He is telling us that this has been done so that the persecution would not be so severe and continuous that none of the Jews or Christians would survive it. The words 'no flesh' in Mark 13:20 do not therefore mean 'no human beings' or 'no animal life' as modern readers might think. They mean that none of the persecuted people would have *physically* survived it, despite the fact that many would still be *spiritually* saved for eternal life.

Whatever you think about this hypothesis, what should not be in doubt is the fact that the 'time, times and half a time' is clearly best interpreted as the interval from Hadrian's expulsion of the Jews (in 136 AD) until the Edict of Toleration in 311. That time of hardship turned out to be exactly 175 years long – which is astonishing in view of the fact that this same number emerges when the 'times' are taken to be the fifty-year Jubilee periods of Leviticus 25:8-10 (the longest of the two or three possibilities that the Law of Moses offers, and the one most clearly supported by Daniel 9:24-27).

The following year, the Roman Emperor Constantine I 'saw the sign of the Son of Man in the sky' according to the fourth century bishop Eusebius of Caesarea who heard it from the man himself, and who tells us that Constantine swore an oath that it was true (*Life of Constantine,* book I, ch.28). After experiencing a dream in which Christ told him "with this sign you will conquer", he had that sign painted onto his soldiers' shields and incorporated into his army's standard, the Labarum, in the hope that it would lead them to victory in his upcoming battle with his rival Maxentius.

I find it quite intriguing that Matthew's version of that prophecy of Christ's actually mentions a 'sign of the Son of Man' appearing in the sky. In Matthew 24:29-30, Christ says,

MATT 24: [29] But immediately after the oppression of those days, the sun will be darkened, the moon will not give its light, the stars will fall from the sky, and the powers of the heavens will be shaken; [30] and then the sign of the Son of Man will appear in the sky. Then all the tribes of the earth will mourn…

The statement that 'the powers of the heavens will be shaken' here could easily refer to the destruction of the pagan gods (who were often identified with celestial bodies). However, if like me you suspect that this prediction was fulfilled by Constantine's victories and his consequent sponsorship of Christianity, the literal meaning of that statement might even have come about. That is because evidence of a modest-sized meteoroid impact in central Italy at around that time (the Sirente crater) has recently been discovered, and ancient oral traditions from the area do appear to associate its conversion with just such a catastrophe. They describe a star getting bigger and bigger, a terrible heat and fire destroying the pagan idols, and finally the sun coming up on the Sirente valley to reveal only the glistening Madonna and child (Santilli et al, *A Catastrophe Remembered*, Antiquity, vol.77, no.296, 2003, p.317).

Some scientists have very reasonably postulated that the sign Constantine described seeing in the sky, and which his whole army also apparently witnessed, could easily have been the arrival of that meteoroid seen from a great distance. However, they usually suggest that this means that the resultant change in the course of history cannot be attributed to God. I do not agree with this suggestion. In fact, I think it is quite misleading because, remember, it was not the sign itself that prompted Constantine to act, if his testimony is to be believed. It was the dream that followed it. And he still had to *defeat* Maxentius.

Constantine's victory that day at the battle of the Milvian Bridge ensured that the eyes of all who came in contact with his legions thence forth would see the sign of the Son of Man. Beginning in the western half of the Roman empire and extending throughout the world, the fortunes of the holy people (or at least those conforming to Constantine's version of Christianity) were transformed in an instant. Churches became powerful institutions, their leaders international statesmen, even the emperors sought their blessing and at times forgiveness, and the people in large numbers gave up their pagan gods and embraced Christianity. They bowed down to the Son of Man just as Daniel 7 – written more than half a millennium before – said they would. And most astonishingly, this bowing to the Son or Man began shortly after the end of a period of exactly *one hundred and seventy-five years* over which the holy people (the followers of the Jewish God) were stateless subjects of pagan Roman Emperors with no legal protection against religious persecution by those emperors. In other words, it fulfilled the most justifiable meaning of the 'time, times and half a time' over which the holy people would be 'given into the hand' of the emperors represented by the eleventh horn on the fourth monster in Daniel 7.

If that isn't divine endorsement of Christianity, what is? Could this level of accuracy in a prophecy written long before the events that fulfilled it really be just chance? If you suspect that might still be a possibility, then read on. In the next chapter I will tell you about another prophecy of Rome's emperors in the book of Daniel where the predicted events are set in an even narrower window of time than those of Daniel 7. And yet, as with Daniel 7, they all came true right on time. Hence, even if you are still sceptical at this stage, I remain confident that by the end of chapter 5 you too, like me, will be a believer. The book of Daniel will have done its job.

CHAPTER FIVE

A lot can happen in Seven Years!

As a child I learned to play the bagpipes. I was inspired by a piper on Pitlochry Dam, and in my mid-twenties they were at times my main source of income! I appeared in thousands of tourist photos and videos, a full page of the *New Woman* magazine, and even a Bollywood movie. Not perhaps the best career move. However, looking back, it now seems part of a very precise answer to prayer.

Around Christmastime in 1995, while working on a PhD I was rapidly losing interest in, a friend asked what I was hoping to do with my life. Having no idea at the time, and feeling that my career was going nowhere, I remember saying quite honestly but without much hope, 'get married, settle down and have a couple of kids'. The following autumn I quit the PhD, fled home to the west coast of Scotland for the winter and returned to St Andrews in the spring, pipes in hand. The previous summer, a large group of Japanese students had come to stay in my hall of residence.

Their interest in my piping, and the fact that one of my friends had started to busk for a living, persuaded me to give it a try. It was the fact that those first brief trials were relatively well-rewarded that brought me back to my university town that spring seeking financial independence.

I played every summer for the next seven years. But that first summer I met my bride to be – the sweetest, humblest and most caring person I have ever met (as well as being stunningly beautiful) – and we were married the following spring. Our first child arrived in 1999 and our second in 2001. A self-fulfilled prophecy? Perhaps. But there's more. While busking away to pay the mortgage on our flat, I am ashamed to say I was somewhat envious of a friend who'd bought his mortgage-free from an inheritance. 2002 was a rocky year as I was a student once again with only a student loan and my bagpipes to support my wife and family, and yet despite this, due to a convenient ripple in the property market and an exceptionally warm summer, by December of that same year we were also mortgage-free homeowners! I still find that very strange. Those seven years were by no means easy, but that is probably why the occurrence of the things I'd prayed for during that time is so surprising. I had walked away from a science career and chosen to busk for a living while pursuing the independent research that has led to this book. It seems God granted the wish I'd voiced seven years before to encourage me in this pursuit–Perhaps even to illustrate the prophecy of this chapter.

As you will see in the rest of this chapter, the idea that God sometimes acts in the future to fulfil something that was uttered in the past is probably the only reasonable way to account for the accuracy of another prophecy in the book of Daniel – a seven-year one, the accuracy of which is just as astonishing as that of the *eleventh king* prediction in Daniel 7, or the *'times' are 'fifties'* interpretation of the time-period in that same passage. But as with those prophecies in Daniel 7, the events that fulfilled the prophecy in this case were not nice ones. In fact, they were pretty horrible ones – deaths, wars, destructions and desolations.

You might at first think that this is something God should be criticised for. After all, he is supposed to be a God of love, isn't he? Why would a God of love ensure the fulfilment of predicted deaths, disasters and desolations?

I think the answer to this is two-fold. Firstly, it is mainly disasters that make the news. These are the events that get noted down in the history books. Hence if God restricted himself to fulfilling predicted births, happy marriages and periods of peace and plenty, it is very likely that there would be no historical record of these events for future readers to be able to test the prophecy against. But secondly, and more importantly, if God limited himself to fulfilling predictions of nice, happy events, people would have no grounds to believe it was God.

Human beings *want* good things to happen; so when those good things do happen, observers will naturally be inclined to attribute them to the acts of human beings rather than to God. Thus the fact that the holy people would not want to be persecuted for 175 years is one of the things that makes the fulfilment of this prediction really interesting. The fact that no king would particularly want to have to subdue three previous kings is one of the reasons the 'eleventh king' prediction in Daniel 7 is so fascinating. And the fact that the Jews would not want their city and temple to be destroyed, their land laid waste, and ancient religious traditions ended by exile, makes it all the more surprising when time-limited predictions of such terrible disasters just happen to get fulfilled within the predicted windows of time, as we shall now see.

The third astonishing prophecy in the book of Daniel is only four verses long. It is located at the end of the ninth chapter of the book after a lengthy prayer and vision, and it comprises only Daniel 9:24-27. Yet, as we shall see shortly, its most obvious and straightforward reading makes several stunningly specific predictions about the future (from Daniel's perspective). And a mere glance at the history books confirms that every single one of them was fulfilled in exactly the way the prophecy specifies.

Moreover, even mainstream critical scholars admit that the predicted events in this case are set at a time long after the latest date at which the prophecy could have been written. They claim that this must be because the writer of the prophecy did not know his history very well. But in view of the relatively accurate knowledge of history demonstrated elsewhere in the book of Daniel, I suspect that they only make this claim because the first prediction in the prophecy is the arrival at Jerusalem of a prince or king called 'Christ' who would get put to death emptyhanded. Evangelical Christian scholars have naturally argued that this was fulfilled by Jesus of Nazareth, and critical scholars do not want to write anything that may suggest they are of the same opinion. Consequently, they refuse to even consider the possibility that this prophecy might have been intended as a genuine prediction of the future – which is a perfectly legitimate hypothesis in this case. As we shall see in chapter 7, those same scholars use this very same hypothesis to account for the content of Daniel 11:40-45 – which is another prophecy where the predicted events are set at a time somewhat later than the time those scholars believe the book of Daniel was completed. They confidently claim that *this* prophecy must be a guess at the future; so why don't they ever consider that the same might be true of Daniel 9:24-27? Could it be merely the fact that in the former case the predicted events never happened, whereas in the latter case they did?

As you will see in the next chapter, that almost certainly *is* the reason this possibility is neglected by critical scholars. Evangelical Christian scholars have shown quite convincingly that the most justifiable interpretation of the time-period in this prophecy happens to predict the arrival of this Christ to within the most likely month in history for the Triumphal Entry and subsequent crucifixion of Jesus of Nazareth. The accuracy of this prediction really is astonishing. And as you will see in chapter 7, the text of Daniel 9 pretty much rules out the possibility that the writer of this passage did not regard this prophecy as a prediction of his future. To demonstrate these things, though, requires a little bit of hard work, and even a little bit of elementary arithmetic. I have therefore left it until the next couple of chapters. In this chapter we shall instead examine the *latter* part of this prophecy – the part which claims to be telling us what will happen to the Jews and Jerusalem *after* the appearance and death of this Christ.

As with the straightforward meaning of Daniel 7, the fulfilment of the latter part of this prophecy has gone largely unnoticed by the early church fathers and other evangelical scholars, who tend to consider it to be a prophecy about *our* future (the so-called 'end-time') that has simply not yet come to pass. They ignore the fact that the destructive king mentioned in the prophecy is a king *of the same people who would destroy Jerusalem after the completion of the time-period in the first part of the prophecy*, and that these people are definitely *the Romans* who destroyed the city in 70 AD, and whose empire ceased to exist in 1453. Instead, they assume that the future will bring about a revival of the specified circumstances, thereby allowing the prophecy to be fulfilled. The problem is that if you interpret the prophecy that way, any suggested fulfilment that may occur in the future is totally unsurprising because it is perfectly reasonable to attribute such a fulfilment to chance.

So why do they interpret the prophecy this way rather than in the obvious and straightforward way that I am claiming was fulfilled by history? As with the time-period in Daniel 7, it is likely they have ignored that obvious fulfilment simply because of their desire to make that prophecy predict something relevant to Christianity. In their view, it cannot just be about the Jews and Jerusalem, even though that is exactly what it *says* it is about! It reads as follows:

> **DAN 9:** [24] "Seventy "sevens" [or 'weeks'] are determined for your people and your holy city, to finish disobedience, and to make an end of sins, and to make reconciliation for iniquity, and to bring in everlasting righteousness, and to seal up vision and prophecy, and to anoint the most holy.

> [25] Know therefore and discern that from the going out of the word to restore and rebuild Jerusalem to the Anointed One, the ruler ['prince' or 'king' – the Hebrew literally means 'exalted leader'], there will be seven "sevens" and sixty-two "sevens". It will be built again, with street and trench, even in troubled times. [26] After the sixty-two "sevens" the Anointed One will be cut off [usually meaning 'put to death'], and will have nothing. The people of the ruler who will come [another 'exalted leader'] will destroy the city and the sanctuary. His end [or '*Its* end' or '*The* end'] will be with a flood, and war will be even to the end.

Desolations are determined. [27] He will confirm a covenant with many for one "seven". In the middle of the "seven" he will cause the sacrifice and the offering to cease. On an overspreading [or 'wing'] he will set up the abomination of desolation even until the full end, that which is determined, is poured out on him. [Some translations render this last sentence, 'On the wing of abominations will come one who makes desolate; and even to the full end, and that determined, wrath will be poured out on the desolate']."

As you can see, the prophecy is meant to be about Daniel's people and holy city (the Jews and Jerusalem). It predicts the rebuilding of that city which took place in the century that immediately followed the date Daniel received the prophecy (539 BC). It then predicts the arrival of an Anointed One who would be a prince, king or other exalted leader, and who would show up after an intriguing time-period of *'seven "sevens" and sixty-two "sevens"'* from the issuing of the word to restore and rebuild Jerusalem. After that, he would get put to death (the traditional meaning of 'cut off') empty-handed. Since the Greek translation of the Hebrew for 'Anointed one' is 'Christ', this prophecy thus predicts a future arrival and subsequent ignominious execution of a kingly Christ at Jerusalem.

That much, however, is not that surprising because it is quite likely that the name Christ was applied to Jesus by his followers precisely because he appeared to them to have fulfilled this prophecy. The really surprising feature is that the arrival of this Christ is predicted with such a specific time interval. As you will see in chapter 6, that time interval is remarkably easy to interpret, and the meaning that is *most justifiable* from the text of the book of Daniel predicted the arrival of this Christ in the spring of 33 AD. Amazingly, that turns out to be the most likely time for the

Triumphal Entry and subsequent execution of Jesus of Nazareth, as judged from the gospel accounts.

Due to the detailed chronological analysis that will be required to establish this fact, I have left it until the next chapter. In this chapter, we shall instead examine what this prophecy says will happen *after* its Christ's death, which is far more straightforward.

The first point to note is that the death of this Christ is only predicted to happen 'After the sixty-two "sevens"' (verse 26). Notice, however, that no starting point is given for those sixty-two "sevens". This means that they simply must be interpreted as following on from the first *seven* "sevens" to make a total of *sixty-nine* "sevens" from the word to restore and rebuild Jerusalem. That is because otherwise the arrival of the Christ will not be predicted to happen in any limited window of time, and any fulfilment of such an interpretation would consequently be unsurprising.

This, however, is not the case for the last "seven" mentioned in the prophecy. That "seven" clearly *is* given a starting point. It begins when 'the ruler who will come' starts to confirm his covenant with 'the many' (the most justifiable meaning of which is easily evident from this prophecy as we shall see shortly). As a result, there is no reason to assume that this last "seven" must be joined onto the end of the previous sixty-nine "sevens". The very fact that the prophecy only says '*after* the sixty-two "sevens"' for the predicted execution of this Christ strongly implies that there is meant to be a gap of undefined duration between the two time periods as evangelical scholars have often suggested. However, for reasons that will be given shortly, that gap cannot possibly be thousands of years in length, as is also often suggested. There is a very clear statement in the prophecy that limits the size of that gap to around a century – which, though still long, is short enough for the occurrence of the very rare event it contains to still surprise us.

The next prediction the prophecy makes is that 'the people of the ruler who will come' will destroy Jerusalem and her Temple. As you will see in the next chapter, there is no justifiable interpretation of the time-period in this prophecy that will make it end any earlier than the first century BC (and as I have said, the *most* justifiable interpretation places its endpoint in 33 AD). Within that long time-period there was only one event that was widely perceived as a destruction of Jerusalem, but that happened way back in 168 BC – a long time before the end of that time-period according to all reasonable ways of reckoning it – and it did not involve the destruction of the Jewish Temple.

The first destruction of Jerusalem to happen *after* the end of that time-period was that which the Roman emperor Vespasian's son Titus brought about in 70 AD. And surprisingly enough, this one did indeed involve the total destruction of both the city of Jerusalem and its Temple. Nevertheless, there is no fixed time in the prophecy for the occurrence of this event, and the only other event that can be definitely set in time is the 'end to sacrifice and offering' that it refers to in verse 27. As St Jerome pointed out in the fourth century, Jewish sacrifice and offering at the Temple site did not end in 70 AD with the Temple's destruction by Titus. It was only finally ended sixty-five years later, around 135 AD, when Hadrian crushed the second rebellion of the Jews in Judea, and made Jerusalem a no-go area for all Jews on pain of death. St Jerome tells us,

> ...After the city of Aelia was established upon the ruins of Jerusalem, Aelius Hadrian vanquished the rebelling Jews in

their conflict with the general, Timus Rufus. **It was at that time that the sacrifice and offering (ceased and) will continue to cease even unto the completion of the age**, and the desolation is going to endure until the very end...

...I am also well aware that some of the Jews assert that as for the statement about the single week, "He shall establish a covenant with many for one week," the division is between the reigns of Vespasian and Hadrian. According to the history of Josephus, Vespasian and Titus concluded peace with the Jews for three years and six months. And the [other] three years and six months are accounted for in Hadrian's reign, when Jerusalem was completely destroyed and the Jewish nation was massacred in large groups at a time, with the result that they were even expelled from the borders of Judaea.

(St Jerome's *Commentary on Daniel*, translated by Gleason L. Archer, 1958, p.109)

St Jerome thus points out that because Jewish sacrifice was ended by Hadrian some of the Jews in his day saw the prophecy of 'the ruler who will come' as being fulfilled by Hadrian. In a moment you will see that they were absolutely right to do so. But first, let us take stock of what the prophecy has so far predicted.

Observing that Jewish sacrifice and offering was ended by Hadrian around 135 AD, we can immediately see that it has accurately foretold a destruction, by invaders, of Jerusalem's city and Temple to within a window of time of around 100 years (Less justifiable views on the time-period might possibly extend that window to 200 years, though these will be found to be quite unacceptable in the light of the evidence I shall present in chapter 6). Although that may not seem very impressive, the same event had only occurred once in the previous *thousand* years, so it was far from guaranteed that such an event was going to transpire in that 100-year time-frame. The really important aspect of this prediction though is the fact that it says '*the people of the ruler who will come* will destroy the city and the sanctuary'. 'The ruler who will come' is the same ruler who will 'put an end to sacrifice and offering', and we know from St Jerome (page 124) that this was the emperor Hadrian.

Hence, we can now say that not only did this prophecy correctly predict the destruction of Jerusalem and her Temple to within a time-period of around a century, it also accurately identified the people responsible: 'The people of the ruler who will come' are *Hadrian's people* – in other words, *the Romans*. Moreover, the fact that it attributes this destruction to those people rather than to 'the ruler who will come', himself (the one who would 'put an end to sacrifice and offering'), suggests that this ruler would not be leading those people at the time they destroyed Jerusalem. Since the Romans destroyed Jerusalem in 70 AD, several years before Hadrian was even born, this obviously also turned out to be true.

But this is just the *first* thing that's predicted to happen after the execution of the exalted Christ (page 120). The next thing is a massive invasion denoted by the common invasion metaphor of 'a flood'. The prophecy says 'His end will come with a flood'. Note that I have used the personal possessive pronoun 'His' in this sentence (making it refer to *the ruler who will come*'s end) where most translations use 'Its' (meaning *the sanctuary's* end) or 'The' (meaning the end *of the age*). All three possibilities are perfectly valid, as most Bibles acknowledge in the footnotes, because the Hebrew pronoun is ambiguous. However, to my mind, 'His end' is the only option that makes sense of what follows. Although this line of the prophecy could be describing how the sanctuary would meet the destruction mentioned in the previous sentence, the very next couple of sentences say, 'War will go on until the end, desolations are decreed. *He* will confirm a covenant with many for one "seven"...' The fact that this part of the prophecy introduces 'the ruler who will come' with a *pronoun,* rather than repeating the phrase 'the ruler who will come', strongly suggests that this ruler, and not the sanctuary, is the subject of the previous sentence. This whole section of the prophecy is about *him.* Hence it is *'His* end' that *'will come with a flood'.* And a glance at what the history books say about Hadrian shows that this did indeed come to pass.

Despite an otherwise relatively peaceful two decades in power, the well-organised rebellion in Judea that erupted in 132 required a vast invasion force of Roman legions to put it down (possibly as much as a third of the entire Roman army). Hadrian appears to have overseen the operation in person until around 134, and it was shortly after this that his health began to fail. He eventually died of the condition or disease he had contracted – passing away in some discomfort, to the delight of surviving Jews, on 10th July 138 AD.

So, the prophecy was right about that invasion. But what about the phrase, 'War will go on until the end, desolations are decreed'. In my opinion, this further supports our conclusion that the 'end' referred to is not that of the sanctuary but that of the ruler who will come. That is because what starting point is this war continuing *from*? The only possibility I can see in the prophecy is the destruction of the city and the sanctuary. If you agree with this, then you will notice that this sentence talks about ongoing war *in between* that moment and the huge invasion predicted by the word 'flood'. And sure enough, the Jews were never really at peace with Rome following the destruction of the Temple. There was sporadic unrest that all came to a head in 115-117 when Jews throughout the empire rebelled against Romans in the widespread but ultimately unsuccessful uprisings that became known as the *Kitos War*.

Hence our observations so far indicate that this prophecy accurately predicted (to within a window of just over 100 years) the Roman destruction of Jerusalem and her Temple in 70 AD. It rightly anticipated that the ruler (Hadrian) who would put an end to Jewish sacrifice and offering would visit Jerusalem in person, and that he would also participate in a huge invasion towards the end of his life. Moreover, in between the destruction of Jerusalem and that huge invasion, according to the prophecy, there would be war (presumably between Jews and Romans) which there indeed was. Already, this prophecy has proven astonishingly successful. However, it is what comes next that really puts this prophecy up among the most astonishing prophecies ever written.

The final verse of the prophecy says,

> **DAN 9:** [27] 'He will confirm a covenant with many for one "seven". In the middle of that "seven" he will cause the sacrifice and the offering to cease. On an overspreading [or 'wing'] he will set up the abomination of desolation even until the full end, that which is determined, is poured out on him.'

In my earlier reproduction of the full prophecy (page 121) I mentioned a somewhat different translation of this verse that's found in some Bibles. I have not mentioned it here because to me that alternative translation does not make much sense. It suggests that 'the end determined' is that of Jerusalem, which isn't likely because verse 26 of the prophecy has already predicted that the destruction of Jerusalem will take place long before the final "seven". And it appears to add in the word 'wrath' so that what is *poured out* on the desolate or desolator is not 'the end determined'. In so doing, this dubious proposal renders that endpoint merely the end of the final "seven". It ensures that the prophecy predicts no significant event at that endpoint (which would make it rather pointless). In contrast, the above translation makes that endpoint *the death of 'the ruler who will come'* – an event that is likely to give rise to a historically recorded date. And what could that alternative translation possibly mean by the strange sentence *'On the wing of abominations will come one who makes desolate'*? That rendering makes no sense whatsoever. Compare it with the corresponding part of the translation above which is found in most Bible translations: *'On an overspreading [or 'wing'] he will set up the abomination of desolation'*. This rendering of the Hebrew is *far more justifiable* because we know from Daniel 11:31 what an 'abomination of desolation' is. As you will see shortly, the use of the phrase 'abomination of desolation' in Daniel 11:31 and 12:11 (and in Matthew 24:15 and Mark 13:14) definitely supports the translation proposed here (the one found in most Bible versions). So let us see what this most defensible translation actually foretold.

Considering that this passage is about Daniel's 'people and holy city', what is the most obvious meaning of a 'covenant with many' that would be confirmed sometime after the *destruction* of that holy city? It surely has to be a promise to *rebuild that city* made to the Jews of Judea! Remember, we are not at liberty to just consider any covenant we choose to be the fulfilment of that prediction. Any fulfilment can only be considered surprising if it is the most *justifiable* interpretation that gets fulfilled. And clearly, a promise to *rebuild Jerusalem* is the only non-arbitrary possibility for that covenant that the content of this prophecy suggests.

Notice that this conclusion is made even more justifiable by the fact that a 'word to restore and rebuild Jerusalem' is used earlier in the prophecy as the starting point for its *first* time-period (the sixty-nine "sevens" that leads up to the 'Christ'). This makes the confirming of a covenant *to rebuild Jerusalem* a very fitting starting point for the last time-period that the prophecy contains.

That time-period is described as *'one "seven"'*. Given the number of major events that are predicted to take place within it, anyone familiar with the Law of Moses will be able to recognise what the most likely meaning of that time-period is. In Leviticus 25:1-7, Moses commands the Israelites to sow and reap for six years but in the seventh year eat only what they have stored and what grows naturally from the land. They were to keep every *seventh year* as a sabbath for the land, just as they kept every seventh day as a sabbath for the people – a day of rest. Although the word translated "seven" here can mean a 'seven-day week', and is often translated 'week' in modern Bibles, the fact that so many major events are predicted to take place within the "seven" in the prophecy strongly indicates that this is not the meaning being applied here. As we have seen, there is only one other meaning of "seven" in Jewish scripture that denotes a time-period: the seven-year week of Leviticus 25. Hence that is what we must assume those "sevens" to be. This view is shared by almost every scholar of Daniel (both critical and conservative). It is by far the most justifiable position.

Hence the prophecy predicts that the Roman ruler who puts an end to Jewish sacrifice and offering will confirm a promise to rebuild Jerusalem *for seven years*. Why only seven years? Verse 27 strongly indicates that it is because he is to *die* at the end of that time. Its final line suggests that 'the end determined' – the end of the seventy "sevens" in the prophecy – is *his* end. This is the view of most Bible translations (and as I said, the other view, that it is the ending of wrath being poured out on the desolate city, makes no sense as a prediction of anything that could be verified). The end determined is definitely intended to be the end of 'the ruler who ends Jewish sacrifice', who we now know was Hadrian.

I find this very interesting because it suggests that this prophecy was designed to give us an *unambiguous window of time* for its latter events. The date of an emperor's death was generally something that was recorded (since it was the date his successor took over), and Hadrian's case was no exception. Scholars are fairly confident that he died on 10th July 138 AD. The reason I say we have an unambiguous window of time is because the words *'he will confirm a covenant with many for one "seven"'* pretty much tell us what the starting point of those seven years has to be. Remember, the only obvious meaning of 'covenant' in the context of this prophecy is a promise *to rebuild Jerusalem*. So the *confirming* of that covenant has to be the start of the actual building work. And since the building of a new Roman city always began with a *foundation ceremony*, the obvious starting point is the date of that foundation ceremony – the foundation ceremony for Hadrian's new Jerusalem, which he renamed *Aelia Capitolina* after himself (*Aelius Hadrianus*) and the Roman god *Capitoline Jupiter*.

Unfortunately, that date was not recorded by the few classical historians who documented these events, and no commemorative coin or plaque has yet been found with that date on it. Nevertheless, we do have a lot of other evidence indicating when this event took place. The early third century historian Cassius Dio, for example, attributes the Jewish rebellion in 132 AD (known as the *Bar Kokhba Revolt*) to the building of this city and its Roman temple (see Dio's *Roman History* 69:12). If he is correct, and many scholars think he is, then the city was founded before the revolt erupted – a view that is largely supported by the discovery of Roman coins depicting the founding of Aelia Capitolina in caves that were used by the Judean rebels. And historians who have traced the movements of Hadrian around his empire do believe he visited Jerusalem in 130 AD prior to a visit to Egypt. A letter he sent to the city of Hierapolis at this time appears to confirm this suspicion. As does part of a commemorative arch recently found in Jerusalem. At the time of writing, (July 2018) the Wikipedia article on the Bar Kokhba revolt says about that latter discovery,

> 'The inscription was dedicated by Legio X Fretensis to the emperor Hadrian in the year 129/130 CE. The inscription is considered to greatly strengthen the claim that indeed the Emperor visited Jerusalem that year, supporting the tradit-ional claim that Hadrian's visit was among the main causes of the Bar Kokhba Revolt, and not the other way around.'

Since Jewish sources claim that it was at the site of Jerusalem that Hadrian promised the Jewish people he would rebuild their city (see *Midrash Genesis Rabbah* 64), this was almost certainly when that happened. And since there is some evidence that the Roman governor Tineius Rufus, rather than Hadrian, presided over the foundation ceremony (see *Talmud, Taanit* 29a) – which must therefore have taken place some months *after* Hadrian's visit – that foundation ceremony looks certain to have taken place in 131 AD.

In fact, this is when Wikipedia now *says* it took place! Though not always the most reliable of sources, Wikipedia is at least updated quickly as new archaeology comes to light, which is important in this case because, as we have seen, significant evidence of Hadrian's visit to Jerusalem and the extent of the Bar Kokhba revolt has been unearthed in recent years. At the time of writing (July 2018) the Wikipedia article on the Bar Kokhba Revolt reads:

> 'The proximate reasons seem to centre around the construction of a new city, Aelia Capitolina, over the ruins of Jerusalem and the erection of a temple to Jupiter on the Temple mount. One interpretation involves the visit in 130 CE of Hadrian to the ruins of the Jewish Temple in Jerusalem. At first sympathetic towards the Jews, Hadrian promised to rebuild the Temple, but the Jews felt betrayed when they found out that he intended to build a temple dedicated to Jupiter upon the ruins of the Second Temple. A rabbinic version of this story claims that Hadrian planned on rebuilding the Temple, but that a malevolent Samaritan convinced him not to. The reference to a malevolent Samaritan is, however, a familiar device of Jewish literature.
>
> An additional legion, the VI *Ferrata*, arrived in the province to maintain order. Works on Aelia Capitolina, as Jerusalem was to be called, **commenced in 131 CE**. [my emphasis] The governor of Judea, Tineius Rufus, performed the foundation ceremony, which involved ploughing over the designated city limits. "Ploughing up the Temple", seen as a religious offence, turned many Jews against the Roman authorities. The Romans issued a coin inscribed *Aelia Capitolina*...'

You've probably done the sum already. **From the summer of 131 until the summer of 138, when Hadrian died, is indeed seven years**. And despite severe opposition from the Jewish rebels, Hadrian confirmed his covenant to rebuild this city *right up until* *his death*. He never gave up. Moreover, in the middle of those seven years he crushed the Jewish revolt and forbade the Jews entry to Jerusalem, thereby putting a true end to Jewish sacrifice and offering (which could only be performed at the Temple site). Although the ending of the revolt was a year or so beyond the midpoint of those seven years, the point at which the Jews no longer had any hope of regaining Jerusalem was almost certainly earlier in the war, and very probably around the midpoint of that "seven" when Hadrian felt sufficiently assured of victory that he could return to Rome and celebrate a *Triumph* (the victory parade of a victorious Roman general). It may well have been then that he had an equestrian statue of himself erected upon the desolate site of the Jewish Temple's *Holy of Holies* (St Jerome, 398 AD, *Commentary on Matthew*, book IV, 24:15). An abomination in the eyes of devout Jews, this was a clear fulfilment of the prediction 'on an overspreading he will raise the abomination of desolation'.

Finally, the word 'overspreading' in this passage is often translated 'wing' and interpreted as a wing of the Jewish Temple. Notice, though, that this prophecy predicted the *destruction* of that temple and gives no hint that any of it would be rebuilt. The reason I prefer the alternative translation 'overspreading', here, is because that word is a surprisingly appropriate description of what had happened to the Temple site in the minds of devout Jews at that time.

As part of the foundation ceremony for Aelia Capitolina, the city limits, including part of the Temple site, had been *ploughed over*. The Jewish rabbinical scriptures known as the *Mishnah* remembers this as a deep sacrilege, and places it on the 9th of the Jewish month of Av (July/August), their saddest day of the year. It may well have been what caused the rebellion. Intriguingly it is actually depicted on Roman coins that were minted in Jerusalem at the time (in fact, the very ones mentioned at the end of my earlier Wikipedia quote – page 132). The front face of that coin contains a portrait of the emperor Hadrian as expected. But its reverse is shown below:

Source: A Dictionary of Roman Coins, Republican and Imperial (1889)

http://www.forumancientcoins.com/numiswiki/view.asp?key=Dictionary%20Of%20Roman%20Coins

© Public Domain

As you can see, it depicts COL[ONIA] AEL[IA] CAPIT[OLINA] COND[ITA] – *'the founding of Colonia Aelia Capitolina'*. And the chosen image is that infamous 'ploughing over' ritual which took place as part of the foundation ceremony to the horror of the Jewish onlookers.

For me, the use of the word 'overspreading' (*not 'wing'!*) to refer to the site of Jerusalem's Temple in a prophecy (page 121) that was so clearly fulfilled by Hadrian's ending of Jewish sacrifice and offering, and subsequent death, is shockingly reminiscent of that most serious of crimes that Hadrian committed in Jewish eyes.

Of course, the really amazing prediction in verse 27 is that from this foundation ceremony – the moment the promise to rebuild Jerusalem started to be kept – until the death of 'the ruler who will come' (he who will *'cause the sacrifice and offering to cease'*) will be *one "seven"* (i.e. *seven years*). This is really amazing because it almost certainly *was* seven years between these two unique events!

Since we can only be confident of that time interval *to the nearest whole year*, it will be interesting to see, as more data gets unearthed, whether or not that prediction proves even more accurate than this. I suspect it will. Due to the stunning accuracy of the most justifiable interpretation of the *first* time-period in this prophecy, the one we are going to examine in the next chapter, I am willing to bet that it will in fact turn out to be just over a month *less* than exactly seven years! In other words, I'll wager that the founding of Aelia Capitolina will turn out to have taken place in *mid-August* 131 AD – maybe even *the 9th of Av* as the *Mishnah* (*Taanit* 4:6) says! To see why, you'll need to read the next chapter.

As with the fulfilment of Daniel 7 described in the previous two chapters, the fulfilment of Daniel 9:26-27 demonstrated here really is surprising. It is surprising, not only because it was a fulfilment of the most *justifiable* meaning of this passage, but because that most-justifiable meaning limits the predicted events to famous ones that would yield historically recorded dates (the foundation of a specific city and the end of a specific national religious practice), and it restricts the time of these events to *very narrow windows in history* (a month or two in the case of the former and a year or two for the latter depending on how fuzzy you consider *'in the middle of that "seven"'* to be). Whilst the precise dates of those events are currently known only to within a year or so, the endpoint of the time-period – the death of the Roman ruler who would end Jewish sacrifice (10th July 138 AD) – is not in dispute. The fact that the predicted events occurred in the very position relative to that recorded endpoint that the prophecy *says* they will occur in (and the fact that no human being could have engineered this) really is astonishing. My amazement at this is only further increased by the spooky relevance of the predicted 'raising of an abomination of desolation *on an overspreading*' to the exact manner in which history fulfilled that final ending of Jewish sacrifice and offering.

Puzzlingly, evangelical scholars at the time of writing seem somewhat oblivious to this astounding miracle. They prefer instead the idea (contradicted by St Jerome) that Jewish sacrifice ended when the Temple was destroyed in 70 AD. It is therefore vital to note that **Christ's *own* reference to this passage** supports the view that it was fulfilled by Hadrian. In Matthew 24 and Mark 13 (page 108) Christ identified the raising of the 'abomination of desolation' as the moment when the Jews would need to 'flee to the mountains' to escape an intense period of oppression the likes of which will never be seen again. Since the slaughter in 135-6 was far *greater* than in 70 AD, of these two tragedies only that later oppression (by Hadrian) could be a fulfilment of this claim. Moreover, judging from the fact that Luke (probably writing in the 70s AD) replaces 'abomination of desolation' with 'Jerusalem surrounded by armies' in his version of this passage (Luke 21:20) we can be fairly certain nothing fitting the former description took place in 70 AD.

Finally it is worth noting that Christ stressed the *imminence* of this event with the words '*this generation* will not pass away until **all these things** are accomplished' (Matt. 24:34). He was referring to signs, including Daniel 9's 'abomination', that 'the coming of the son of man on a cloud' (which in Daniel 7 symbolises the victory of the holy people's *religion*) is 'near, right at the door'. Now, the only meaning of 'generation' that works in this context is 'humans alive today'. So the implication is that *after these initial signs* the people alive when Christ said this around 33 AD *will **all** be dead!* In other words, he wasn't talking about *40* years from then, but just over *100*. Judging from what we will discover in chapter 6, these claims of Christ's should be considered of *utmost* relevance.

CHAPTER SIX

The Perfect Timing of the Holiest Christ

I was very dubious when I first heard the claim that Daniel 9 predicted the Triumphal Entry of Jesus Christ *to the very day*. In fact, I was so dubious I dismissed this claim out-of-hand and didn't even bother at the time to look into it. My thinking was that if such a claim were really true it would be so famous we'd all know about it by now. After researching its origin, though, I am now not so sure. My findings positively support this claim.

Whilst I don't think our knowledge is yet sufficient to conclude that the claim is definitely correct, I am now convinced that the approach that led to this claim is the most justifiable way of interpreting the passage. I am also persuaded that the gospel-based arguments for locating the Triumphal Entry of Jesus Christ in 33 AD are trustworthy, and that the starting point of the time-period has been identified correctly to within a month or so. Consequently, I can say with relative confidence that Daniel 9 does predict a triumphal arrival at Jerusalem of a famous and most holy Christ (who'd get executed shortly afterwards) to within a narrow window of time, only around a month long, in the spring of 33 AD. And I am pretty certain that the event we now associate with that description *did indeed happen within that month*, despite the fact that the prophecy was definitely in existence in its current form around two hundred years before. Here is why:

The prophecy in question is Daniel 9:24-26, which reads as follows:

> **DAN 9:** ²⁴ Seventy "sevens" are determined for your people and for your holy city, to finish disobedience, and to make an end of sins, and to make reconciliation for iniquity, and to bring in everlasting righteousness, and to seal up vision and prophecy, and to **anoint** the Most Holy.
>
> ²⁵ Know therefore and discern that **from the going out of the word to restore and rebuild Jerusalem until the Anointed One** ['**Christ**' in Greek]**, the *ruler*** [the Hebrew means '*exalted leader or king*']**, there will be seven "sevens", and sixty-two "sevens"** [i.e. 69 "sevens"]**. It will be built again with street and trench** [or 'moat' – i.e. surrounding defences]**, even in times of trouble.**
>
> ²⁶ **After the sixty-two "sevens", the Anointed One [the 'Christ'] will be put to death and will have nothing.**

It is important to remember that this prophecy was in existence at least as early as the second century BC. So it definitely pre-dates Christianity by more than a hundred years. Indeed, the fact that Jesus of Nazareth appeared to fulfil certain aspects of the Anointed One in this prophecy is probably why he came to be referred to as

'Christ' in the first place ('Christ' being Greek for 'Anointed One'). The gospels all describe a public anointing of Jesus; and he was hailed as "King" when he entered Jerusalem riding on a donkey on the day of his Triumphal Entry. His mode of transport was itself a statement of that claim to kingship. It was deliberately chosen by Jesus, according to John 12:14-15, to fulfil a prediction elsewhere in the Old Testament (Zachariah 9:9) that says of Israel,

> "Rejoice greatly, daughter of Zion! Shout, daughter of Jerusalem! Behold, **your king comes to you**. He is righteous and having salvation; lowly and **riding on a donkey**, even on a colt the foal of a donkey."

And of course, Jesus was put to death shortly afterwards, having been deserted by all his disciples and having seemingly gained nothing, just like the Christ predicted in this prophecy.

The fact that the time-period in this prophecy ends simply with 'Christ, the king' has been taken by some to mean that provided it ends at any significant moment in Christ's life, one can count that part of the prophecy as being fulfilled. However, as I have emphasised before, we are not looking for the fulfilment of just any interpretation of the prophecy. We want to find out whether or not its most *justifiable* interpretation has been fulfilled by history. Since this prophecy is specifically about the city of Jerusalem, the endpoint of its time-period should indeed be understood to mean an important arrival of this Christ (the anointed king) *at Jerusalem*.

Although Jesus visited Jerusalem a few times *before* his Triumphal Entry, he had arguably not yet been anointed on these occasions, and he had certainly not been proclaimed 'king'. The prophecy (verse 24) definitely appears to require a *physical* anointing carried out by *Daniel's people* (not a spiritual one carried out by the Holy Spirit – this is the main message of verse 24), and the only physical anointing of the head of Jesus of Nazareth mentioned in John's gospel takes place in Bethany (near Jerusalem) shortly before his Triumphal Entry (see John 12:3). In Matthew and Mark it takes place a couple of days *after* the Triumphal Entry (Matthew 26:7 and Mark 14:3) which is still supportive of the view that this final arrival of Jesus of Nazareth at Jerusalem has to be the one that fulfils the prediction of the 'Anointed One' if the prophecy is to be considered fulfilled. Only Luke has his anointing of Christ take place miles away in Galilee at the beginning of Christ's ministry (Luke 7:38). But Luke's version probably refers to a different event (as opposed to the same event in a mistaken setting) because it seems to be cited in John 11:2 and is not an anointing of Christ's head. The fact that this event does not take place in the vicinity of Jerusalem makes it hardly supportive of any previous arrival at Jerusalem being the fulfilment of that 'anointed one' prophecy.

A far more important observation about this prophecy is that it describes its predicted Christ as 'king' (or 'exalted leader'). Jesus of Nazareth was only proclaimed 'king' on the day of his Triumphal Entry. His crown of thorns and the sign nailed to his cross bear gruesome witness to the reality of that proclamation.

But the most obvious piece of evidence that makes the Triumphal Entry the only reasonable moment in Christ's career that could possibly be a fulfilment of the end of the time-period in this prophecy is the fact that the predicted arrival at Jerusalem of 'Christ the king' is to be followed by the *execution* of this Christ. Since that execution is the first thing to happen *after the end of the time period*, it ought to be *immediately* afterwards. Obviously, none of the previous visits of Christ to Jerusalem got immediately followed by his execution, so the Triumphal Entry definitely fits all the inferred aspects of that starting point.

The question that many scholars have tried to answer over the centuries that followed is this: Did that Triumphal Entry to Jerusalem of the most famous Christ in history happen at the *time* that this prophecy predicts? And I would like to add a second important question: If it did, could Jesus of Nazareth have *deliberately* fulfilled this prophecy as he did the donkey one mentioned earlier? If the answer to the second question is "yes" then even if the Triumphal Entry did happen at the right time, there is no need to invoke a God to explain it.

The first question here looks relatively easy to answer. Just identify 'the word to restore and rebuild Jerusalem', work out the date it was issued, count forward sixty-nine-times-seven years and see where in history you arrive. If it isn't the date of the Triumphal Entry the prophecy has failed. If it is, then the prophecy came true.

However, there are a couple of tiny problems we must overcome before we can do this. One is the rather surprising fact that the year of the Triumphal Entry (and subsequent crucifixion) of Jesus of Nazareth is not precisely known. Various years from 27 AD (when Pontius Pilate, the Roman prefect who tried Jesus, became prefect of Judea) right up until 36 AD (when Pilate was recalled to Rome) have been defended, and no real consensus has yet been reached.

This lack of consensus, though, is probably more due to an unwillingness on the part of many scholars to consider the gospel accounts as reliable witnesses. That is because, as the evangelical scholar Harold Hoehner showed in his book *Chronological Aspects of the Life of Christ* (1973), the political situation evident in the gospel accounts strongly favours a Triumphal Entry relatively late in the governorship of Pontius Pilate. In fact, it rules out all the years prior to 18th October 31 AD when the captain of Rome's Praetorian guard, Sejanus, the most powerful man in the empire apart from emperor Tiberius himself, was executed for treason.

This Sejanus had risen to be the emperor Tiberius' most trusted advisor. He had risked his own life to save that of the emperor and had thereby earned his total confidence. As the emperor's advancing age made him less able to handle the day-to-day work of running the empire, he began to entrust this more and more to Sejanus. In 26 AD he retired completely from public life in Rome and settled on the island of Capri, leaving the city and empire effectively under the control of Sejanus. Although not the emperor, Sejanus controlled the information the emperor received, making him effectively the man in charge. He also set about purging the Senate of his enemies – an act that probably led to his eventual denunciation and execution in October of 31 AD.

Sejanus was notorious for his anti-Semitic policies, as was Pilate early in the ministry of Jesus of Nazareth. Luke 13:1 mentions how Pilate 'mixed the blood of the Galileans with their sacrifices', and Josephus records various instances where Pilate deliberately provokes the Jewish leaders. This policy would almost certainly have been adopted to please Sejanus who despised the Jewish people. Pilate may even have been appointed to his prefect post by Sejanus (rather than by Tiberius) since his appointment does appear to coincide with Tiberius' retirement to the island of Capri which left Sejanus in more-or-less complete control of the empire's government. But whether that was the case or not, Pilate's ruthlessness towards the Jews prior to Sejanus' death, as documented by several historians, would clearly have been encouraged by his knowledge that he had Sejanus' blessing for such provocation and cruelty. He would happily free the people the Jewish leaders wanted dead, and condemn those they wanted freed.

Pilate's attitude to the Jews at Jesus' trial, in contrast, is not that of a governor who cares nothing about offending the Jewish leaders, or who believes such offences would be ignored by his superiors in Rome. For example, he doesn't *release* Jesus. He clearly believes Jesus to be innocent (or at least not deserving of capital punishment). Yet he chooses not to release him. This is quite out-of-character for someone who in the past had gone out of his way to provoke and cause offence to the Jewish elite. It suggests he was afraid of negative reports about his treatment of the Jews getting back to Rome, and this is confirmed by John's gospel. John 19:12-16 actually makes out that Pilate's decision not to release Jesus was the result of the Jews saying that if he released Jesus he would 'be no friend of Caesar'. Had Sejanus still been in charge in Rome, that threat would have carried no weight whatsoever because Sejanus despised the Jewish elite and controlled what information got to Caesar. So Jesus' trial has to have taken place *after* Sejanus' downfall, when Pilate, in fear for his life, was doing everything in his power to distance himself from Sejanus' policies. Only then was he going out of his way to make friends with the Jewish leaders, and avoid drawing the Emperor's attention, as we find him doing at Jesus' trial.

That, of course, narrows down the time of this world-changing event to the interval 32-36 AD. But assuming that Jesus was crucified on the eve of the Jewish *Passover Feast*, as it says in John's gospel, the fact that the day after the crucifixion is a Sabbath (and therefore a Saturday) allows us to do even better than this. It is important to note that the Jews reckoned their days from sunset to sunset, so in John's account, the Passover began in the evening of the Friday on which Jesus was crucified and finished on the Saturday evening. The reason this allows us to come up with a most probable year for these events is that the likelihood of the Jewish Passover Feast ending on a Saturday can be determined from astronomical retro-calculation. That is because the Jews used a *lunisolar calendar* where their months always began with the appearance of the new moon (or the day after the thirtieth day of the previous month – whichever was sooner). The Passover Feast was always held fifteen days after the new moon that began the first month of the Jewish year, and the dates when new moons would have become visible over Jerusalem can be calculated by a computer program that traces the moon's orbit back in time. Such calculations rule out every one of those possible crucifixion years except 33 AD and 36 AD. But 36 AD is too late. That is because Luke 3:1-2 says that John the Baptist commenced his short ministry 'in the fifteenth year of the reign of Tiberius Caesar', which was 28-29 AD. Since Jesus almost certainly began his own ministry in the same year, and since the gospel accounts allow one to argue for at most a *four*-year duration for Jesus' ministry, they only support the 33 AD possibility. We can therefore conclude that, judging from John's gospel, 33 AD is *by far* the most likely year for the Triumphal Entry and crucifixion of Jesus of Nazareth.

Of course, the other three gospels may suggest a different year based upon the fact that Jesus appears to celebrate the Passover with his disciples *before* his crucifixion. There is a tendency among evangelicals to explain this away as being due to the possibility that the Galileans used a different calendar from the one used by the priests in Jerusalem, or that the last supper wasn't really a Passover meal. The former proposal seems to me to be quite improbable, and in need of documentary evidence. However, I think the latter proposal is quite likely. The writers of the so-called 'synoptic gospels' (Matthew, Mark and Luke) could easily have added in the word 'Passover' to give what otherwise seems to be an ordinary evening meal a day or two before the Passover greater spiritual significance. Christ could still have secured the upper room under the pretence of eating the Passover there the day after. Alternatively, Christ may simply have wanted to celebrate this joyful feast with his disciples a little earlier than normal, knowing what lay ahead. Hence, I still think the date of 33 AD is by far the one best supported by the gospel accounts.

This means that for us to claim a successful fulfilment of the 'Christ' prediction in Daniel 9:24-26, the time-period in that prophecy would have to end a week or so before the time of the Passover in 33 AD. Let us therefore find the starting point of that time-period and count forward to see if this is the case. But here is where we encounter the second tiny problem with this prophecy. What is meant by 'the going out of the word to restore and rebuild Jerusalem' (page 138)?

Four separate royal decrees have been proposed as this starting point, together with two or three Old Testament prophecies. Those prophecies I think we can dismiss without further discussion due to the fact that they were issued even before Daniel is supposed to have received this vision. If they really had been the intended 'word to restore and rebuild Jerusalem', one would have expected the author of the vision to have added 'as spoken through the prophet Isaiah', or 'as spoken through the prophet Jeremiah', or at least to have said '*my* word to restore and rebuild Jerusalem' (or '*this* word...' if he meant Daniel's prophecy itself as some have even suggested). Since no such language is used, I think it is safe to assume that the author was indeed referring to a future, non-divinely-authored command – a word to restore and rebuild Jerusalem that would be issued sometime after Daniel received this vision. And of course, for that command to have any authority (and therefore significance), it would almost certainly have to be the decree of a king or powerful governor whose power extended over Judea.

As I have said, there are four royal decrees in the Old Testament that are relevant to the restoration of Jerusalem: All of these were issued by Persian emperors (since for the two centuries after the fall of Babylon it was Persia that ruled the whole of the Middle East, together with Egypt and much of Asia). The first and most famous of those decrees is the *Edict of Cyrus* (c. 538 BC), recorded in Ezra 1:1-4, which permitted the Jews to return home and rebuild the Temple of Jerusalem. The second is the *Decree of Darius I* (c. 520 BC) in Ezra 6:1-12, which basically reconfirmed the Edict of Cyrus at a time when the legality of the Temple building in Jerusalem was being challenged. The third is the permission to restore correct Jewish worship and Mosaic Law in Jerusalem, which was granted to a scribe called Ezra by Artaxerxes I around 457 BC (see Ezra 7:12-25). And the fourth is the permission to rebuild the wall and fortifications of Jerusalem that was granted to Nehemiah by that same Artaxerxes I in 444 BC. Notably, it was only the last of these (in Nehemiah 2:1-8) that resulted in the extensive rebuilding of the city indicated by the words 'It will be built again with street and trench' in Daniel 9:25.

The next thing to notice is that in each of the first three decrees the emphasis is on rebuilding and restoring *the Temple*, which Daniel 9:25 refers to as 'the sanctuary'. Not one of these decrees mentions the restoration or rebuilding of anything else in the city.

Surely if the author of this prophecy had intended one of these decrees to be the starting point for his time-period, he would have written 'the word to restore and rebuild *the sanctuary*'? As he specifically mentions the rebuilding of *the city*, and emphasises this in the very next sentence, it is far more likely that the decree he is referring to is the one given to Nehemiah by Artaxerxes I which really did permit the building of a city. That decree is cited in Nehemiah 2:1-8, which says the following:

> **NEH 2:** [1] In the month Nisan, in the twentieth year of Artaxerxes the king, when wine was before him, I picked up the wine, and gave it to the king. Now I had not been sad before in his presence. [2] The king said to me, "Why is your face sad, since you are not sick? This is nothing else but sorrow of heart."
>
> Then I was very much afraid. [3] I said to the king, "Let the king live forever! Why shouldn't my face be sad, when the city, the place of my fathers' tombs, lies waste, and its gates have been consumed with fire?"
>
> [4] Then the king said to me, "What is your request?"
>
> So I prayed to the God of heaven. [5] I said to the king, "If it pleases the king, and if your servant has found favor in your sight, I would like you to send me to Judah, to the city of my fathers' tombs, that I may build it."
>
> [6] The king said to me (the queen was also sitting by him), "How long will your journey be? When will you return?"
>
> So it pleased the king to send me, and I set a time for him. [7] Moreover I said to the king, "If it pleases the king,

let letters be given me to the governors beyond the River, that they may let me pass through until I come to Judah; [8] and a letter to Asaph the keeper of the king's forest, that he may give me timber to make beams for the gates of the citadel by the temple, for the wall of the city, and for the house that I will occupy."

The king granted my requests, because of the good hand of my God on me.

The letters of Artaxerxes I that this passage refers to are the only royal command in the Old Testament that specifically permitted Jerusalem to be rebuilt after its destruction by the Babylonians, and they are therefore *by far* the most likely meaning of 'the word to restore and rebuild Jerusalem' in Daniel 9. At the end of this chapter, I will be revealing some very convincing evidence that this was definitely what the person who put the book of Daniel together thought too. So we really have no justification for considering anything other than the issuing of this permission to Nehemiah to be the starting point of our time-period.

It is important to remember that this royal permission would have been extremely well-known to the Jews from the moment they began the rebuilding process onwards because it was the proof of their legal right to do so. Rebuilding the walls of a city was no trivial matter. If not permitted by the emperor, it would constitute rebellion. Hence the population at the time would have had to be convinced. And I am pretty certain that copies of Nehemiah's letters would have been kept as insurance in case their right to do this was later disputed by neighbouring nations. With a constant visual reminder in the form of Nehemiah's wall, this permission would have been frequently talked about. If the author of this prophecy had not meant his 'word to restore and rebuild Jerusalem' to be this permission, one would therefore expect some indication in the text of Daniel 9 that this most obvious and well-known possibility was not the one intended. As you will see later in this chapter, the rest of Daniel 9 strongly supports the view that this permission *was indeed* the intended beginning of the time-period, which is what the wording of Nehemiah's request to *'build it'*, where 'it' is the city of Jerusalem, so clearly suggests .

So, when was that permission issued?

The book of Nehemiah tells us that it was in the Jewish month of *Nisan* in the twentieth year of the Persian king *Artaxerxes I.* Scholarly textbooks and commentaries usually reckon this to be March-April 445 BC. But this view has been proven wrong. In *Chronological Aspects of the Life of Christ* (1973, p.127) Hoehner makes a very simple observation about the book of Nehemiah that forces the date of his permission to be one year later. He points out that, in Nehemiah, the Jewish month of *Tishri* (September-October) comes *before* the Jewish month of Nisan (March-April) in the twentieth year of king Artaxerxes I. This is strange because Nisan (March-April) is usually the *first* month of the Jewish year. The only reasonable explanation for this is that Nehemiah was reckoning the king's years according to a different calendar (one that is attested to in the reign-lengths of kings elsewhere in the Bible, and in contemporary writings by Jews in Egypt), where the first month was Tishri (September-October).

As you will now see, this definitely makes the date of Nehemiah's permission March-April 444 BC. That is because Artaxerxes I came to the throne in December 465 BC, and his accession year (from December 465 BC until Sept-Oct 464 BC on Nehemiah's calendar) would most probably have been counted as his *first year*. Hence, his *twentieth year* would go from Sept-Oct 445 BC until Sept-Oct 444 BC. As a result, since the month of Nisan of that twentieth year was in March-April, it would have to be the March-April of 444 BC (rather than the March-April of 445, as it would have been had Nehemiah been reckoning the new year from the month of Nisan as scholars had originally assumed).

Let us now count on the 'seven "sevens" and sixty-two "sevens"' of the time-period to see where it takes us. Remember, we are only interested in the most justifiable interpretation of this prophecy. In other words, we want the view that can be most easily justified from the rest of the book of Daniel, not the one that best fits one's religious hopes or scholarly biases.

For this reason, we can ignore the suggestion of some mainstream scholars that the seven "sevens" and the sixty-two "sevens" are time periods that start, both together, at the issuing of the decree to restore and rebuild Jerusalem and run in parallel. In that view, the first one supposedly leads to an anointed prince forty-nine years later, and the second to the 'cutting off' of *another* anointed one 385 years after that (62 "sevens" = 434 years, 434 − 49 = 385).

That view is not supported by the text of the prophecy (page 138) because in the list of things that Daniel's people and city were to accomplish within its seventy "sevens" time-period, the last one mentioned is to 'anoint the most holy'. Translators often add in 'place' after the words 'most holy' in this verse to make it suggest the Jerusalem Temple's *inner sanctuary* (known as the *Holy of Holies*), but there is no good reason for such an insertion. Since 'anointing' was usually something done to a *person* (not a place), it is quite probable that the writer was not thinking of the

Temple at all in this case. And this is made all the more likely by the fact that the two references to anointed ones that follow are each references to a *human individual*. Although there are commands in the Law of Moses about anointing the holy vessels, one would expect those object anointings to have been routine practice in the Temple, and not something reserved for those seventy "sevens". So the vast weight of evidence favours the view that the Most Holy in verse 24 is a *person*.

It is worth noting here that St Jerome's *Commentary on Daniel*, written around 407 AD, tells us that the Jews of St Jerome's day did not see this verse as a reference to the Temple's inner sanctuary either (see Gleason L. Archer translation, 1958, p.108). If Jerome was accurately representing the opinion of the Jewish *experts* of his day (which is more than likely), they thought it referred to a *person* too. And since we are only interested in the most justifiable interpretation of this prophecy, we must here follow suit. The context strongly favours the view that the Most Holy of verse 24 is a *person*, so that is the view we have to take.

The problem for the parallel time-intervals suggestion is that the appearance of Anointed One in verses 25 and 26 (page 138) is not explained in these verses. This makes it almost inevitable that the reference to an **'anointing'** in verse 24 is the *explanation* for the mention of **'Anointed One'** in those following two verses. And since it is a single person called 'the Most Holy' who gets anointed in verse 24, we should expect that the same person is the 'Anointed One' of verses 25 and 26. If the two parts of the time-period were really meant to start from the same moment and end at some event in that individual's life, that individual would have to be alive for at least 385 years! Hence, we can safely reject those interpretations that consider the two parts of the time-period to run in parallel.

There is therefore only *one* Anointed One; and the seven "sevens" and sixty-two "sevens" describe *a single time interval of sixty-nine "sevens"* (expressed poetically like 'four and twenty blackbirds' in the English nursery rhyme – a view strongly asserted by the Jews in St Jerome's day [see *Commentary on Daniel,* p.109]). Beginning at the issuing of Nehemiah's permission to rebuild Jerusalem in March-April 444 BC, it is this well-defined time interval that predicts the arrival of this Anointed One *as king* at Jerusalem.

Sixty-nine "sevens" is, of course, 483 years. Beginning in March-April of 444 BC and going forward 483 years takes us to March-April of 40 AD (remember there was no year zero). Since Jesus almost certainly rode triumphantly into Jerusalem in 33 AD, it seems that the prophecy has failed to predict the Triumphal Entry by seven years. But wait a minute! What if the 'years' implicit in the word "seven" were not normal (solar) years? What if the Jews reckoned each year as a *specific number of days*, and the word "seven" actually meant the unit of time consisting of seven times the number of days the Jews thought a year to contain? Provided we could find a reference in the book of Daniel that tells us what number of days that was, this would be an *equally justifiable* way of reckoning the endpoint of that time-period.

Fascinatingly, there is indeed a couple of verses in the book of Daniel that gives us precisely this information. Those verses are Daniel 12:11-12. They appear to be an interpretation of the phrase 'a time, times and half a time' – in fact they are *two* interpretations of that phrase. Both of these seem designed to indicate the length of a three-and-a-half year persecution of the Jewish faith that took place from 168-164 BC. For reasons I will explain in the next chapter, most mainstream scholars think that this persecution was actually ongoing when this part of the book of Daniel was written, and that the additional time in the second interpretation is a consequence of this. Those two verses say the following:

> **DAN 12:** [11] "From the time that the continual burnt offering is taken away, and the abomination that makes desolate set up, there will be one thousand two hundred and ninety days. [12] Blessed is he who waits for, and comes to the end of the one thousand three hundred and thirty-five days."

As many scholars have noted, the repeating year-like unit that makes sense of these time intervals is a unit of 360 days.

1290 days is 3.5 times **360**, plus another 30 days.

1335 days is 3.5 times **360**, plus 2.5 times 30 days.

The extra whole and half multiples of 30 are not surprising due to the fact that they come from the lunar month (clearly rounded to 30 days) and the time from new moon to full moon (15 days). The fact that they thought of a month as 30 days is probably why they interpreted a year as 360 days (twelve months).

With this evidence it becomes perfectly reasonable to consider that the time-period was actually meant to consist of *69 times 7 times 360 days*. In fact, this may be even *more* justifiable than interpreting the "sevens" as seven *solar (*or *calendar)* years. That is because anybody with access to an accurate king list (or who knew the age of the wall that Nehemiah built round Jerusalem) could have worked out that the latter interpretation of the time-period was going to end in March-April 40 AD. Had a Christ appeared at that time, it would therefore have been no surprise. Interpreting each "seven" as 'seven years of 360 days', as Daniel 12:11 suggests, makes it far harder for any would-be

Christ to work out when exactly to stage his arrival, and he is far more likely to opt for the 40 AD fulfilment. It would indeed be quite astonishing if the most famous Christ in history fulfilled the '483 times 360-day' interpretation of the time-period, which as I have shown is perfectly justifiable from the text of Daniel. Let us therefore see where that interpretation takes us.

$$69 \times 7 \times 360 = 483 \times 360 = 173880 \text{ days}$$

To see how many solar years (complete cycles of the seasons) this is, we need to divide those 173880 days by the number of days in a *mean solar year* over the period from the fifth century BC to the first century AD. The mean solar year in 1900 was measured to be 365.24219879 days. But mathematical models of the solar system show that the mean solar year gets just over half a second shorter every century. Although such a slow rate of change makes little difference to our calculation (reducing the time-period by merely an hour or two), we shall use the corrected value of 365.242328 days (approximated using 'Newcomb's formula') instead of the 1900 AD value to avoid an obvious source of criticism.

Dividing by the mean length of the solar year over the period in question thus gives:

$$173880 \div 365.242328 = 476.0674946 = \textbf{476 solar years}$$

plus $0.0674946 \times 365.242328 = 24.651872 = \textbf{24.65 days}$

Or a total of **476 solar years *to the nearest whole day***

and an extra 25 whole days.

In other words, the fully justifiable "360-day years" interpretation gives a total length for the time period of

476 solar cycles and 25 days (The 476 solar cycles brings you to exactly the same *time of year and time of day* – though not necessarily month – as you started from).

Counting forward 476 years from 444 BC (and remembering that there was no year zero) requires splitting the 476 years into **444 years + 32 years** and adding them on separately as below:

444 BC + **444 years** = 1 AD, 1 AD + **32 years** = 33 AD

So, we are in exactly the right year for the Triumphal Entry of Jesus Christ!

Now, you might think the 25 days would be a problem. If Nehemiah received his permission to rebuild Jerusalem in Nisan 444 BC, as the text of Nehemiah indicates, and the 476 years takes you to Nisan 33 AD, then surely the 25 days will take you past the 14th Nisan when Jesus was crucified? (Jesus was crucified on the eve of the Jewish Passover Feast, according to John's gospel, and the Passover Feast was always on 15th Nisan). But that is to neglect the fact that the Jews used a *lunisolar calendar*. Each month began with the first glimpse of the new moon (or the day after the 30th day of the previous month, whichever came sooner) and lasted for either 30 days or 29 days (depending upon when the next new moon was sighted). Since the lunar year (twelve lunar months) is only a little over 354 days long, the Jewish months would get 11 days earlier (relative to the seasons) every year.

This was a bit of a problem for the Jews as they had festivals that needed to take place at particular times of year due to the availability of the food or other produce that was required on those occasions. Consequently, they regularly corrected this drift by adding an extra 30-day month onto the previous year (in the modern Hebrew calendar it goes just in front of the last month). They did this every two or three years, and in Nehemiah's day there was probably not any fixed system. The priests would simply look at how well the crops were growing, and decide on that basis whether to add an extra month or let the new year begin. As a result, it was possible for the month of Nisan to drift more than a full month earlier relative to the seasons before the addition of an extra month to the previous year shifted it forward again.

The interesting thing for us is that one can determine from astronomical retro-calculation when the new moons would have been visible from Jerusalem, and therefore whether a given year was likely to involve the addition of the extra month or not. And it turns out that 444 BC is likely to have been one of those years, whereas 33 AD was not. If 444 BC did involve the High Priest adding an extra month to the previous Jewish year, and Nehemiah knew of this in Babylon, then Nisan would have been shifted forward (i.e. futureward) by a month, and the 25 days would indeed be a problem. On the other hand, it is possible that a mild winter could have caused the High Priest to delay the insertion of the extra month until the following year – or, alternatively, that word of the intercalation did not reach Nehemiah before he set off from Babylon, and he forgot to amend his notes (or could not re-date his royal permission) when he did learn of it. Either way, we then find that the month of Nisan in 444 BC is indeed early enough for the 476 solar years and 25 days to take us to the tenth Nisan in 33 AD (Monday 30th March 33 AD according to Hoehner), which was very probably *the actual day of the Triumphal Entry*.

Now, you might be thinking that in allowing this last possibility I have veered away from considering only the most probable scenario, and that I have done this to prevent the prophecy from failing by a week or two. You might indeed have a point there. Nevertheless, I think it is important to show you that there is a very reasonable chance that this prophecy is *precisely correct*. I find this fact utterly astonishing. There should not be any way in which a prophecy of this specificity, written long before the time of the event it predicts, could be correct, unless of course its fulfilment was deliberately brought about at that time. Jesus of Nazareth was very much in the business of fulfilling ancient prophecies, and he would have been well aware of this one, so perhaps that is the explanation. The problem is that without a precise record of the number of months in each of the years since Nehemiah received his royal permission, it is difficult to understand how anyone at the time of Jesus could have worked out the right time to stage his Triumphal Entry. The length of the solar year was not known precisely enough to do the calculation we have done, so the only way would have been to work out the number of days that had gone by since the month of Nisan in 444 BC (which would have required those records).

Another criticism that has been levelled at those who claim this accuracy is astonishing, is that they have just made the prophecy work by selecting 360-day years instead of normal years. I think that would be a fair criticism if it were anything other than 360 days that had worked. As we saw earlier, the use of 360-day units of time is attested to *elsewhere in the book of Daniel*. We find it in the numbers stated in Daniel 12:11-12 (see page 153). That makes it perfectly justifiable to interpret the "sevens" as a unit of 'seven times 360 days'. Only by interpreting the year as a whole number of days could the "sevens" all be the same length, and this evidence from Daniel 12 provides a non-arbitrary means of doing this. And don't let's forget, 360 days is twelve full 30-day months. It was very much the number of days that people with a lunisolar calendar would have understood the year to consist of (since they would be well aware that it was over twelve lunar months long).

I recently found support for this assertion in the work of the first century Roman historian Livy. In documenting the deeds of one of the kings of Rome during the city's 'Monarchy Period' (when she was a small Italian city-state ruled by elected kings), Livy writes:

> 'First of all, he divided the year into twelve months, according to the courses of the moon; **and because the moon does not fill up the number of thirty days in each month**, and some days are wanting to the complete year, which is brought round by the solstitial revolution, **he so regulated this year, by inserting intercalary months**'
>
> (Livy, *The Rise of Rome*, 1:19, translated by John Henry Freese, Alfred John Church, and William Jackson Brodribb) [The bold typeface is my emphasis]

In other words, the king that Livy was describing thought the difference between the Lunar Year (twelve lunar months) and the Solar Year (solstice to solstice) was due to the fact that the months were not all *thirty days long!* Since when Livy wrote this in the late first century BC the Romans used a solar calendar with a 365-day year, I hardly think this could have been Livy's own view. However, the fact that he doesn't make this clear suggests to me that the idea that a complete year was twelve thirty-day months in length (360 days) was probably fairly common even at that time.

A totally different justification for those 360-day years comes from chapter 5. Recall the rabbinical *9th of Av* date for the founding of Aelia Capitolina (page 133). One of the two possibilities for this is

20th August 131. From four days earlier (to include preparations), one "seven" will only reach up to Hadrian's death on 10th July 138, as Daniel 9:27 requires, if it is *seven times 360 days!* See page 309.

For those who are still suspicious about the choice of 360-day years, it is worth considering what alternatives the proponents of this view could have chosen in an effort to make the prophecy work. Obviously, 'calendar cycles' (averaging 365.242328 days) is one of them, but are there any others?

As far as I can see there are only three, none of which is attested to anywhere in the book of Daniel. They could have argued for "Sabbatically-perfect" years of *364 days* – years that were a whole number of weeks – as something the Jewish God might find pleasing. Alternatively, they could have argued that God might instead use *365-day* years because that was the number of whole days in the solar year, or even *354-day* years because that was the number of whole days in a *lunar* year and he might not be in favour of the intercalation process. But that is all. No other option seems in any way justifiable. The only obvious meaning of the "sevens" in this context are the seven-year periods of Leviticus 25:1-8, and there are now only five possibilities for the meaning of 'year' implicit in those seven-year periods (360 days, 365.242328 days, 364 days, 365 days, or 354 days). Each of these would make the time-period predict the Triumphal Entry within a different window of a month or so between 25 and 40 AD.

To take into account the uncertainties over the intercalation process, we should actually assume *two* adjacent windows for each possibility due to the two possible positions of the month of Nisan. But that is it! When all those remotely justifiable possibilities for making this prophecy work are taken into account, they together predict the arrival at Jerusalem of a holy exalted leader called 'Christ', who would later get executed empty-handed, in at most *ten separate month-long intervals* out of the whole of history (roughly March or April 33 AD, March or April 40 AD, August or September 38 AD, November or December 39 AD, or November or December 25 AD). And in one of these – one of the two obtained by what seems the *most* justifiable meaning of 'year' in the book of Daniel – an event of major historical significance that perfectly fulfilled that prediction almost certainly did take place!

Since there has been only one famous Christ who meets all the criteria of the Most Holy of Daniel 9:24-27, the odds in favour of this happening by chance are extremely low. One might think one could improve them by arguing that there are other possibilities for the *starting point* of the time-period – e.g. the other three royal decrees that the Bible mentions. But as we saw earlier, Nehemiah's permission is the only royal command we know about that specifically allowed *the rebuilding of Jerusalem*. This fact is frequently brushed aside by critical scholars as though it were somehow unimportant. They tend to lump Nehemiah's permission together with the other three decrees as though they are all equally likely to be 'the word to restore and rebuild Jerusalem' that the writer of Daniel 9 was referring to. However, there is very strong evidence in the book of Daniel which all but proves that this impression, which critical scholars appear to me to be trying to create, is not only misleading but completely *false*. The evidence I am about to reveal shows that Nehemiah's Permission *has to have been* 'the word to restore and rebuild Jerusalem' that the person who wrote the final text of Daniel 9 was thinking of. And as such, it is *indeed* the only justifiable possibility for the starting point of that prophecy's sixty-nine "sevens" time-period.

The evidence I am referring to is the fact that there is considerable similarity between the prayer in Daniel 9 and a prayer found in Nehemiah 1:5-11. In fact, it is the very prayer that Nehemiah prays shortly before he receives his 'word to restore and rebuild Jerusalem'. In the next chapter, you will discover the full extent of that similarity, and find out why it is so significant. In short, it is significant because most critical scholars believe that the prayer and prophecy in Daniel 9 came from separate sources. In other words, in their view somebody either wrote that prayer to go with this prophecy or decided that this prophecy and that prayer went well together. But if this was the case, the resemblance of that prayer to the prayer of Nehemiah is not likely to be a coincidence. It is very powerful evidence that whoever combined these two texts really did believe that 'the word to restore and rebuild Jerusalem' that the prophecy refers to *was* that permission given to Nehemiah soon after he prayed his very similar prayer. Even if that person didn't compose the prayer in Daniel 9 himself, he couldn't have failed to *notice* its resemblance to the prayer in the book of Nehemiah, so the same conclusion applies.

Now, I should mention at this point that, in the view of most critical scholars, this person was a Judean (almost certainly male) who lived over two hundred years *after* Nehemiah. As a result, that prayer of Nehemiah's and its historically momentous answer would have been well-known to him. Having rebuilt the wall of Jerusalem, Nehemiah was a national hero, and his successful prayer would have been widely read as an example to the Jewish Nation to remain faithful to their God. Consequently, the most likely explanation for him choosing to combine a very similar prayer with this prophecy, if that is what happened, is because he saw a link to that part of the book of Nehemiah within this prophecy. And of course, the only obvious such link is the 'word to restore and rebuild Jerusalem' that begins its time-period.

As you will see in the next chapter, critical scholars are decidedly reluctant to talk about the similarity between these prayers. They come across as overly eager to convince us that the word to restore and rebuild Jerusalem was the Edict of Cyrus (c. 538 BC) or some much earlier prophecy of Isaiah or Jeremiah, or even Daniel 9:24-27 itself, and they hardly mention the permission given to Nehemiah as though it were somehow irrelevant.

We have seen in this chapter how weak and indefensible such a position is. In the next chapter I shall explain why it is that critical scholars don't budge on this issue. From what I can see, the reason is political rather than evidence-based. Were they to defend the view that the word to restore and rebuild Jerusalem is most likely to refer to the permission given to Nehemiah, their peers would be likely to accuse them of being 'conservative' or 'religiously motivated' (which would not be good for their career in critical scholarship). The problem is that if one admits that the prophecy refers to Nehemiah's permission, it becomes all but impossible to argue in favour of an interpretation of the time-period in the prophecy that supports the current 'critical consensus' on the book of Daniel. Instead, the time-period inexorably points to the first century AD and the time of Christ, as we have seen in this chapter.

But, you might be thinking, if critical scholars were really avoiding the most defensible view, it would be easy for other scholars to prove them wrong. Doesn't the fact that all critical scholars pretty much agree that the 'word to restore and rebuild Jerusalem' wasn't Nehemiah's permission mean that it probably wasn't? Surely reason and evidence would ultimately triumph over politics.

Well, one would hope so, but perhaps that is being overly optimistic. During my own research into the book of Daniel I have studied the claims on both sides of the divide. I have examined them as impartially as I can, looking for the most likely explanation for the content of each prophecy the book contains, and from what I can see, the most likely position has not yet been stated in the literature. I don't believe for a minute that it is because those scholars haven't thought of it. Hence, I am at present of the opinion that the politics is indeed preventing its publication.

As I mentioned before, critical scholars are wary of appearing to be siding with the conservative views of evangelical scholars. But I also think evangelical scholars are equally wary of appearing too critical (or liberal) in their assessment of scripture in the eyes of the institutions that fund their research. As you will see in the next chapter, it is this that prevents them posing a serious intellectual challenge to the critical consensus on Daniel 9 (and also Daniel 2 and 7). As far as certain *other* prophecies in the book of Daniel are concerned (namely Daniel 8 and Daniel 11), the critical consensus that we will explore next *does* make a lot of sense. It explains their content *extremely well*. Hence, when evangelical scholars draw attention to the serious flaws in the critical consensus on Daniel 9, critical scholars merely point out the indefensible claims that evangelical scholars are making about Daniel 8 and 11 – thereby discrediting their very reasonable claims about Daniel 9:24-26.

As you will see in the next chapter, were evangelical scholars to accept the critical explanation for the content of Daniel 8 and Daniel 11, they could mount an extremely robust case against the critical views on Daniel 9, Daniel 2 and Daniel 7. Remember, these are the astonishingly accurate prophecies we have been discussing over the last five chapters, and they are the only ones in the book of Daniel that predict Christ and Christianity. If evangelical scholars were to accept the critical explanation for Daniel 8 and Daniel 11, they could convincingly refute the strange mainstream claim that these amazingly accurate prophecies of Christ (Daniel 2, 7 and 9:24-27) were erroneous impressions of the past that just happened to predict the future accurately by pure chance. We have already seen how the similarity of the prayer in Daniel 9 to that of Nehemiah 1 *completely destroys* the mainstream assumption that the 'word to restore and rebuild Jerusalem' in the ensuing prophecy was not intended to be the permission to do just that which was given to Nehemiah soon after he prayed his prayer. But it only destroys that assumption if you are willing to accept the mainstream critical claim that the prayer in Daniel 9 was written *after* that of Nehemiah 1 by someone who was not the prophet Daniel! It could not have been the prophet Daniel because Daniel died at a ripe old age in the 530s BC, and Nehemiah's prayer was prayed in the late autumn of 443 BC and is thought, even by mainstream critical scholars, to be a part of a genuine memoir written by Nehemiah himself during his governorship of Judea.

The implication that Daniel's prayer was not written by Daniel himself seems to be just too much of a deviation from traditional views on scripture for conservative (evangelical) institutions to accept. The fear is that evangelical Christians will be offended by the thought that certain passages of scripture would then have been written by a liar (or at best a fantasist) – someone masquerading as the prophet Daniel, for example, in the case of the prayer in Daniel 9. Would the Christian God really allow such a thing?

I personally consider myself an evangelical, and for the record, I do not think of scripture in such a black-and-white way. I have great confidence that much of the Bible (such as the prophetic dreams we have been discussing) was genuinely inspired by God. However, I am willing to allow for the fact that God might also have chosen other texts, ones that came from imperfect human minds, and which were perhaps even written for ignoble purposes, to accomplish his purposes in the Bible. The prayer in Daniel 9, for example, is powerful evidence that the person who compiled the book of Daniel believed that 'the word to restore and rebuild Jerusalem' was the one given to Nehemiah (and not Cyrus' Edict or anything else). Hence, I think God selected it and encouraged its inclusion for precisely this purpose. It may well be a lie (or at least an imaginative reconstruction). But it has been included to reveal an important truth to those who might otherwise not be able to see that truth. And as you will see in the next chapter, there are equally strong reasons for God to include the other parts of the book that the critical consensus satisfactorily explains. In fact, had those other parts been written at the time of Daniel, they could not possibly have served the important purpose that they now serve. They would also have been unable to serve that purpose if their writer had been honest about who he really was.

Hence in my view, the book of Daniel is an astonishingly effective work of the Christian God. But Christians will only be able to see this if they are prepared to remove the blindfold of traditional views on scripture – unjustifiably restrictive doctrines on what God was and wasn't allowed to include – that are now quite indefensible. God doesn't lie. But he is allowed to use any lies and falsehoods that were written by human beings as tools to accomplish his noble purposes, should he choose to do so. For this reason, insisting that everything in the Bible has to have been written by exactly the person it says it was written by is very likely to prevent you from fully appreciating the work that God has done in constructing and preserving this remarkable collection of texts, and it could even give you the wrong impression of what God is like.

If you are prepared to dispense with this blindfold, and look instead for the most likely explanation for the content of Daniel's prophecies, I believe that you, like me, will come to appreciate what an effective tool for evangelism God has created in this book. You will perfectly understand the point of the long prophecies in Daniel 11 and Daniel 8. And you will realise that the God in whom you trust probably does not despise individual human beings, even if they are world leaders who attacked his people, and he probably does not delight in lions tearing up women and children even if they do happen to be related to the political enemies of his favourite prophet. In fact, you will discover evidence that God really is a loving heavenly father who wants us humans to realise his existence and recognise his endorsement of the Christian gospel so that we can thereby gain everlasting life.

If you would like to have what is in my view an *enlightened* understanding of the book of Daniel, which harnesses its true power as a tool for evangelism, then by all means read on. But just be aware that the next four chapters very much support the view on scripture I have outlined here. They reject the doctrine that there are no falsehoods in the Bible because that doctrine is inconsistent with the perfectly reasonable view that the Christian God is allowed to use false claims written by imperfect human beings as a means of accomplishing his loving and noble purposes whenever and wherever he decides that this is the best way to achieve those desirable outcomes. After all, he uses imperfect *human beings,* acting for imperfect reasons, to accomplish his purposes all the time if the Christian gospel is correct.

CHAPTER SEVEN

God's Seal, Daniel's Prayer and Our Wake-up Call

Consider the sentence below:

*I prayed to **Yahweh** my God, and made confession, and said, "Oh lord, **the great and awesome God, who keeps his covenant of love with those who love him and keep his commandments…***

Does this sound to you somewhat like this?

*I beg you, **Yahweh**, the God of heaven, **the great and awesome God, who keeps his covenant of love with those who love him and keep his commandments…***

You may be surprised to learn that they are not different translations of the same Bible verse. Nor are they attributed to the same biblical character. The first is from the ninth chapter of the book of *Daniel*. It is the opening line of a prayer that the prophet

167

Daniel supposedly prayed around 539 BC, after much mourning and fasting, concerning how long the desolate state of Jerusalem in his day was going to last (the city having been destroyed by the Babylonians almost fifty years previously). The second, on the other hand, is found in the first chapter of the book of *Nehemiah*. It is the opening line of a prayer that Nehemiah (cupbearer to the king of Persia) prayed around 444 BC, almost a century later. Yet it was also prayed in response to the desolate state of Jerusalem at the time, and like that prayer of Daniel's it was also preceded by mourning and fasting. Moreover, just as Daniel's prayer is followed by a prophecy of Jerusalem's rebuilding that begins with 'the issuing of the word to restore and rebuild Jerusalem', this prayer of Nehemiah's is followed by – you've guessed it! – the issuing to Nehemiah of a permission to restore and rebuild Jerusalem (which he duly undertook to the best of his abilities).

Could it be mere coincidence that the prayers of both these heroes just happen in those similar circumstances to begin in almost exactly the same way?

Perhaps, you may be thinking, that opening verse was just a common way of addressing God that both Nehemiah and the writer of Daniel 9 had adopted independently. But if you compare the next couple of verses of those prayers we again find considerable similarities (highlighted in bold typeface). Daniel 9:5-6 says,

> **DAN 9: [5] ...we have sinned, and have dealt corruptly, and have done wickedly, and have rebelled, even turning aside from your commands and from your laws. [6] We have not listened to your servants the prophets**, who spoke in your name to our kings, our princes and our ancestors, and to **all the people of the land**.

Compare this with the third verse of Nehemiah's prayer which constitutes an almost identical confession of national guilt,

> **NEH 1: ⁶...[we] have sinned. ⁷We have dealt very corruptly against you. We have not obeyed the commands, nor the decrees, nor the laws that you gave your servant Moses.**

Moreover, the *second* verse of Nehemiah's prayer (Nehemiah 1:6) – the verse immediately *preceding* this confession of guilt – appeals to God to **'Let your ear now be attentive, and your eyes open, that you may listen to the prayer of your servant, which I pray before you, at this time, day and night for the children of Israel your servants, while I confess the sins of the children of Israel, which we have committed against you. Yes, I and my father's house have sinned...'** The 'children of Israel', here, are what the third verse of Daniel's prayer (bottom of page 68) refers to as **'all the people of the land'**, and it is notable that later in Daniel's prayer (Daniel 9:18, page 174), Daniel also appeals to God to **'turn your ear, and hear, open your eyes and see, our desolations and the city which is called by your name.'** So far, the two prayers are saying almost exactly the same thing!

But what I find most astonishing is that the *fourth verse* of Daniel's prayer appears to be acknowledging the fulfilment of the very punishment mentioned in the *fourth verse* of Nehemiah's prayer, as you can see below. Nehemiah's fourth verse (Nehemiah 1:8) reads,

> **NEH 1: ⁸Remember, I beg you, the instruction you gave your servant Moses, saying, 'If you are unfaithful, I will scatter you among the peoples;**

whilst Daniel's fourth verse (Daniel 9:7) reads,

DAN 9: ⁷Lord, righteousness belongs to you, but to us shame, as it is today—to the men of Judah, and the inhabitants of Jerusalem, and to all Israel, both near and far off, **in all the countries where you have scattered us, because of our unfaithfulness to you.**

How likely is that to be just chance? When I first noticed it, I began to suspect that those two prayers were not independently composed. Reading on, I saw even more similarities between them.

The very next verse of Nehemiah's prayer focusses on God's mercy and forgiveness:

NEH 1: ⁹but if you return to me, and keep my commandments and do them, though your outcasts were in the uttermost part of the heavens, **yet I will gather them from there, and will bring them to the place that I have chosen, to cause my name to dwell there** *[or 'as the dwelling place of my name'].*

And likewise, so does the next couple of verses of Daniel's prayer:

DAN 9: ⁸ Lord, to us belongs shame, to our kings, to our princes, and to our fathers, because we have sinned against you. ⁹**To the Lord our God belong mercies and forgiveness**; even though we have rebelled against him.

It is also worth noting that Nehemiah 1:9, above, describes Jerusalem as **'the dwelling place of God's name'.** This is framed as a quote from scripture, and a very similar description of Jerusalem appears in Daniel 9:18 (compared earlier with Nehemiah 1:6 on page 169). There Jerusalem is **'the city which is called by your name'**, which may well allude to that very same scripture.

Admittedly, Daniel's prayer is considerably longer than Nehemiah's. However, much of its extra length seems to involve the repetition and amplification of the same themes encountered in Nehemiah's prayer. For example, its next few verses re-emphasise Israel's national guilt and the justness of its consequences; and they refer explicitly to the Mosaic instruction and warning cited by Nehemiah 1:8, which was only *alluded to* earlier in Daniel 9:7.

> **DAN 9:** [10] We haven't obeyed our God Yahweh's voice, to walk in his laws, which he set before us by his servants the prophets *[the theme of Nehemiah 1:7]*. [11] Yes, all Israel have transgressed your law, turning aside, that they should not obey your voice *[the theme of Nehemiah 1:6]*. Therefore, **the curse and the oath written in the law of Moses the servant of God has been poured out on us** for we have sinned against him *[the theme of Nehemiah 1:8]*. [12] He has confirmed his words, which he spoke against us, and against our judges who judged us, by bringing on us a great evil; for under the whole heaven, nothing has been done like what has been done to Jerusalem *[the motivation for Nehemiah's prayer]*. [13] **As it is written in the law of Moses, all this evil has come on us. Yet we have not entreated the favour of Yahweh our God,** that we should turn from our iniquities and have discernment in your truth *[the theme of Nehemiah 1:9]*.

It is interesting to see Daniel referring explicitly to the instructions of **Moses**, here, just as did Nehemiah (see **NEH 1:7-8**), whereas earlier in his prayer (**DAN 9:5**) he referred generally to 'the prophets'. It is almost as if the writer has added this extra detail because he *wants* those close similarities between this prayer and the famous prayer of Nehemiah to be recognised by his readers.

When I first heard about those similarities, I was very eager to know what mainstream scholars of Daniel made of them. However, there seemed to be a wall of silence. Some of them did mention in passing that this prayer was similar to prayers in the book of Nehemiah. However, their example was usually Nehemiah 9:5-38 – a later prayer – not Nehemiah 1:5-11 (though some did mention that one too). None of them went into any details in the articles and books that I read, so I had a look at that later prayer in the book of Nehemiah myself. To my surprise, I found it far *less* similar to Daniel 9:4-19 than Nehemiah 1:5-11 was. True, it is long and rambling like Daniel 9, but it does not begin in the same way and does not contain anything like the correspondences in structure and content that I have so far pointed out. Moreover, it is not even the confessional appeal of an individual seeking Jerusalem's restoration. It is in fact more like a public expression of praise that finishes with an oath of commitment to God's law. Nevertheless, I did find some intriguing correspondences with Daniel 9 in this prayer also. For example, Daniel 9:14 says,

> **DAN 9: [14]** Therefore **Yahweh has watched over the evil, and brought it on us; for Yahweh our God is righteous in all the things he does, and we have not obeyed his voice.**

And Nehemiah 9:33 says almost the same thing:

> **NEH 9: [33]** **you** [O Yahweh our God] **are just in all that has come on us; for you have dealt truly, but we have done wickedly.**

But as I said, Daniel 9:4-19 is far more like Nehemiah 1:5-11. It seems to me that the similarities with Nehemiah 9 are merely the statements in Daniel 9 that embellish those themes of Nehemiah 1. I found an absolutely astonishing example of this when I compared the very next verses of the two prayers.

Daniel 9:15 describes God as the redeemer of the people of Israel using the following words:

> **DAN 9**: ¹⁵ Now, Lord our God, **who brought your people out of the land of Egypt with a mighty hand**, and **gained a name for yourself, as it is today**; we have sinned. We have done wickedly.

Compare this with Nehemiah 1:10, which says:

> **NEH 1:** ¹⁰ Now these are your servants and your people, **whom you have redeemed** by your great power, and **by your mighty hand.**

When you remember that 'redemption' for the Jews was their freedom from slavery in Egypt, you suddenly realise that these verses are also saying the same thing. But there's more. That redemption is specifically described as the freedom from slavery in Egypt *in Nehemiah 9:10*, and there, amazingly, we also find the phrase **'and gained a name for yourself as it is today'** – the very same phrase that appears in this context in Daniel 9:15 (above).

Even the 'righteous acts' and 'object of scorn' phrases in Daniel 9:16 (below) seem to point to sections of Nehemiah 9. God's righteous acts are listed in detail in Nehemiah 9:27-31 (a long passage that I shall not reproduce here); and Nehemiah 9:36-37 (which I shall also not reproduce) quite clearly portrays the Israelites as an object of scorn. The section of Daniel's prayer that might allude to those verses of Nehemiah 9 reads as follows:

DAN 9: ¹⁶ Lord, in keeping with **all your righteous acts**, please let your anger and your wrath be turned away from your city of Jerusalem, your holy mountain. Because for our sins, and for the iniquities of our fathers, Jerusalem and your people have become an **object of scorn** to all who are around us.

Finally, compare the conclusions of the two prayers:

DAN 9: ¹⁷ Now therefore, our God, **listen to the prayer of your servant, and to his petitions.** For your sake, lord, cause your face to shine on your sanctuary that is desolate. ¹⁸ My God, **turn your ear, and hear. Open your eyes, and see** *[Nehemiah 1:6]* our desolations, and **the city which is called by your name** *[Nehemiah 1:9]*; for we do not present our petitions before you because of our righteousness, but **for the sake of your great mercy** *[the theme of Nehemiah 1:9]*. ¹⁹ Lord, listen! Lord, forgive! Lord, hear and act! Don't defer, for your own sake, my God, since **your city and your people are called by your name.**

NEH 1: ¹¹ Lord, I beg you, **let your ear be attentive now to the prayer of your servant, and to the prayer of your servants,** who delight to fear your name; and please prosper your servant today, and grant him compassion in the sight of this man.

Although Daniel's conclusion is considerably longer than that of Nehemiah, it is largely a summary of the themes already mentioned earlier in his prayer. As we have just seen, these are remarkably similar to those of Nehemiah 1:5-11. Moreover, its emphasis on appealing for God to listen to his servant is exactly the same as we find in Nehemiah 1:11. Thus, not only does Daniel 9:4-19 emphasize the fact that Jerusalem is *the place of God's name* (the very definition found in Nehemiah 1:5-11), but it begins with *the same words* as Nehemiah 1, includes a very similar *confession of national guilt*, makes its fourth verse respond to *the very same Mosaic instruction* that Nehemiah refers to in the fourth verse of his prayer (Nehemiah 1:8), and mentions the redemption of Israel by God's 'mighty hand' in the build-up to its concluding petition, *exactly like Nehemiah 1:10*. Both prayers also use the same name for God, Yahweh (a name not used elsewhere in the book of Daniel), and implore him to *open his eyes and ears*.

For reasons that will become clearer later in this chapter, the conclusion to which these observations inexorably direct us is that the prayer in Daniel 9 was inspired by – perhaps even *derived from* – that prayer in the book of Nehemiah. The fact that it has been placed in front of the prophecy in Daniel 9:24-27 therefore makes it quite unreasonable to claim that 'the word to restore and rebuild Jerusalem' to which that prophecy refers was not meant to be the permission that Nehemiah received in 444 BC to do precisely that.

As we discovered in chapter 6, when you interpret the 'years' implicit in the "sevens" of that prophecy as the units of 360 days evident in Daniel 12:11-12, the time-period beginning with Nehemiah's permission in 444 BC reaches precisely to the very month of Christ's Triumphal Entry in AD 33 (the most probable year for that world-changing event). When I first read this in the book *Chronological Aspects of the Life of Christ* by Harold Hoehner, I was amazed. The 360-day years are perfectly justified by the text of the book of Daniel. The numbers in Daniel 12:11-12 show that time was being measured, at least by the author of that prophecy, in terms of a unit of 360 days. And as we have seen, the similarity of Daniel's prayer to that of Nehemiah is powerful evidence that 'the word to restore and rebuild Jerusalem' in the prophecy was indeed the royal building warrant given to Nehemiah in 444 BC.

The one major missed opportunity in Hoehner's work is that he did not exhibit this extremely powerful piece of evidence. That would have persuaded me instantly. The problem is that evangelical scholars like Hoehner have their hands tied as far as such evidence is concerned. They simply cannot exhibit it because it clashes with the conservative views of their institution or readership on how God created the Bible. As you will see in the rest of this chapter, if evangelicals were to be more openminded on this issue, and less willing to put limits on what God is allowed to do, they would soon discover that the book of Daniel offers extremely powerful objective evidence endorsing the view that Christianity really is God's kingdom on Earth as Jesus claimed.

We have so far examined the prophecies in Daniel 2, Daniel 7 and Daniel 9 which appear to be amazingly accurate predictions of Christ and Christianity. In the rest of this chapter we shall examine the evidence found in other parts of the book of Daniel which all but confirms that these three prophecies were included in that book long before the events that fulfilled them took place, and which shows quite clearly how they were interpreted by that book's earliest readers.

No matter how critical scholars attempt to explain away the content of these prophecies, there is no escaping the fact that when compared with the history that has come down to us, the most justifiable meaning of Daniel 2:31-45, Daniel 7 and Daniel 9:24-27 accurately predicted specific events in early Christian times that could not have been deliberately brought about by human beings. Due to the time-limited nature of these predictions, and the fact that critical scholars will not date them any later than the second century BC, this is an astonishing observation. But you might be wondering why critical scholars are so reluctant to date these prophecies to Christian times. If they could have been edited after the events that fulfilled them their stunning accuracy could easily be accounted for as hindsight. So why don't critical scholars suggest this?

Part of the reason is that fragments of these prophecies dating from pre-Christian times are present amongst the Dead Sea Scrolls, and there are what appear to be references to them in works that date from before the events that fulfilled them took place. But then again, the scrolls are only fragmentary. Not much of each prophecy has survived, and one could surely make a hypothetical case that the existing references to those prophecies, and early copies of them, were gradually "improved" by Christian copyists until they formed those perfectly accurate predictions that our Bible now contains. Of course, it would then be hard to explain why the Jews accept the current book of Daniel as their scripture. But maybe that could be put down to the ravages of time and early suppression and persecution erasing memories and records of how those prophecies originally read.

Perhaps the strongest argument against such a scenario is the fact that the early church fathers simply *did not notice* how accurate these prophecies were. They didn't realise that the most obvious interpretation of Daniel 7 accurately predicted the rise of Vespasian in the Year of the Four Emperors. They thought that the most obvious interpretation of this prophecy had failed, and were very puzzled about what the prophecy meant, each interpreting the imagery a different way. The same was the case with the 'time, times and half a time' in Daniel 7, the only really justifiable meaning of which reveals an amazing fulfilment only when combined with that most obvious interpretation of the rest of the prophecy. Only the fulfilment of Daniel 9 was fully recognised. The extraordinary prediction of its final "seven" was recognised by the Jews of Jerome's day as being fulfilled by the actions and death of Hadrian (see page 124), and its first prediction was recognised by the early Christians as being fulfilled by Jesus of Nazareth, though even then the importance of interpreting the "sevens" as 'seven years of 360 days' wasn't realised until the Scotland Yard detective and theologian Robert Anderson penned *The Coming Prince* in the late nineteenth century.

However, the main reason critical scholars will not consider a date later than the second century BC for these prophecies is because of the content of the two other long-term prophecies that the book of Daniel contains. These are Daniel 8 and Daniel 11-12, which we will now examine. Both of these prophecies present a relatively detailed account of history. But unlike Daniel 2, 7 and 9, the accuracy of those accounts extends only as far as the Judea-based activities of a Seleucid king of Syria known as Antiochus IV Epiphanes (the fourth 'king Antiochus' of the Seleucid succession – the succession of Macedonian kings that began with Alexander the Great's general Seleucus), and these took place in 168-167 BC.

As a Macedonian king of the Seleucid dynasty, Antiochus IV Epiphanes ruled one of the four parts of the Greek empire of Alexander the Great (which Jews in his day were bound to see as the four-headed leopard in Daniel 7). He came to the throne in 175 BC, launched two invasions of Egypt (ruled by the young Macedonian king Ptolemy VI), and when the second of these was prematurely curtailed by the Romans in 168 BC, he vented his frustration on the Jews of Judea whose religion he disliked.

Daniel 8 and Daniel 11 (page 221 and 323) accurately record how he attacked Jerusalem and slaughtered thousands of her people, plundered her holy Temple, abolished Jewish sacrifice, forced the Jews to sacrifice to Greek gods, and set up an altar to the Greek god Zeus within their Temple's inner sanctuary. The latter took place in 167 BC, and these prophecies contain no further predict-ions about this king that were fulfilled by events after that date. Nevertheless, in one of them his story does appear to continue.

Daniel 11:40-45 (page 324-325) appears to predict a campaign that will be undertaken by this king *after* his attack upon Jerusalem. The problem is that this future campaign is a third – and very successful – invasion of Egypt. All scholars agree that Antiochus IV Epiphanes *did not undertake such a campaign*. There is no sign of it in the history books, and such a successful campaign at that time in history would almost certainly have been documented. Moreover, the king in the prophecy is predicted to die soon afterwards, seemingly in Judea, which is not where Antiochus Epiphanes died according to reliable classical historians.

Critical scholars point out that these facts are best explained by the very reasonable hypothesis that Daniel 8 and Daniel 11-12 were written from hindsight between 167 and 164 BC (the year Antiochus Epiphanes really died) by someone pretending to be the prophet Daniel. Fearing his deception would be too obvious if all the events his prophecies predicted had already come to pass, this person made a guess at the future and added it to the end of Daniel 11, making it as detailed as he dared in order to fool the sceptics. It is the fact that this guess *didn't come true* that shows us when the book of Daniel was put together. It really only shows us when Daniel 10-12 (the continuous section containing this prophecy) was written. However, the prophecy in Daniel 8, though much less detailed than Daniel 10-12, covers exactly the same ground as that final prophecy and has the same emphasis on the Judea-based activities of Antiochus Epiphanes, making it very likely to be the work of the same person. It also consists of animal imagery with accompanying interpretation, which strongly suggests it was modelled on Daniel 7, and which thereby indicates the existence of Daniel 7 at that time. Moreover, Daniel 10-12 uses the obscure 'abomination of desolation' phrase that features in Daniel 9:24-27, and it also appears to have borrowed the strange 'time, times and half a time' phrase from Daniel 7.

All this points to the view that those other prophecies were in the possession of the writer of Daniel 10-12 at the time he wrote this section of the book (the mid-160s BC judging from the inaccuracy of Daniel 11:40-45). When one considers why this writer might want to create this detailed prophecy of Antiochus Epiphanes at that time, one quickly realises that the whole book was probably put together – though not necessarily written – by this writer.

The time 167-164 BC when Daniel 8 and Daniel 10-12 were written according to this very plausible mainstream theory was a time of terrible hardship for devout Jews in Judea who sought to hold onto their religious traditions. King Antiochus Epiphanes had issued decrees making it illegal to follow the law of Moses on pain of death. He even insisted that Jews must break their religious law by making offerings that it disallowed as a demonstration of loyalty to him, and many Jews chose the ultimate sacrifice rather than submit to Antiochus' demands. But the oppression was so severe that faithful Jewish leaders would undoubtedly have worried that it was likely to succeed in its aims. They needed something that would strengthen the morale of the faithful and make them willing to resist.

Enter: the book of Daniel! What would work better than a "re-discovered" collection of morale-boosting stories about a "perfect" religious hero forced to work for foreign kings, but who would never compromise his faith even when not doing so appeared to mean certain death – a fate he always miraculously survives, resulting in rewards and riches being heaped upon him by the foreign kings desperate to appease his God. If anything was going to boost the morale of the faithful this was it! But the Jewish leaders needed some way to convince the Jewish nation that it had really happened and that their God expected the same from them. The writer's stroke of genius was to make this perfect hero receive prophetic visions that predicted Antiochus IV Epiphanes and their current sufferings…and beyond.

The 'beyond', here, is perhaps the most important part. And in my view, it hardly gets considered by the scholars who subscribe to this very plausible theory. If all the prophecies in the book of Daniel extended only as far as the time of Antiochus Epiphanes, this was bound to raise suspicions (especially if almost everything they predicted had already come to pass). Hence the writer had a very strong incentive to include prophecies that predicted events that still lay in the very distant future of his own time.

As I have already mentioned, most critical scholars think the totally inaccurate part of Daniel 11 (verses 40-45) was that writer's attempt to satisfy the sceptics with a *real prediction* – a third invasion of Egypt by Antiochus IV Epiphanes – and I find this hypothesis quite reasonable. Antiochus Epiphanes had already invaded Egypt successfully twice, and the latter attempt had been thwarted only by Antiochus' reluctance at that time to challenge Rome's hegemony. Political circumstances could easily change, and if they did Antiochus would be sure to swiftly finish the campaign that had been so humiliatingly curtailed.

However, the writer may not have cared too much whether the prophecy came true or not. Provided the length of time before it failed was sufficient for the book of Daniel to serve the immediate purpose he intended it for, all that mattered was that the prediction was plausible. He did not want the historical predictions in the prophecy to end in the past because sceptics would immediately denounce the book as a forgery. But neither did he want them to be immediately perceived as guesswork. Critical scholars see Daniel 11:40-45 as a clever attempt to give the sceptics enough reason to hold back on their denouncement while the book of Daniel worked its magic with the more-gullible populace.

But as we have seen in chapters 2-6, there are other parts of the book of Daniel where the history portrayed seems to extend beyond the time of the Judea-based activities of Antiochus Epiphanes: Daniel 2:31-45, Daniel 7 and Daniel 9:24-27. It seems very strange to me that those scholars are never willing to postulate that similar motives may account for the inclusion of these passages too. Although the predictions that these passages make stretch much further into that writer's future than Daniel 11:40-45 does, the goal of convincing the sceptics would seem to me to be made vastly more achievable by the inclusion of predictions of this nature too. After all, if every one of Daniel's prophecies were about Antiochus Epiphanes the sceptics would almost certainly suspect the book was just propaganda. It clearly needed prophecies that its readers would think were *not* about that reigning king.

For me, this is the only satisfactory explanation for why that proposed writer would include Daniel 2, Daniel 7 and Daniel 9:24-27. As we saw in the previous chapters, these prophecies do not predict events in the second century BC, and were never designed to do so. The Jews of that time could not have failed to notice this.

Even if we ignore the fact that the sequence of empires in Daniel 7 contains one too many for the fourth to be the Greek or Seleucid Empire, the prophecy still makes no sense as a prediction of Antiochus Epiphanes. That is because it says that the blasphemous king who attacks the Jews is the *eleventh* king of his nation, and that he would *subdue three previous kings* of that same nation during his rise to power. Antiochus Epiphanes was the *eighth* Seleucid king – ninth if you include a non-Seleucid usurper called Heliodorus who attempted to seize the throne just before him – and he did *not* subdue three previous kings of that empire.

Critical scholars tend to claim that the three kings the writer must have been thinking of were (1) the failed usurper Heliodorus, (2) an infant son of the previous king Seleucus IV (Antiochus probably did have this child secretly murdered), and (3) Seleucus IV himself, whose death was nothing to do with Antiochus Epiphanes. The problem of Seleucus' death doesn't bother them much because the writer might simply have *thought* Antiochus Epiphanes was involved. However, to my mind that is the smallest of the problems this view faces. The more serious problems are the fact that the eleventh king is represented by a *little horn*, and the fact that even with the inclusion of Seleucus' infant son (no mention of whom appears in Daniel 11) Antiochus Epiphanes would still only be the *tenth* Seleucid king. Why would he be given a *little* horn if one of the ten previous horns represents an uncrowned infant, and another a usurper? And why the *eleventh?*

To make Antiochus Epiphanes an eleventh king of the Greek Empire, those same scholars claim the writer was including Alexander the Great in his king list. But the problem is that Alexander the Great left an unborn son when he died in 323 BC; and that boy reached his teenage years before being murdered, and he was even regarded as a king by some of the Greeks. Moreover, this happened *prior to the crowning of Seleucus I* (the first king of the Seleucid line of kings that led to Antiochus Epiphanes). Surely if that writer saw Seleucus IV's infant son as a king of the Greek Empire, and considered Alexander the Great to be its *first* king, he would see Alexander the Great's son as its *second* king! Thus, even if he did ignore all the Ptolemaic, Antigonid and Attalid kings of the Greek Empire, and chose instead to include murdered infants and unsuccessful usurpers in its line of kings, he would *still* not perceive Antiochus Epiphanes as the eleventh.

Critical scholars appear now to be admitting this. The most recent suggestion I have come across is that the number eleven was only chosen because it may have symbolised illegitimacy!

Other critical scholars, however, have tried to account for the ten kings a different way. They argue that the prophecy was probably written at the beginning of the Greek Empire (333-323 BC), or the early years of the Seleucid Empire (founded in 312 BC), as a prediction of its *future longevity*. They claim it was merely *edited* during the 160s BC to make it depict Antiochus Epiphanes.

But if that were the case, one wonders why the person who edited it didn't do a better job. One also wonders why the scholars who are making this suggestion aren't considering the possibility that it was instead included in the early *second* century BC as a prediction about the *Roman* empire's longevity. Remember, Rome became indisputably the dominant empire in the world after she defeated the Seleucid Empire in 189 BC at the Battle of Magnesia (twenty-one years before Antiochus attacked Jerusalem). Surely, therefore, that possibility is by far the one most favoured by the imagery of the sequence of empires. Not only was Rome obviously the fourth distinct empire in the sequence beginning with Babylon, but everyone in the second century BC would have identified the Greek Empire that gave rise to Antiochus Epiphanes (and which split in four) as the *third* empire in that sequence due to the four heads and four wings on the *third beast* in the vision. As this would mean that the fourth empire was intended to be Rome and *not* Greece, the prediction of the eleventh king of that empire subduing three before him wouldn't have been about Antiochus Epiphanes at all, so the fact that it doesn't fit the facts about Antiochus Epiphanes need not worry those scholars any longer!

Even the prophecy in Daniel 9 does not fit the actions of Antiochus Epiphanes. As we saw in chapter 5, the time-period that sets the predicted events in history is far too long for this. But ignoring that minor inconvenience the sequence of events itself is extremely problematic. For a start, it predicts a destruction of Jerusalem *and her Temple*. Although Antiochus Epiphanes destroyed parts of Jerusalem in 168-167 BC, he did not destroy the Temple. He merely rendered it unclean by devoting it to Greek worship. But even if some zealot at the time regarded this as the end of the Temple (it being no longer fit for purpose), the timing of events in the prophecy is far from consistent. Antiochus' destruction of Jerusalem was followed *only weeks later* by his ending of Jewish sacrifice and offering. However, the ending of sacrifice and offering in Daniel 9:27 is predicted to take place *at least three-and-a-half years* (half the final "seven") – and probably a lot longer – after the destruction of Jerusalem and her Temple! I think it is inconceivable that a writer who had just experienced those terrible events would portray them so inaccurately.

Needless to say, critical scholars claim not to hold this opinion. In their view, all three of these prophecies were intended by this writer (the book's compiler) to predict events in the 160s BC. They claim that each is a deliberately muddled vision of Antiochus Epiphanes, and that all three have been inserted into the book in their current order so that, in combination with Daniel 8 and Daniel 11, they give the impression of a vision of the future (i.e. the writer's present) getting clearer and clearer as the book progresses.

When I first heard this claim, I became very suspicious. Deliberately muddled prophecies are prophecies that *haven't come true*, or which have so much obscure symbolism they can mean anything at all! Neither of Daniel 2, Daniel 7 or Daniel 9:24-27 fits either of these categories. But if it did, it would be counter-productive in a book of this nature. It would leave the reader confused and disappointed with the book's hero, or with God himself, and would certainly go nowhere towards removing his worries about the future or strengthening his resolve to stand up to Antiochus' henchmen. So why else were these prophecies put in?

As far as I can see, the theory that *best* explains the inclusion of Daniel 2, Daniel 7 and Daniel 9:24-27 in the book of Daniel is that these prophecies were included to predict the distant future of the writer's day – the distant future from the perspective of a Jewish writer in the mid-160s BC. That writer already had two very good prophecies of Antiochus Epiphanes. He didn't need any more. What he really needed was predictions of the future, far beyond his day, that sceptics would recognise as such and as a result be more cautious about denouncing his book as a forgery. He really needed to persuade those sceptics. And for this reason, it was far better to select suitably ancient prophecies from a source whose work appeared to have started coming true than to make up such prophecies himself. That way the sceptics would not be able to argue that the writing in the book was of a modern style, and they might even recognise the writing style as that of the prophet Daniel from whom those genuine prophecies almost certainly came, thereby reducing their suspicions.

Of course, this plan would not work if he couldn't persuade those sceptical readers to take an interest in those three genuine prophecies. Hence he has designed the book in a way that draws the reader's attention to them. This, in my view, explains why Daniel 10-12 is placed immediately after Daniel 9:24-27, and Daniel 8 is placed next to Daniel 7. The use of the phrase 'abomination of desolation' in Daniel 10-12 is calculated to draw the reader's interest back to Daniel 9:24-27, and the use of animal imagery to represent specific nations in Daniel 8 is designed to make the reader look back in more detail at the animal imagery of Daniel 7. In fact, in view of the obvious similarity of Daniel 8 to Daniel 7, and the fact that the detail in Daniel 11 makes it a far clearer prediction of Antiochus Epiphanes than Daniel 8 is, it seems to me that the only benefit of including Daniel 8 in this book is the fact that it makes the reader reconsider Daniel 7. I therefore suspect that Daniel 8 was composed for this very purpose.

We shall look in more detail at my reasons for thinking this in chapter 9. In the next chapter, I shall consider the mainstream views on the content of these prophecies, and show why that content is far better explained by the position I have outlined here. First, though, I want to emphasise the role of God in all this.

You might think that if Daniel 8 and Daniel 11 were written by a person pretending to be Daniel for propaganda purposes then they cannot be the work of God. However, remember what I said earlier about God being perfectly at liberty to use the imperfect creations of human minds to serve his purposes should he see fit to do so. Well, I don't know if you have noticed, but there is a very important purpose that Daniel 8 and Daniel 11 now serve in the Bible, which they could not have served had they not been the work of someone pretending to be Daniel (or imagining a vision Daniel might have had). They provide us with a very early date at which we can be quite sure the book of Daniel was completed. Moreover, their content tells us quite clearly that the genuine prophecies found in Daniel 2, 7 and 9 were already included in that pre-Christian book of Daniel. They thus act as a datable *seal* – an easily datable package that was clearly made to contain these prophecies, and which thereby proves their existence two centuries or more *before* the events that fulfilled them took place.

If this is indeed what Daniel 8 and Daniel 11 are for, God never ever meant us to believe they were genuine. The very fact that Daniel 11 contains a section that didn't come true proves that it isn't, and both Daniel 8 and Daniel 11 contain other features that ought to make us convinced that their content wasn't from God. For example, they identify the predicted empires by *naming* the nations responsible. If they really had been predictions, this would have needlessly put those nations at serious risk of invasion or eradication by the previous empires. And they also make nasty remarks about Antiochus Epiphanes, which suggests more the biases of an embittered human mind than the all-seeing mind of God. Moreover, the history in Daniel 11 (see Appendix) is so detailed that had it been a genuine prophecy it would have been utterly famous in no time at all. Yet, as critical scholars take pleasure in reminding us, there is no evidence for the existence of the book of Daniel before the second century BC. That, in my opinion, is very strong grounds to believe that any book of Daniel that was around at that time did not include Daniel 11.

In view of all this evidence of the human origin of Daniel 11 and Daniel 8, for God to include these prophecies in the book of Daniel was not misleading. If we have been misled by this, we have only ourselves to blame. These prophecies were put there, not to predict the future, but because they provide an unambiguous date of completion for the book of Daniel – a date that anyone with a cursory knowledge of ancient Jewish history can see was long before the events that fulfilled the three prophecies of Christianity in that book came to pass. They allow later readers open-minded enough to look for the most likely explanation for the content of each prophecy in that book to realise that Daniel 2:31-45, Daniel 7, and Daniel 9:24-27 were definitely predictions of the distant future when they were first written, and to thereby understand just how astonishing the miracle of their perfect fulfilment by subsequent history really is.

Intriguingly, Daniel 11 and Daniel 8 also provide clues as to how their writer would have interpreted Daniel 2, 7 and 9:24-27, and those clues suggest that his interpretation would not have been anything like what mainstream critical scholars assure us he believed. As you will see shortly, it would be much more like the straightforward historically-accurate interpretation of these prophecies that I have argued to be the most justifiable one. The justifiability of the interpretations that I have put forward in this book is greatly *supported* by what that writer wrote in Daniel 8 and Daniel 10-12 about time, theology, and above all his nation's history. In fact, the historically-accurate interpretations of the prophecies of Christ and Christianity in the book of Daniel are so well-supported by these late additions that I suspect this was another reason God wanted these late additions included. Like the prayer in Daniel 9, they act as a key to the correct interpretation of those genuine predictions. They make it quite unreasonable to argue that the writer of these prophecies had a completely mistaken understanding of history, as mainstream scholars today insist. So let us now examine that key in detail and be amazed at the wonderful miracle that its presence in the book of Daniel thereby constitutes.

NOVEL CONCLUSIONS FROM CHAPTER 7:

The prayer in Daniel 9:4-19 was derived from the prayer in Nehemiah 1:5-11 with some obvious embellishment from Nehemiah 9:5-38. As a result, its inclusion immediately prior to the prophecy of Daniel 9:24-27 has profound implications. It ensures that Nehemiah's permission to rebuild Jerusalem (issued by Persian Emperor Artaxerxes I in the Jewish month of Nisan in 444 BC) is incontestably the most justifiable interpretation of 'the word to restore and rebuild Jerusalem' in that prophecy. Daniel's prayer thus tells us that Nehemiah's permission was the intended starting point of that prophecy's time-period, a time-period that ends with the arrival at Jerusalem of a most holy Christ the king who would get put to death shortly afterwards having nothing. The fact that this prayer mirrors Nehemiah's in so many ways makes it inconceivable that the person who completed Daniel 9 didn't think its time-period began from Nehemiah's Permission.

Starting from the moment when that word to restore and rebuild Jerusalem was issued in 444 BC, the most justifiable meaning of that sixty-nine "sevens" time-period reaches precisely to the most likely year and month for the Triumphal Entry and crucifixion of Jesus of Nazareth (30th March 33 AD with the crucifixion on 3rd April according to Hoehner's Chronological Aspects of the Life of Christ, 1973). In view of this astonishing accuracy, the inclusion of that pseudonymous prayer was very probably allowed by God as a way of ensuring that future readers cannot reasonably claim that the starting point of the time-period was anything other than Nehemiah's Permission.

The inaccuracy of Daniel 11:40-45 (its failure to come true) confirms that the excessively detailed prophecy of Antiochus Epiphanes in Daniel 10-12 was a human construct written around 165 BC. Its inclusion in the Book of Daniel, however, was very probably allowed by God in order to provide a date from which we can be certain the three genuine prophecies the book contains (Daniel 2:31-45, Daniel 7 and Daniel 9:24-27) were already in existence, long before history fulfilled their most justifiable meanings.

The inability of evangelical scholars to openly consider this possibility (due to peer pressure from overly conservative institutions) is almost certainly preventing people from appreciating the full extent of God's creative genius and thoughtful provision that the structure and content of the book of Daniel so clearly reveals.

CHAPTER EIGHT

The Key, the Clock and the Kindness

I was first informed of the astonishing similarity between the prayer in Daniel 9 and the prayer of Nehemiah by an anonymous blogger on an internet forum who said he thought scholars of Daniel ought to look into this. It was a long time before I realised why they don't.

It is perhaps obvious in the case of evangelical scholars. They have no wish to appear as though they are being critical of their institution's conservative views on scripture. If Daniel's prayer was inspired by Nehemiah's, then it wasn't written by Daniel as it claims. But as for critical scholars, I didn't at first understand why they wouldn't embrace this evidence as strong grounds to believe that the time-period in Daniel 9:24-27 begins with Nehemiah's Permission – the permission to restore and rebuild Jerusalem given to Nehemiah by the Persian Emperor Artaxerxes I soon after Nehemiah prayed the prayer that is so similar to Daniel's.

I knew there was the small problem that well-respected evangelical scholars like Harold Hoehner had reckoned the time-period from that very moment and found that it reached precisely to the day of Christ's Triumphal Entry (page 154-5). But that shouldn't really matter too much to critical scholars. After all, their explanation for this passage was that its writer had little idea of his nation's chronology anyway. In their view, he was trying to construct a prophecy of the Greek king Antiochus Epiphanes' prohibition of Jewish sacrifice (167 BC), and, having no idea how much time had gone by from whatever starting point he had in mind, simply made an important-sounding guess. He supposedly multiplied the seventy years of Jeremiah's prophecy (a prophecy to which Daniel refers at the beginning of Daniel 9) by the symbolic number seven and hoped for the best. According to this hypothesis, he then slotted the evil deeds of Antiochus into the final "seven" and separated it from the rest (just in case he hadn't allowed for enough time!).

In view of this, it shouldn't really matter to them what starting point he had in mind because they are assuming he was making no attempt to be in any way accurate, and they make that same assumption even when considering the starting point to be one of the earlier decrees. They have to make that assumption in these cases too because the time-period still takes them well beyond the time of Antiochus. So why don't they just admit that he had Nehemiah's Permission in mind? They can still argue that the writer simply thought that this permission had been granted to Nehemiah much earlier than was actually the case – *four hundred and eighty* years previously instead of the correct two hundred and eighty years (from 444 BC to 164 BC) – can't they?

Well, no! They can't. As you will see later in this chapter, by making Nehemiah's permission the starting point of this time-period (via the words 'it will be built again with street and trench' and the addition of the prayer that is so like Nehemiah's) the true author of the book of Daniel has provided his readers with a clock that would have told them exactly how much of that time-period had passed by their day. The setting of that clock, which I will identify later in this chapter, is clearly evident in the book of Nehemiah; and the Jews of Jerusalem in the second century BC would all have known where to go to read its dial. It is this that I think makes critical scholars reluctant to discuss the similarity of those prayers, or even contemplate that the writer of Daniel 9 may have been thinking of Nehemiah's famous permission when he included the *Seventy "Sevens"* prophecy. If they were to accept this, their claim that this writer had no idea how much of that time-period had passed by his day would be very implausible indeed.

However, God's purpose in adding that fairly conclusive evidence into Daniel 9 was not to make critical scholars uncomfortable. It was to ensure that those prepared to look for the most justifiable interpretation of the prophecy would be led to the one that endorses Christianity. They would be led to the interpretation of the prophecy's time-period that makes it predict the triumphal arrival at Jerusalem of the holiest Christ – a king who was to be executed having nothing – *to the very month (and possibly day) of the Triumphal Entry of Jesus of Nazareth,* the most famous and most holy Christ in history. The prayer in Daniel 9, although written no doubt much later than the prophecy, is thus there to serve a very important purpose which it could not have served had it been composed when the prophecy was written (i.e. in the sixth century BC, long before Nehemiah was born).

But that prayer in Daniel 9 did not lead us to the historically accurate interpretation of the prophecy's time-period *on its own.*

193

It merely pointed to the correct *starting point*. For the most justifiable interpretation of that time-period we needed evidence of what the years in each "seven" ought to consist of. And you may be surprised to recall that we discovered that evidence in Daniel 10-12 – a part of the book of Daniel that we now have good reason to believe was *also* written much later than the sixth century BC (see page 179).

That evidence was the 1290 days and the 1335 days that we found in Daniel 12:11-12 (page 153). In chapter 6, we analysed these uncontroversially as '*3.5 times 360 days plus one 30-day month*' and '*3.5 times 360 days plus two-and-a-half 30-day months*' respectively. This analysis is widely accepted, even by critical scholars. However, it was in that simple and obvious analysis that we found year-like units of time that were a fixed number of days in length (360 days), and therefore ideal for interpreting the "sevens" of Daniel 9 as a fixed number of days. And it was when the "sevens" were interpreted as seven of those year-like units used by the writer of Daniel 10-12 that the time-period in Daniel 9 turned out to be the perfect length for predicting the arrival of a most holy Christ at Jerusalem – a prince who would be put to death emptyhanded – to at least within a month of the likeliest date for the Triumphal Entry of Jesus (the most famous Christ in history, whose ignominious execution is perhaps his most famous feature).

Whenever I am reminded of that incredible accuracy I am always overcome with amazement. What is so amazing is the fact that the interpretation of this prophecy which subsequent history fulfilled is its most *justifiable* one. Yet its justification from the text of the book of Daniel results from the inclusion within Daniel 12:11-12 of those time-periods containing units of 360 days. In other words, it depends on a passage that we have every reason to believe was added to the book of Daniel (see page 180-181) as part of a piece of wartime propaganda created in the second century BC, long after the time of Daniel (but still long before the time that Daniel 9 predicts for the coming of Christ). Since it is so incredibly unlikely that this vital key to the meaning of this prophecy would be included by pure chance, it seems to me that this is further evidence of the involvement of the God of Jesus Christ in the development of that book. It is another amazing miracle.

As far as pointing the reader in the direction of that historically-accurate interpretation of Daniel 9 is concerned, this very same short passage (Daniel 12:11-12) has even more to offer. It also provides a defensible view on the meaning of the phrase 'abomination of desolation' in Daniel 9:27. Moreover the view that it provides makes that phrase perfect for predicting the idol (an equestrian statue of himself) that Hadrian raised on the overspreading of the Temple site around 134-5 AD (see page 133). Daniel 12:11 says:

> **DAN 12:** [11]'From the time that the continual burnt offering is taken away, and the abomination that makes desolate set up, there will be one thousand two hundred and ninety days.'

We know from its context that this sentence is talking about the foreign object of worship that Antiochus Epiphanes ordered erected in the Jerusalem Temple in 167 BC when he stopped the Jews sacrificing to their God. He made them sacrifice to the Greek god Zeus instead, and installed an altar or statue for this purpose. The term 'abomination of desolation' thus obviously refers to a foreign object of worship. Due to its occurrence in this context in the book of Daniel, that is its most *justifiable* meaning.

Since the time-period in Daniel 9:25 of sixty-nine "sevens" from 'the word to restore and rebuild Jerusalem' takes us more than a century *beyond* the date of Antiochus' abomination of desolation (167 BC) – and this is the case whichever of the four royal decrees you start from – we can be very confident that *his* erection of an idol in the Jerusalem Temple cannot be regarded as the fulfilment of the reference to 'abomination of desolation' in Daniel 9:24-27. It is not the event that Daniel 9:27 refers to. (Whether or not the writer of Daniel 10-12 *thought it might be* is another matter we will consider shortly). But the interesting thing is that the use of this 'abomination of desolation' phrase by the writer of Daniel 10-12 not only tells us this writer had access to the text of Daniel 9:24-27 (the content of which is very clearly *not* based upon Daniel 10-12), it also tells us that it is reasonable to consider this phrase as referring to a *foreign idol* – thus making Daniel 9:27 *perfectly fulfilled by Hadrian's statue* (as I argued on page 133).

Another feature of this text that I find very intriguing is that its abomination of desolation is used as the beginning of a time of persecution. This is not the case in Daniel 9 as we now have it. But recall from chapter 4 (page 108-9), when the time-period for the persecution *in Daniel 7* was interpreted the most justifiable way, we discovered that the raising of Hadrian's abomination of desolation coincides closely with its starting-point. Of course, the persecution in Daniel 12 is the one instigated by Antiochus Epiphanes (three centuries *before* Hadrian). And it could just be a coincidence that the writer of Daniel 10-12 saw this period as beginning with the raising of an abomination of desolation. I can't help wondering, though, if there was once an extra verse or two after the prophecy in Daniel 9 where the prophet made further enquiries about the vision, and God told him something like,

"From the ending of sacrifice and the raising of the abomination of desolation there will be a time of trouble, such as never was since there was a nation even to that same time. It will be for a time, times and half a time. And when they have finished breaking in pieces the power of the holy people, all these things will be finished. Blessed is he who awaits and sees the end of those days", thereby linking that prophecy to Daniel 7. After all, the prophecy in Daniel 9 does end rather abruptly. Would Daniel really have been silenced by its final "seven"? This is just speculation but perhaps the writer of Daniel 10-12 cut off the ending of that passage and adapted it for the time of Antiochus. If so, he would thus have followed God's plan to save his elect from annihilation expressed by Christ (in Mark 13:12-20) with the words,

> **MARK 13:** [12] "Brother will deliver up brother to death, and the father his child. Children will rise up against parents, and cause them to be put to death. [13] You will be hated by all men for my name's sake, but he who endures to the end, the same will be saved. [14] But when you see the abomination of desolation, spoken of by Daniel the prophet, standing where it ought not (let the reader understand), then let those who are in Judea flee to the mountains, [15] and let him who is on the housetop not go down, nor enter in, to take anything out of his house. [16] Let him who is in the field not return back to take his cloak. [17] But woe to those who are with child and to those who nurse babies in those days! [18] Pray that your flight won't be in the winter. [19] For in those days there will be oppression, such as there has not been the like from the beginning of the creation which God created until now, and never will be. [20] Unless the Lord had shortened the days, no

flesh would have been saved; but for the sake of the chosen ones, whom he picked out, he shortened the days."

It is interesting to note from this that Christ definitely did *not* see the abomination raised by Antiochus around 167 BC (as recorded in Daniel 11:31 and 12:11) as the fulfilment of Daniel 9:27. As far as he was concerned, in 33 AD that fulfilment *still lay ahead*. Moreover, in the above passage he is almost certainly predicting the time of persecution indicated by the 'giving into the hand' in Daniel 7:25 (page 72). We know this because he says it will precede 'the Son of Man coming on the clouds with power and great glory' (Mark 13:26) which is the same imagery as Daniel 7:13-14 (page 66). Christ is saying that this oppression is a future event in 33 AD – it is not what Daniel *12* refers to. Yet intriguingly, it is also to be heralded by the raising of an *abomination of desolation*. This is not clear from Daniel 7 as we now have it. We were only able to find this out *from hindsight* by ending the most obvious meaning of 'a time, times and half a time' (175 years) at the official ending of the persecution of Christians (311 AD) and counting backwards. Christ must have known this some other way.

Even if Christ based his prophecy on Daniel 12, he was definitely predicting a very *long* persecution. Its 'shortening' suggests it exceeded all previous times of trouble (some lasting tens of years). As I shall now explain, the persecution that *Daniel 12* refers to was very much shorter (though probably equally severe). Daniel 12:1 describes it as 'a time of trouble, such as never was since there was a nation even to that same time', which sounds remarkably like Christ's description of that much later persecution in Mark 13:19.

Although the ending of the time-period of 1290 days in Daniel 12:11 isn't stated, we can infer that it is the time over which foreign worship took place in the Jerusalem Temple before it got rededicated to the Jewish God Yahweh. In other words, it was the time over which the Jews of Jerusalem were being persecuted by Antiochus' soldiers (167-164 BC). How do we know? One reason is that Daniel 12:11 is given in answer to Daniel's earlier query (verse 8), 'What will be the outcome of these things?' – where 'these things' clearly refers to the persecution of the Jews by Antiochus Epiphanes portrayed in the previous few verses. But further evidence of this is found in the next sentence which reads,

> **DAN 12:** [12] 'Blessed is he who waits for, and comes to the one thousand three hundred and thirty-five days'

The blessedness here implies that something good is to happen, and the context strongly suggests this must be the Temple's rededication. That was accomplished in 164 BC, around three-and-a-half years after Antiochus defiled it by raising his abomination of desolation therein (167 BC). It was brought about by a successful Jewish rebellion led by a freedom fighter called Judas Maccabeus and his brothers, one of whom eventually came to rule Judea.

The view that the blessing to come after the 1335 days was the Temple's rededication is most strongly supported by a statement in Daniel 8 (which for reasons that will be given in chapter 9, was probably written by the same person). At the end of the dream imagery with which Daniel 8 illustrates its very similar prediction of Antiochus Epiphanes, we read, 'then the sanctuary will be cleansed' (Daniel 8:14, page 221). The blessing here is preceded by a longer time-period than in Daniel 12:12 (2300 days instead of 1335 days). However, that is easily accounted for by the fact that the start of that time-period also appears to be somewhat *earlier* than is suggested by Daniel 12:11-12. It includes the time for 'the army to be trodden underfoot because of disobedience' (Daniel 8: 13). Hence it is the *disobedience* the writer is talking about that constitutes the start of this somewhat longer time-period (not the stopping of Jewish sacrifice). And since this disobedience is being claimed to be the *reason* God allowed Antiochus to destroy Jewish resistance in the city and slaughter large numbers of her inhabitants, it has to come *before 168 BC* when that happened.

There is no point in us getting into the detail of what particular disobedience the writer had in mind in this case because it is largely irrelevant whether or not this prophecy came true. Any fulfilment could be self-caused. What matters is that the time-period it defines is to end with the Temple being cleansed – a very happy event for the Jewish nation, and therefore most probably the one hinted at in Daniel 12:12. The 2300 days could just have been a guess that placed this predicted blessing in the writer's future. In fact, since no specific details of the Maccabean revolt that led to the Temple's rededication are alluded to in either prophecy, many critical scholars assume that this final prediction *was* a guess rather than hindsight. Perhaps it is indeed an instance of *self-fulfilled prophecy* as I hinted earlier. Its prediction in the recently circulated book of Daniel may actually have *inspired* the Jews to fight back, and thereby ensured the predicted cleansing took place.

Whatever it was, though, the interesting thing for me is that the duration of the persecution that's going to be followed by this blessing is being described by the writer of Daniel 10-12 as 'a time, times and a half' (from Daniel 7:25); and it is going to start from the raising of an 'abomination of desolation' (from Daniel 9:27). Does this mean that the writer of Daniel 10-12 thought that the actions of Antiochus Epiphanes were the *fulfilment* of Daniel 7 and Daniel 9:24-27?

Critical scholars are adamant that it does. However, I am not so sure. You see, all that writer has really done is borrow two obscure phrases, one from each of these prophecies, interpret them to suit the time of Antiochus, and fit them into his "prophecy" of that time. Had he used two more-common words from these prophecies instead, no-one would claim he was trying to interpret them. If he were really trying to demonstrate that he thought Antiochus Epiphanes had fulfilled the 'ruler who will come' prediction in Daniel 9, one would surely expect some hint of the 'seventy "sevens"' time-period. And if he really believed that the 'time, times and half a time' period of persecution alluded to in Daniel 7 was the one ongoing at the time of writing, why would he not indicate four distinct empires in that prophecy, and identify the eleven kings of the fourth one, and show how three of them were subdued by the eleventh? As you will see shortly, the history he does present in Daniel 11 seems to be making it crystal clear that Antiochus Epiphanes *cannot be* the fulfilment of Daniel 7.

I am therefore very doubtful of this tempting conclusion that critical scholars so quickly jump to. I think it is reading far too much into the use of two obscure phrases. For me, the lack of any attempt to show the fulfilment in Antiochus Epiphanes of the rest of these two prophecies suggests entirely the opposite conclusion – that Daniel 7 and 9 were *never* thought to be about Antiochus. But if so, why did the writer use these two phrases in Daniel 11-12?

I think the answer follows from our earlier explanation (pages 186-7) for why such a writer would want to include Daniel 2, Daniel 7 and Daniel 9:24-27 in this book when he was creating it as a work of propaganda designed to fire up the Jewish faithful to resist Antiochus Epiphanes' demands (as critical scholars all believe). Remember, the most obvious interpretations of these prophecies all predict events a long time after the time of Antiochus Epiphanes. And remember also that this writer was intending to pass off his work as the work of the prophet Daniel who lived three-and-a-half centuries before his time. If he simply proclaimed the discovery of these ancient prophecies that appeared to foretell exactly what had recently happened to Jerusalem in considerable detail, sceptics were bound to denounce the book as a forgery. And if the people believed them, his efforts would almost certainly not succeed. He had to come up with a book that would not only convince the ordinary folk that God was on their side but would satisfy the experts too. It had to be good enough to persuade the priests, rabbis and aristocracy that it might actually be genuine – or at least give them reason to doubt their sceptical assumptions long enough for the book to become widely accepted. That perfectly explains why he would want to include within it three genuine ancient prophecies, most probably written by the very prophet Daniel to whom he was attributing the book.

You can imagine the learned debates among the experts who were not in on the ruse. On the one side would be sceptics angrily announcing that the book was most probably a forgery due to its recent discovery and to the fact that the predictions in Daniel 11 had almost all come to pass. On the other side would be experts in ancient texts calmly pointing out that three of the book's chapters contained prophecies that predicted events that lay a long time in the distant future, and swearing that they were genuine works of Daniel. And in the middle, would be the fence-sitters who would point out that Daniel 11 wasn't yet completely fulfilled. Antiochus Epiphanes was still alive. Let's just wait and see if he invades Egypt again before we dismiss this potentially extremely important find.

But to ensure such debates would take place, our writer had to make certain that people paid attention to the content of the prophecies in the earlier sections of the book. He had to make sure they bothered to read those earlier prophecies and work out what they predicted. This, for me, is the most probable reason for why he used the dramatic words 'abomination of desolation' from Daniel 9:27 in the prophecy of Daniel 10-12 (the one he wrote himself), and for why he took the obscure time-phrase 'a time, times and half a time' from Daniel 7:25, reinterpreted it to suit his own ends, and inserted it along with that abomination phrase into Daniel 12. The 'abomination' phrase would make the experts look back at Daniel 9 in detail, and they would soon work out that the sixty-nine "sevens" from the permission given to Nehemiah placed the events of that prophecy a long way off in their distant future. The obscure time-phrase would then cause them to look back at Daniel 7 where it also occurs. For reasons we will consider in the next chapter, they would have no difficulty noticing that the same time-phrase in that prophecy referred to a time of persecution that lay a long time ahead of them, and which cannot therefore be the one the Jewish people were then suffering. The sceptics, who would probably have just assumed that these prophecies were also about Antiochus Epiphanes, would have been totally silenced when those observations were demonstrated to them.

In my opinion this hypothesis is far more satisfactory than the mainstream claim that the writer of Daniel 10-12 believed Daniel 7 and Daniel 9 to be about Antiochus Epiphanes. Unlike that popular mainstream view, it doesn't suffer from the unsolvable problem that no careful reader in the 160s BC would have interpreted Daniel 7 as a prediction of Antiochus. Remember, they perceived the Greek empire as having split into four parts (as is clearly evident from Daniel 8:22, page 222). Consequently, they would have interpreted the four-headed, four-winged leopard in Daniel 7 as Greece; and since the Seleucid Empire of Antiochus Epiphanes was one of those four parts of the Greek empire (as Daniel 8 also makes clear) they could not possibly have associated Antiochus with the totally distinct *fourth* empire that the dream predicted.

But the strongest evidence in favour of this hypothesis is the fact that the person who compiled the final version of the book of Daniel has allowed a prayer that is very clearly derived from the prayer of Nehemiah to be inserted into Daniel 9, and he has created, or at least permitted, Daniel 8 to go after Daniel 7. For reasons I will now explain, the inclusion of that prayer in Daniel 9 tells us that whoever included it *cannot possibly have understood Daniel 9 to be a prediction of Antiochus Epiphanes.* And whoever added Daniel 8 to the book of Daniel was making it crystal clear that the same also applies to Daniel 7.

Of course, these parts of the book of Daniel may have been the work of other contributors and not the person who put the whole book of Daniel together. However, given the secrecy that would need to have surrounded the creation of this work of propaganda, the most likely scenario is that the same writer was responsible, and very probably the writer of Daniel 10-12. But even if the final form of the book was decided by several individuals, they would have to have been working together with the same goal in mind. As a result, what we can reasonably infer about their beliefs is very likely to apply to the final compiler as well.

The prayer in Daniel 9 is, as I have said, very clearly derived from the first prayer in the book of Nehemiah. I demonstrated this in chapter 7. Critical scholars, for obvious reasons, do not draw such a strong conclusion about it. The closest they come to it is saying that Daniel's prayer is very similar to 'other Old Testament prayers such as Nehemiah 1:5-11 and Nehemiah 9:5-38.' Sometimes they even add Ezra 9, which in my opinion is much less like it than those prayers of Nehemiah. But if you compare it closely with Nehemiah 1 and 9, as we did at the beginning of chapter 7, you can almost see the derivation process in action.

The key point to remember is that the presence of such a prayer in Daniel 9 was bound to remind the Jewish reader of Nehemiah's prayer, and consequently his famous permission to restore and rebuild Jerusalem. Since Nehemiah built the wall of Jerusalem in the same year he received that permission, anyone who knew the age of that wall also knew how many years had elapsed since that famous 'word to restore and rebuild Jerusalem' went out. Due to the fact that the residents of the city relied upon that wall for their protection, I suspect that its age, and therefore how long ago the event of its building took place, would have been regularly recollected in conversations. That wall, and the conversations that kept its age fresh in Jewish minds, would thus have served as a public clock ticking down the years that had passed since that famous permission kickstarted the long countdown to the Messiah.

This is especially likely when you consider that the building of that wall involved many residents of the city (all of whom are recorded in Nehemiah 3). The descendants of those original wall-builders would frequently recall and discuss their ancestor's role with great pride, thereby preserving the memory of the wall's age (or at least a means of working it out). Consequently, it is difficult to believe that in those days of few distractions the age of that wall would get forgotten with time. As a result, many residents of Jerusalem in the 160s BC would have had no trouble noticing that

Daniel 9's prophetic time-period of 'sixty-nine-times-seven years' from Nehemiah's permission was nowhere near completed in their day. Nehemiah's wall had only stood for 280 years, whereas that time-period amounted to 483 years. They would thus realise that the events in Daniel 9:26-27, which seemed so reminiscent of the actions of Antiochus Epiphanes, *could not be those recent events.* They were merely similar events that were not to happen for another two centuries.

But they could only come to this conclusion if they were reminded of Nehemiah's permission. It is this that perfectly explains why the person who completed the book of Daniel would include a prayer so like Nehemiah's in Daniel 9. And if you are willing to accept that he was probably also the writer of Daniel 8 and Daniel 10-12, we can be fairly confident that the use of the phrase 'abomination of desolation' in Daniel 11 and Daniel 12 was not because the writer of those passages thought Daniel 9 predicted the same events. On the contrary, it was because he wanted to draw his readers' attention back to Daniel 9 so that they would discover that the events it predicted lay a long way into their future. They lay so far in their future that they couldn't possibly involve king Antiochus Epiphanes, who would be long dead and gone by then.

But why on earth would that writer want to write a prophecy like Daniel 8? It is, as I have said, a prediction of the very same events predicted in parts of Daniel 11 – the conquest of Persia, the four-way splitting of Greece, and the evil deeds of Antiochus Epiphanes – and they are predicted with far more clarity in Daniel 11. It is true that Daniel 8 explicitly predicts the Temple rededication, whereas Daniel 11 does not. However, it would have been much easier for that writer to simply squeeze that prediction into Daniel 12 rather than write a whole new prophecy for that purpose.

As you will see in the next chapter, the only explanation for the inclusion of Daniel 8 that makes any sense at all is that it was included for the very purpose of helping readers of the book of Daniel in the mid-160s BC arrive at the historically-accurate interpretation of the beasts in Daniel 7. As we saw in chapter 3, that really obvious interpretation of Daniel 7, where the sequence of four empires is *Babylon-Persia-Greece-Rome*, was stunningly fulfilled by the Year of the Four Emperors in 69 AD and the later conquest of Rome by Christianity. Of course, the writer of Daniel 8 in the mid-160s BC could not have known this would happen. What was important to him was that this historically-accurate sequence of empires placed the events predicted by Daniel 7 *a long time in his distant future*. The narrow window of time in which those events had to occur for a successful fulfilment of this prophecy was not likely to come about *for many generations*, and he wanted contemporary readers of this prophecy to recognise that fact. Only this would stop the sceptics among them denouncing the book of Daniel as being only concerned with recent events and personalities, and therefore most probably a forgery.

The writer of Daniel 8 was almost certainly the same writer who wrote Daniel 10-12 (or at least he was part of the same team), and he desperately wanted the readers of the book of Daniel to recognise that Daniel 7 was a prediction of *their distant future*. He knew that if they thought all the prophecies in the book were about Antiochus Epiphanes and his recent persecution of their religion, some of them would become highly sceptical about the book's authenticity, and would no doubt voice their misgivings. For his book to stand any chance of being accepted as a product of the sixth century BC, he had to give these people some grounds to hold back. And one obvious way to do this was to ensure that it contained prophecies predicting events so far in the distant future that they could not possibly be about Antiochus Epiphanes.

However, his readers needed to recognise this fact. If the timing of the events in those prophecies was not clear to them, they would probably still think they were about Antiochus – or even worse, they might think they had failed come true. Hence he had to make his own understanding of those time-periods crystal clear to his readers in a way that would not be obvious as the work of a contemporary writer.

As we have seen in this chapter, in the case of the *Seventy "Sevens"* prophecy in Daniel 9, he added a prayer closely derived from the well-known prayer of Nehemiah. This was to ensure they understood that Nehemiah's permission to rebuild Jerusalem was *'the word to restore and rebuild Jerusalem'* in that prophecy. They would then have no difficulty recognising that this prophecy spoke of their distant future. In the next chapter, I will try to show you that in the case of the "Four Kingdoms" prophecies in Daniel 7 and Daniel 2, he was attempting to achieve this very same goal via his creation and inclusion of Daniel 8.

Of course, in doing so at that time in history, he was (perhaps unknowingly) providing a key by which all later readers of the book of Daniel can understand what those prophecies predict. That key makes it quite unreasonable for anyone to claim that at the time they were written Daniel 2, Daniel 7 and Daniel 9:24-27 were not genuine and specific predictions of the future. With a little historical research, those who want to know can thereby easily find out that these prophecies were all surprisingly fulfilled, exactly as predicted, in the first, second and fourth centuries AD by the rise of Christianity and associated world events.

The astonishing historical fulfilment of the most justifiable interpretations of these prophecies is objective evidence that the gospel of Jesus Christ is endorsed by the God of Daniel. That is why I think God allowed – and perhaps even inspired – the inclusion of Daniel 10-12, Daniel 8, and the prayer in Daniel 9. These pseudonymous additions, written in the second century BC, clearly show later readers what the most-justifiable interpretation of each prophecy is. Without them, that interpretation could be reasonably challenged as being merely a consequence of our far-more-objective perspective on history. Way back in second-century-BC Palestine the Jews may well have had an entirely different perception of their history than we have now.

As we have seen from Daniel 12 and the prayer in Daniel 9, that was not the case – or at least, not in terms of the details needed to arrive at the historically-accurate interpretation of Daniel 9:24-27. The 360-day years in Daniel 12:11-12 and the similarity of the prayer in Daniel 9 to that of Nehemiah 1 are clear indicators of this. But just in case you're thinking that this might not be true of Daniel 2 and Daniel 7, let us now examine Daniel 8. As you will see, the way Greece is split-in-four in Daniel 8 and 11 supports my view that Daniel 8 is a key designed by the writer of Daniel 10-12 in the mid-160s BC to lead the reader to the historically-accurate interpretation of Daniel 7 and 2. He wanted his readers to see that the most justifiable interpretation of these prophecies predicted the distant future far beyond their time because they would then be much less willing to dismiss his book as a recent forgery.

More than two hundred years later, it was that same interpretation that got miraculously fulfilled by the Year of the Four Emperors and the rise of Christianity, which is why I think this key was not merely the work of man.

NOVEL CONCLUSIONS FROM CHAPTER 8 (WITH SUPPORT FROM CHAPTER 9):

The content of Daniel 11 and Daniel 8 – especially the fact that both these prophecies emphasise the four-way splitting of Greece – makes it totally unreasonable to argue that the sequence of empires in Daniel 7 and 2 was ever meant to be anything other than the historical sequence of distinct conquering nations: Babylon-Persia-Greece-Rome. That is because only the third beast in Daniel 7 is split in four. This fact was bound to make the intended readers of the completed book of Daniel around 165 BC recognise it as Greece; and the content of Daniel 11 and Daniel 8 clearly shows that the person who completed the book of Daniel with these readers in mind had exactly the same view. Like his intended readers, he too regarded that third empire as Greece. The four-way splitting of Greece in Daniel 11 confirms this. Moreover, his allusions to Rome's victories over the Greeks means he undoubtedly identified the fourth as Rome. This is not surprising as Rome already ruled the world in his day, and had done so for the previous two decades.

His inclusion of Daniel 7, 2 and 9 in a book that was essentially about his own time is easily explained as a device designed to fool the sceptics, or at least delay their denouncement of his book by giving them a few ancient prophecies of the really distant future, written by Daniel himself, to get their teeth into. His use of certain key phrases from Daniel 7 and 9 within Daniel 10-12 is therefore not an attempt at interpreting those genuine predictions, but a means of drawing his sceptical readers' attention to them.

As a result, the content of Daniel 11 and Daniel 8 reveals the existence of Daniel 7 and 9 at that very early date in history, long before the highly specific predictions in the latter two started to come true. At the same time, it acts as a key to their meaning, making it unreasonable to argue that Daniel 2, 7 and 9 represent a perception of history that is radically different from the one that has come down to us today. In view of the astonishing accuracy of Daniel 2, 7 and 9, it is thus reasonable to infer that God allowed those genuine prophecies to be put together with Daniel 11 and 8 for this very purpose.

Daniel 12 may also be a part of this divinely-permitted key. That is because the numbers of days it gives for the oppression by Antiochus Epiphanes clearly imply multiples of 360, making 'seven times 360 days' by far the most justifiable meaning of the "sevens" in Daniel 9. It thus supports the interpretation of Daniel 9:24-27 that was perfectly fulfilled by the Triumphal Entry and subsequent execution of Jesus Christ, the destruction of Jerusalem by Rome, Hadrian's final ending of Jewish sacrifice and offering, and the time from the founding of Aelia Capitolina (9th Av 131) until Hadrian's death (10th July 138).

Further support for that interpretation of Daniel 9:24-27 is the similarity of Daniel's prayer to the prayer in Nehemiah 1. That similarity clearly suggests that the starting point of the time-period in Daniel 9 was Nehemiah's Permission. Granting this, the walls of Jerusalem would have served as a clock counting down the years that had passed since that time-period began, making it highly implausible that residents of Jerusalem in the 160s BC would have had no idea how much of that time-period had elapsed by their day.

The use of Daniel 7's 'time, times and half a time' to mean three-and-a-half years by the writer of Daniel 12 probably prevented the Romans later discovering the most justifiable meaning of that phrase (175 years based upon Leviticus 25:8 as implied by Daniel 9:25). It thereby prevented Daniel 7 being used as grounds to annihilate the holy people after their rebellion of AD 66-74. It was probably allowed by God for this very purpose as suggested by the words of Christ in Matthew 24:22 and Mark 13:20. With these words, Christ confirmed the true meaning of that phrase over a hundred years before the raising of Hadrian's abomination of desolation heralded the 175-year period of statelessness and persecution that the holy people really did endure before they gained the kingdom.

CHAPTER NINE

God's Thoughtful Provision

The finishing touches to my presentation were now complete, so I went back and flicked through my slides. I read their content out-loud to an imaginary congregation and practiced embellishing it where necessary. I knew the point I was making was good. Not only was it highly defensible from a critical, scientific standpoint, but it also squared with the approach to prophecy advocated by Deuteronomy 18:22. This passage says that you know a prophecy isn't from God if the events it predicts *do not come to pass*. The events in Daniel 11:40-45 had not come to pass.

Although my intended audience would not like the implications of this observation, my talk showed them that it did not have to mean that the inclusion of this prophecy in the book of Daniel was not God's work. The prophecy in Daniel 10-12 (see Appendix) may not have *come* from God, but that did not mean God hadn't selected it for inclusion in this book. My talk would show them that the text of this prophecy performed a very important purpose in the book of Daniel that it could not have performed if it had been God-inspired (and thus perfectly accurate). It was there to show the reader exactly when the book of Daniel was put together.

Even the style of this prophecy was different from the others. It was long and rambling and full of historical detail, not short and compact like Daniel 9:24-27, and it did not consist of dream imagery with accompanying interpretation like Daniel 2, 7 and 8. I made a mental note to explain how the shortness and compactness of Daniel 9 with its easily memorised numbers, and the dream imagery of Daniel 2, 7 and 8, would have made these visions far easier to remember accurately when the prophet awoke. That was very probably what such imagery and compactness was for.

I flicked through to my slides on Daniel 2 and Daniel 7, admiring the beautiful rendering of the statue and the four beasts that I'd found on the Web. I rehearsed what I was going to say about these dreams, and how I would demonstrate the astonishingly unjustifiable way in which mainstream accounts of the book of Daniel try to hide the fact that these dreams came true. I was going to emphasise that readers in the 160s BC, when mainstream scholars claim the book of Daniel was written, would never have understood the four-headed four-winged leopard in Daniel 7 to be anything other than the Greek Empire of Alexander the Great. Only that empire had split into four kingdoms ruled contemporaneously by four Greek dynasties. A writer composing the book of Daniel for these readers could not possibly have failed to appreciate this. Hence, the four-headed four-winged leopard had to have been intended to represent Greece. It cannot have been Persia as those scholars all claimed. In fact, God had used an animal with four-part symbolism in Daniel 8 to represent Greece explicitly, so the mainstream requirement that the leopard be Persia could not be rescued by the remote possibility that the Jews of the 160s BC might not have *perceived* the Greek Empire as split in four.

I flicked forward to my slide on Daniel 8. The dramatic image I'd found on the Web of the powerful one-horned billy goat of Greece skewering the two-horned ram of Medo-Persia appeared before me, and I examined the sequence of smaller pictures around its edge which showed the dream's progression. I planned to draw attention to the snapping off of the goat's single horn (Alexander's death), and the four large horns growing up in its place, and how out of one of these branched a single horn for Antiochus Epiphanes (not an eleventh horn uprooting three before it). God had clearly made certain that rational readers of Daniel's genuine prophecies would understand Daniel 7 as a prediction about the kings of the Roman empire. And He had done this with a dream where the imagery was so simple and dramatic that the prophet Daniel would have had no difficulty remembering it when he woke up. To make absolutely sure the imagery was not misunderstood, God had even *named* the empires it depicted. It was then that I realised my error.

My argument for the authenticity of Daniel 2, 7 and 9 rested on the fact that the specific and astonishingly accurate predictions in these prophecies were set in windows of time that lay far beyond the 160s BC, when the book of Daniel was put together (according to the best explanation for the content of Daniel 10-12). That was not the case with Daniel 8. The events it predicted ended around that very time (see page 222). In fact, they seemed to be much the same as certain events portrayed in Daniel 10-12 (page 323). Although God could have inspired Daniel 8 long before the 160s BC, I had no evidence that this was the case. Indeed, the fact that the empires in Daniel 8 were identified *by name* (unlike those in Daniel 7 or 2) suddenly made me very suspicious. It also occurred to me that had Daniel 8 existed before the writing of Daniel 10-12, the writer of the latter would have had no *need* to write it. Daniel 8 would have worked perfectly well on its own. The portrayal of Antiochus Epiphanes' actions and death in Daniel 8 (page 222) was so clear that this prophecy *on its own* would have been sufficient to inspire the Jews to resist Antiochus Epiphanes. Its authenticity would have contributed to its power. Why risk undermining this gift by combining it with a forged prophecy of the same events?

So it was back to the drawing board for me. In the end, this realisation did nothing to shake my confidence that the book of Daniel was a work of God. Indeed, it made my case for this all the stronger because it showed for definite that the person who put the book of Daniel together in the 160s BC really did see the Greek empire as split in four. The leopard with four heads and four wings in Daniel 7 could *not* be justifiably interpreted as Persia as critical scholars today insist. It had to stand for Greece (just as a comparison of that prophecy with our modern understanding of history quite clearly suggests). The fourth empire could therefore only be Rome. Hence, the inexplicably accurate predictions of Christianity and The Year of the Four Emperors in Daniel 7 and 2 (see chapters 2-3) were indeed genuine prophecies of the future far beyond the 160s BC. You can see this from the diagram opposite.

Only one question remained. We have already seen that Daniel 10-12 was most probably written *before* Daniel 8 because otherwise there'd have been no point in it being written at all (it is after all far less convincing an example of Danielic prophecy than Daniel 8 is). But why did Daniel 8 then get written and included in the same book as Daniel 10-12? What was the writer intending by inserting this less-detailed prophecy of Antiochus Epiphanes into a book that already contained a prophecy of him that nobody would have had any difficulty interpreting correctly? It can't have been to make the book seem more authentic because otherwise he would have abandoned Daniel 10-12 entirely. Nor can it be due to the need to predict something that wasn't included in Daniel 10-12 because both prophecies cover exactly the same time-period, as you can see from the diagram below, making it far more sensible to simply add any extra predictions into Daniel 10-12.

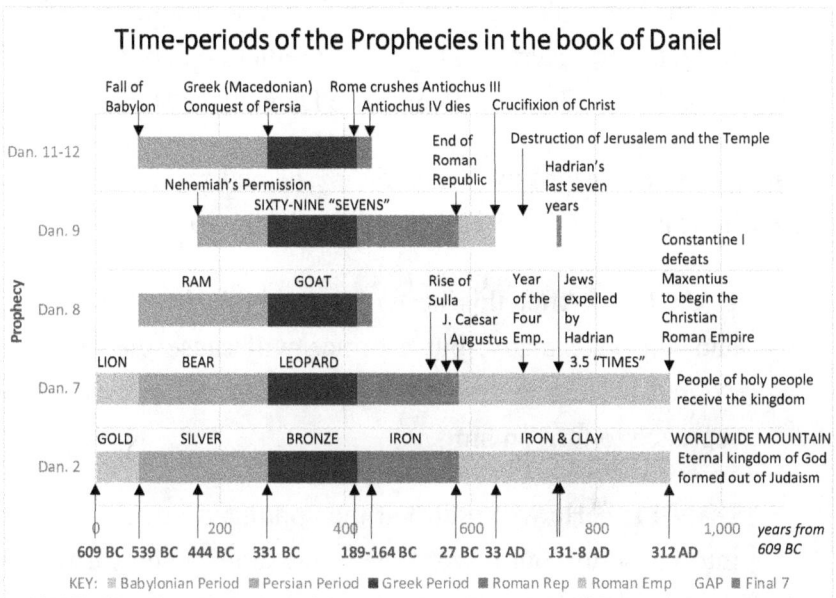

Time-periods of the Prophecies in the book of Daniel

In my effort to understand why the compiler (or last major editor) of the book of Daniel included Daniel 8, I first examined the content of Daniel 8, and I noted how it emphasised certain aspects of the content of Daniel 11. Obviously one of those aspects is the deeds of Antiochus IV Epiphanes in the early 160s BC, but there are several others. As you will see shortly, the other aspects of Daniel 11 that it emphasises are the four-way splitting of the Greek

(Macedonian) empire of Alexander the Great, and the relative weakness of the divided phase of that empire in comparison to its united phase under Alexander. It also points out that the divided phase of that empire at the time of king Antiochus Epiphanes (i.e. when that writer almost certainly lived) was its *latter time*.

Now, one might postulate, as critical scholars do, that this was because its writer believed in an impending conquest of the Greek empire by the Jewish nation. However, I could find no sign of such a conquest in Daniel 8 (page 220-22) or in Daniel 10-12 (page 317-326). In fact, the 'eternal kingdom' prediction, so evident in Daniel 2 and Daniel 7, doesn't appear in Daniel 8 or Daniel 10-12.

What that writer meant by 'latter time' seemed to me to be very clearly indicated by Daniel 11:18, and Daniel 11:29-30, below:

> **DAN 11:** [18] After this he will turn his face to the islands, and will take many; but a prince will cause the reproach offered by him to cease. Yes, moreover, he will cause his reproach to turn on him…

> **DAN 11:** [29] He will return at the appointed time, and come into the south; but it won't be in the latter time as it was in the former. [30] For ships of Kittim [a term generally used for the western Mediterranean coastlands] will come against him. Therefore he will be grieved, and will return, and have indignation against the holy covenant, and will take action. He will even return, and have regard to those who forsake the holy covenant.

Due to the context in which the former passage occurs, all scholars accept that it alludes to the defeat of the Seleucid king Antiochus III (the father of Antiochus Epiphanes) by Rome at the

Battle of Magnesia in January 189 BC. This was no minor setback. A vast Seleucid army drawn from all parts of the Seleucid empire had been decisively defeated by the Roman legions. For the rest of its existence, the Seleucid empire was entirely subordinate to Rome. She paid a vast quantity of tribute to the Senate every year and had restrictions placed upon her armed forces. To ensure compliance, the Romans from then on held the heir to the Seleucid empire as a political hostage in Rome. Even Antiochus Epiphanes served as a hostage of the Senate, and he was only released when his nephew Demetrius became the empire's legitimate heir.

This power and dominance is clearly indicated by the second quote, above. Daniel 11:29-30 alludes to the famous 'line in the sand' incident that put an end to Antiochus Epiphanes' hopes of conquering Egypt in 168 BC. He was met by a Roman ambassador Gaius Popillius Laenus on the banks of the Nile who delivered the Senate's demand that he withdraw from Egypt immediately. When Antiochus asked for time to discuss this demand with his generals, Laenus drew a circle in the sand around him and insisted he give his answer before stepping across it. Totally humiliated, Antiochus wisely accepted the Senate's wishes and pulled out of Egypt, attacking the Jews in Jerusalem on his way home.

Clearly, the writer of Daniel 11 was very much aware of the political reality of his day. The world-dominance of the Greek kingdoms was at an end, and an extremely strong and extremely different nation had now risen to dominance. Residents of Jerusalem in the mid-160s BC knew this very well. Although they lived far away from the centre of Rome's sphere of influence, the Jews of Judea were not nearly as ignorant of international politics as critical scholars of Daniel make out. They were well aware that Rome ultimately ruled their world and had done so for the previous two decades. The reason Rome is not named in this prophecy is not likely to be because the writer thought she was irrelevant. It is far more likely to be because his people (the Jews of the mid-160s BC) were hoping to make an alliance with Rome against Antiochus Epiphanes (as indeed they were at that time). To mention Rome explicitly in this book that was soon to be widely circulated in their propaganda efforts was likely to seriously jeopardise their chances of success in this endeavour. That is because it would be identifying the fourth empire in Daniel 7, which, though portrayed as more powerful than all the others, is also predicted to get conquered by the holy people – or at least by their God. Such an identification would be a gift to their enemies who could simply reveal the book of Daniel to the Romans, scuppering any chance of that hoped-for alliance.

A notable feature of Daniel 8 is that its writer sticks to the same policies as the writer of Daniel 10-12. Both Greece and Persia are named in both prophecies; Rome is not mentioned explicitly in either (though it is alluded to in Daniel 11 as we have seen); and both cover precisely the same period of history. They begin with Persia at its strongest, introduce a portrayal of its conquest by Alexander and the four-way splitting of his empire, and then arrive at a detailed portrayal of the rise of Antiochus Epiphanes, his actions against the Jews, and his longed-for death (though Daniel 11, due to its narrative structure, takes a while to get there).

At the very least this shows that one of these prophecies was based upon the other. Given the secrecy that the creation of this work would have demanded, I think we can be fairly confident that both these prophecies were written by the same person, or at least by people working in the same team. Hence the writer of Daniel 8 was most probably the writer of Daniel 10-12. And if he wasn't, he was almost certainly somebody who shared the same views on history and current affairs. As we have seen, one of those views was the dominance of Rome over the Seleucid kingdom and the other remaining remnants of Alexander's Greek empire.

I thus came to the conclusion that the reason the writer of Daniel 8 puts the reign of Antiochus Epiphanes in 'the latter days' of the four Greek kingdoms is because he was well aware of the fact that the world was now ruled by Rome. Shortly before her recent intervention in Egypt (168 BC), Rome had defeated the king of Macedon, the Antigonid wing of Alexander's Greek empire, and replaced his government with four independent republics. Judging from this, the writer of Daniel 8 had very good reason to expect that the days of the Seleucid Empire and the other two surviving Greco-Macedonian kingdoms were numbered. It was only a matter of time before they would suffer a similar fate.

But before he wrote Daniel 8, that writer had already made this same point in Daniel 10-12 (page 322). In view of the straight-forward narrative form of that final prophecy, it is reasonable to believe that it was written *before* Daniel 8; and this view is further supported by its obvious propaganda elements. Daniel 12:1-3 (page 325), for example, predicts a resurrection of the dead, and eternal life (or enduring fame) for those who keep the faith under the persecution by Antiochus Epiphanes. Those predicted rewards do not appear in Daniel 8. Yet they would have been one of the book of Daniel's most important features as far as its purpose as propaganda was concerned, and therefore presumably incorporated into the prophecy its writer wrote first. So why did that writer then write Daniel 8, and why did he write it in the form of interpreted animal imagery and not bother including within it those same promises of hope and salvation that we find in Daniel 12?

To find out, we must first read the whole prophecy, despite its rather lengthy nature. Daniel 8:1-26 reads as follows:

> **DAN 8:** [1] In the third year of the reign of king Belshazzar a vision appeared to me, even to me, Daniel, after that which appeared to me at the first. [2] I saw the vision. Now it was so, that when I saw the vision, I was in the citadel of Susa, which is in the province of Elam. I looked in the vision, and I was by the river Ulai. [3] Then I lifted up my eyes, and looked, and behold, there stood before the river a ram which had two horns. The two horns were high; but one was higher than the other, and the higher came up last. [4] I saw the ram pushing westward, northward, and southward. No animals could stand before him. There wasn't any who could deliver out of his hand; but he did according to his will, and magnified himself.
>
> [5] As I was considering, behold, a male goat came from the west over the surface of the whole earth, and didn't touch the ground. The goat had a notable horn between his eyes. [6] He came to the ram that had the two horns, which I saw standing before the river, and ran on him in the fury of his power. [7] I saw him come close to the ram, and he was moved with anger against him, and struck the ram, and broke his two horns. There was no power in the ram to stand before him; but he cast him down to the ground, and trampled on him. There was no one who could deliver the ram out of his hand. [8] The male goat magnified himself exceedingly. When he was strong, the great horn was broken; and in its place there came up four notable horns toward the four winds of the sky. [9] Out of one of them came out a little horn, which grew exceedingly great, toward the

south, and toward the east, and toward the glorious land. ¹⁰ It grew great, even to the army of the sky; and it cast down some of the army and of the stars to the ground, and trampled on them. ¹¹ Yes, it magnified itself, even to the prince of the army; and it took away from him the continual burnt offering, and the place of his sanctuary was cast down. ¹² The army was given over to it together with the continual burnt offering through disobedience. It cast down truth to the ground, and it did its pleasure and prospered.

¹³ Then I heard a holy one speaking; and another holy one said to that certain one who spoke, "How long will it take to fulfill the vision about the continual burnt offering, and the disobedience that makes desolate, and to give both the sanctuary and the army to be trodden under foot?"

¹⁴ He said to me, "To two thousand three hundred evenings and mornings. Then the sanctuary will be cleansed."

¹⁵ When I, even I Daniel, had seen the vision, I sought to understand it. Then behold, there stood before me something like the appearance of a man. ¹⁶ I heard a man's voice between the banks of the Ulai, which called, and said, "Gabriel, make this man understand the vision."

¹⁷ So he came near where I stood; and when he came, I was frightened, and fell on my face; but he said to me, "Understand, son of man; for the vision belongs to the time of the end."

¹⁸ Now as he was speaking with me, I fell into a deep sleep with my face toward the ground; but he touched me, and set me upright.

¹⁹ He said, "Behold, I will make you know what will be in the latter time of the indignation; for it belongs to the appointed time of the end. ²⁰ The ram which you saw, that had the two horns, they are the kings of Media and Persia. ²¹ The rough male goat is the king of Greece. The great horn that is between his eyes is the first king. ²² As for that which was broken, in the place where four stood up, **four kingdoms will stand up out of the nation, but not with his power**."

²³ "In the latter time of their kingdom, when the transgressors have come to the full, a king of fierce face, and understanding dark sentences, will stand up. ²⁴ His power will be mighty, but not by his own power. He will destroy awesomely, and will prosper in what he does. He will destroy the mighty ones and the holy people. ²⁵ Through his policy he will cause deceit to prosper in his hand. He will magnify himself in his heart, and will destroy many in their security. He will also stand up against the prince of princes; but he will be broken without hand. ²⁶ The vision of the evenings and mornings which has been told is true; but seal up the vision, for it belongs to many days to come."

When I first read this passage, I was struck by its powerful depiction of Alexander the Great, his conquest of the Persian Empire (which is clearly depicted as a *Medo*-Persian Empire in this dream), and the break-up of the empire that he founded into four separate Macedonian kingdoms. I was so taken with its powerful Daniel-7-like combination of imagery and interpretation that I held onto the view that this prophecy was genuine for some time after I had reached the conclusion that Daniel 11 was essentially a forgery. I had always been somewhat suspicious of the rambling series of detailed allusions to the wars and marriages and treaties of the Seleucid and Ptolemaic kings that Daniel 11 consists of, and I had doubted very much that God would call even Antiochus Epiphanes a 'contemptible person' (Daniel 11:21, page 322). In contrast, I had accepted Daniel 8 on face value. When I found out that Daniel 11:40-45 (pages 324-325) hadn't come true, and realised that the rest of that prophecy was almost certainly written from hindsight, it still took a while before I was forced to accept that the latter was almost certainly true of Daniel 8 as well.

It was in composing a talk that I wanted to do on the book of Daniel that I realised my error. Daniel 8 covered *exactly the same historical ground as Daniel 11*, including much the same emphasis on Antiochus Epiphanes' actions in Judea. Although its history wasn't as detailed as that found in Daniel 11, the fact that it covered the same ground and had the same historical emphasis should have left me in little doubt that it came from the same source. I had been fooled by Daniel 8's powerful imagery and its similarity to Daniel 7. The irony is that I had immediately understood Daniel 7 to be a genuine prediction of Christianity because of the fact that its four-headed leopard so obviously symbolised Alexander's empire, which I knew to have split into four kingdoms *because it was depicted that way in Daniel 8!*

I suspect that the effect of Daniel 8 on me when I first read the book of Daniel was not all that different from how its writer intended it to affect his target audience. Like me, the Jews of Judea in the mid-160s BC were meant to notice the four-way splitting of Alexander's empire as depicted by the four large horns that grew out of the stump of the horn representing Alexander in that vision of two beasts. They were *meant* to realise that this means that the four-winged, four-headed leopard in Daniel 7 definitely also stood for that empire – Greece – and thereby deduce that the empire to follow had to be Rome.

This four-way splitting of Greece was clearly important to the writer of the book of Daniel because it is also emphasised in Daniel 11:3-4, below. These verses occur near the beginning of the book's long final prophecy which, due to many similarities, was probably the work of the same writer as Daniel 8. It is clear from their context (page 319) that the 'mighty king' they refer to is Alexander the Great – the only king of Macedon and Greece who subdued every power he fought against. They tell us,

> **DAN 11:** [3] A mighty king will rise, who will rule with great power, and do according to his will. [4] When he has risen, his kingdom will be broken, and will be divided toward the four winds of the sky, but not to his posterity, nor according to his power with which he ruled…

But Daniel 8 goes much further than this in its support for the historically-accurate interpretation of Daniel 7 because it also makes clear that, as Macedonians, the kings of those new kingdoms should be regarded as belonging to *separate bits of the same distinct empire*. The powerful imagery of the shaggy he-goat whose horns depict Alexander followed by all the Seleucid, Ptolemaic, Antigonid and Attalid kings up to the time of Antiochus Epiphanes is there to emphasise this historical truth. The fact that all these horns grew out of the same animal tells the reader that all these kings, including Antiochus Epiphanes, belong to the *same empire* – the empire represented by that four-headed leopard in Daniel 7. As a result, the fact that there is a fourth beast (standing for a *fourth* distinct empire) in Daniel 7, and the fact that this beast has horns representing kings, means that Daniel 7 *has to be a prediction about the distant future.* It has to be about a time long after the 160s BC when Daniel 8 was written (and when the fourth empire, Rome, was a *republic*). This was the conclusion the writer of Daniel 8 wanted his readers to reach because it meant they'd be less likely to dismiss his book as a forgery. They would want to hold onto it to see whether or not those predictions came to pass.

Although the target audience would undoubtedly have recognised that fourth beast as Rome, which was by far the dominant nation of their world, they would still interpret it as a prediction of the future. That is because in their day Rome was a republic. She was not ruled by kings and hadn't been for centuries. The ten kings represented by the horns of the fourth beast could therefore only be understood as a prediction of a *future phase* of Rome's empire.

But in order for them to reach this conclusion, they would have to be convinced that the four-headed leopard *was Greece.* Would its four heads and four wings be enough? To make absolutely certain, the writer of Daniel 8 has chosen to symbolise the Greek empire in his prophecy using a male goat. Like the leopard, the goat was another animal widely used as a symbol of the Greek god Dionysus – protector of the Macedonians, and a god whom popular traditions asserted once actually took on the form of a goat.

Intriguingly, it seems the same writer may also have selected a religion-based animal to represent the Persian Empire as well. The Persians were Zoroastrians, and a ram with two long horns was a popular symbol of the Zoroastrian protective deity *Verethragna* (who is called 'the best armed of the heavenly gods' in a popular Persian hymn). And in case you think the choice of animals might just be arbitrary, it is interesting to note that in Daniel 10:20-21 (page 318) the writer of Daniel 10-12 (who was probably also the writer of Daniel 8) explicitly reveals a belief in national guardian angels fighting a heavenly war for their chosen nations. In fact, he presents it as a sort-of explanation for how particular nations rise to dominance over other nations.

In Daniel 10:20-21, the angel who gives Daniel the detailed prophecy of the Syrian wars that we find in Daniel 11, says to him,

> **DAN 10:** [20]…"Do you know why I have come to you? Now I will return to fight with the prince of Persia. When I go out, behold, the prince of Greece will come. [21] But I will tell you that which is inscribed in the writing of truth. There is no one who holds with me against these, but Michael your prince."

The reference to 'princes' here is not a reference to human leaders like Cyrus of Persia and Alexander the Great, as it may at first seem. The princes in this passage *fight with this angel*. Hence, they are clearly intended to be heavenly beings – gods who guarded the respective nations.

The view that the choice of animals in Daniel 7 and Daniel 8 symbolise the religions of the associated nations is thus clearly supported by this otherwise strange and seemingly unnecessary piece of additional information. This view is important from God's perspective because it is what allows the killing and burning of the fourth beast in Daniel 7 to represent the destruction of the Roman *religion* and its replacement by Christianity.

As we saw in chapter 3, it also explains how the first three beasts in Daniel 7 could still be alive after the conquest of the nations they represent (see Daniel 7:12 on page 66). It may well be to help his readers understand this puzzling claim that the writer of

Daniel 8 and Daniel 10-12 went out of his way to include that religious symbolism and theological explanation.

But in case the reader isn't familiar with that religious symbolism, the same writer has added an even more obvious feature to Daniel 8 that makes it totally irrational, in my opinion, to defend the view that this writer thought the four-headed four-winged leopard in Daniel 7 was anything other than Alexander's empire. He makes the two horns on his ram stand for *the Medes* and *the Persians*, and he tells us that one horn was 'higher than the other'.

Since the bear in Daniel 7 has 'one side higher than the other', he reckoned that his target audience were now sure to equate that bear with his ram. They didn't need to recognise the bear and ram as standing for the Persian *religion*. The asymmetry depicted in each case would convince them that the bear was to be equated with the ram, which he explicitly interprets as 'the Medes and the Persians'. Since Greece famously conquered the Persian empire, as Daniel 8 explicitly reminds us, they would therefore have no problem recognising that the four-headed leopard which follows the bear in Daniel 7 stood for *Greece* (Alexander's four-part-divided Macedonian empire). They couldn't possibly reach any other view! And since the fourth empire in Daniel 7 was to be 'different from all those before it' (and thus *not Greek*), he felt confident that no-one could successfully argue that the predicted eleventh king of that empire was a portrayal of the Greek king Antiochus Epiphanes.

I think he would be shocked to discover that, two thousand years after his time, mainstream scholars, despite all his efforts, have concluded that the four-headed four-winged leopard must actually be *Persia*, not Greece! Why, you may wonder? Because otherwise the fourth beast *cannot be a prediction of Antiochus Epiphanes!*

I am thus convinced that the whole point of Daniel 8 was to ensure that the intended readers of the book of Daniel did not make the *mistake* of thinking that the eleventh horn in Daniel 7 was Antiochus Epiphanes (the Greek king who was at that time persecuting them). The writer of Daniel 8 knew full well that Daniel 7 was a prediction of the distant future, and he wanted his readers to recognise it as such (because this would make them less likely to dismiss the book of Daniel as a forgery). That was why Daniel 8 was written. It is also why God has allowed that chapter to remain in the book of Daniel. It serves wonderfully well as a guide to the correct interpretation of Daniel 7.

Readers unfamiliar with the history portrayed in Daniel 7 are pretty much presented with that history in Daniel 8. They are presented with it in a form that allows them to unambiguously identify the middle two empires of Daniel 7 as *Persia* and *Greece*, and recognise that the fourth empire has to be founded by a *distinct people*. A glance at the history of Alexander's empire (history that was so recent it would have been a topic of conversation in the writer's day) is then enough to reveal the identity of that fourth empire. Only Rome had subdued all four of the Macedonian kingdoms. Since Rome was a totally distinct beast from all the empires before her, the fact that she is so clearly portrayed as such in Daniel 7 may account for why the writer included that prophecy in his book. He was quite convinced his readers would not mistake that fourth empire for one of the four Greek kingdoms that were now either completely conquered by Rome or completely subservient to her.

The beast representing Rome is described as follows:

> **DAN 7:** [7] "After this I saw in the night visions, and, behold, there was a fourth animal, awesome and powerful, and

exceedingly strong. It had great iron teeth. It devoured and broke in pieces, and stamped the residue with its feet. It was different from all the animals that were before it. It had ten horns."

I was very surprised when I first read through mainstream commentaries on the book of Daniel and found that critical scholars never concede that this might be a prediction of Rome. As Daniel 11:18 and 11:29-30 showed (see page 216), Rome's power at the time the book of Daniel was put together was well-known to the Jews of Judea. Twenty years previously at the Battle of Magnesia she had soundly defeated the vast Seleucid army of Antiochus III (Antiochus Epiphanes' father). Judean men of the Jewish faith may well have fought on Antiochus' side in that battle, and survivors would have come home with plenty of stories about Rome's powerful legions (almost certainly the iron teeth of the monster). Moreover, Jewish merchants trading all over the Mediterranean would have come across the hated tax collectors that extracted tribute from the nations Rome defeated. These are very appropriately represented by the monster's bronze claws. They would also no doubt have heard that the Seleucid heirs were being held as political hostages by the Roman Senate to ensure the payment of vast sums of tribute by the Seleucid crown. At one time those hostages had even included Antiochus Epiphanes himself. It was the fact that Rome still held his nephew Demetrius, the rightful heir, that allowed him to continue to rule.

But for readers in the mid-160s BC the most convincing evidence that Rome was the fourth empire in that sequence was the fact that, only a few years before, she had destroyed one of the four wings of Daniel 7's leopard, and cut off its associated head. Perseus, the Antigonid king of Macedon, had rebelled against Rome in a hard-fought war that ended in 168 BC with his defeat at Pydna and subsequent imprisonment. The Romans had then broken up his empire into four independent republics. Although no explicit reference to this event is found in the book of Daniel, it was almost certainly the outcome of this war that gave Rome the confidence to demand that Antiochus Epiphanes withdraw from Egypt or become an enemy of Rome. As Daniel 11:29-30 indicates (see page 216), the Jews were fully aware of Antiochus' humiliation in front of his whole army in 168 BC when an old Roman senator ordered him to take that army out of the country he had almost conquered, and Antiochus felt he had no option but to comply.

The fact that the writer of Daniel 11 alludes to the dominance of Rome in such an obvious way made me very surprised that no critical scholar takes seriously the possibility that the world-dominant fourth empire in Daniel 7 could be a portrayal of Rome. The writer of the book of Daniel knew full well that Rome was the dominant world power, and he needed to include prophecies that extended into his future to make his book less vulnerable to criticism from sceptics. A portrayal of Rome was a perfect means of doing this.

My surprise, however, gave way to suspicion when I discovered that, in spite of this evidence, the majority of critical scholars suggest that the dominance of Rome was either *unrecognised* or *unimportant* to the Jews of Jerusalem at that time in history. It seemed to me that they were forgetting to mention that Rome had dominated the Greek-speaking world *for more than twenty years* prior to that time, and that this was well-known to the writer of Daniel 11. They were also forgetting that the Jews for whom the book of Daniel was written were under serious threat of annihilation. Such a powerful potential ally as Rome – strong enough to defeat their oppressors or even end their oppression with a single command – was *bound* to be of interest to that nation.

Although Rome is not identified by name in the book of Daniel, that seemed to me much more likely to be the result of diplomatic concerns rather than any sense that the power of Rome was somehow irrelevant to the book's intended message. The writer of Daniel 8 and Daniel 10-12 had no wish to write anything that could jeopardise his people's chances of being on friendly terms with that superpower in the west. Those same diplomatic concerns might also account for why Daniel does not *recognise* the fourth beast in Daniel 7. Perhaps in an earlier version of this prophecy that fourth beast was an animal that all would recognise as symbolic of *Rome's* religion – just as the leopard so obviously symbolises the religion of Greece, and the winged lion that of Babylon – and the editor in the second century BC, or God himself, thought that this was far too dangerous to leave in. Of course, we cannot now know whether that was the case or not. What we can be absolutely sure about is that the writer of Daniel 11 was well aware of Rome's dominance, and his decision to not refer to that nation explicitly need not be because he thought the most powerful nation in the world was somehow irrelevant to the message of his book, as modern critical scholars often suggest.

As well as emphasising the power of Rome, which is not alluded to in Daniel 8, the writer of Daniel 11 also emphasises the weakness of the divided phase of the Greek empire in comparison to its united phase under Alexander the Great (see Daniel 11:4, page 224). As I pointed out at the beginning of this chapter, this is also emphasised in Daniel 8 (see Daniel 8:22, page 222), so it must be important. It is, I suspect, the main reason critical scholars nowadays tend to avoid the hypothesis that the fourth empire in

Daniel 7 was meant to be the divided Greek empire, or the Seleucid kingdom on its own.

That hypothesis was first proposed by the Greek philosopher *Porphyry of Tyre* in the third century AD. Writing against the claims of the Christians of his day, Porphyry is widely hailed by critical scholars of Daniel as the founder of their field. However, his views on Daniel 7 were quite different from those of modern critical scholars. Unlike them, he did *not* argue that the writer must have mistakenly imagined that Babylon fell to an unhistorical resurgent Median Empire, or that Persia was the four-headed four-winged leopard (a claim that would have made him a laughing stock in the empire that had defeated the four Greek kingdoms that Alexander's empire became). Instead, he conceded that the four-headed four-winged leopard *was indeed* Alexander's empire, but proposed that the fourth beast had been intended to represent, not Rome, but the *divided phase* of that Greek empire.

This was a tempting conclusion for early critical scholars desperate to disprove the claim that this prophecy predicted Christianity. That is because it seemed to allow the third beast – the four-headed leopard – to stand for Alexander's empire (as everyone in the second century BC would have thought) *without* preventing the eleventh king of the fourth empire from constituting Antiochus Epiphanes (a Greek king rather than an emperor of Rome).

However, as soon as one assumes that the fourth empire was meant to be the Seleucid kingdom or any combination of the four Greek kingdoms that emerged from Alexander's empire, it becomes very hard to understand why anyone would see that fourth empire as *totally distinct from*, and *far more powerful than*, the ones before it, as Daniel 7:3 (page 68) emphasises. After all, under this hypothesis, the *third* empire (the united phase of the Greek Empire) would be ruled by a king of the *same nation* (Macedon) that gave rise to the rulers of the fourth empire. That fourth empire *would not be distinct at all*. Moreover, if that fourth empire were really meant to be just the empire of Seleucus, or the divided Macedonian Empire of which the Seleucids were part, Daniel 7's claim that the fourth empire was more powerful than the ones before it would be *contradicted* by those references to the relative weakness of the four Greek kingdoms that we find in Daniel 11:4 and Daniel 8:22 (pages 224 and 222 respectively). These details were sufficient to convince me that the writer of Daniel 11 and Daniel 8 *cannot possibly have thought this*.

In this chapter I have hopefully shown you why I think the writer of Daniel 8 and Daniel 11, who was probably responsible for putting the whole book of Daniel together in the mid-160s BC, has taken great pains to ensure that Daniel 7 (and therefore also Daniel 2) were seen as predictions of the distant future in his day. For me this requirement perfectly explains why he wrote Daniel 8. That otherwise unnecessary prophecy of the deeds of Antiochus Epiphanes, which were already documented in Daniel 11, uses two fully-interpreted beasts exhibiting symbolic features that are directly analogous to the primary features of the second and third beast in Daniel 7. By positioning it immediately after Daniel 7, this writer was almost certainly ensuring that his book's careful readers used it as a guide to the meaning of the prophecy they had just read, and they would thereby understand that prophecy as a prediction of the distant future of their time.

Since that writer's hopes for this book pretty much rested on his audience noticing prophecies within it that had not yet been fulfilled, I find it quite surprising that critical scholars never discuss this possibility. They are, after all, quite willing to accept that Daniel 11:40-45 (page 324-325) – the prediction in Daniel 11 that didn't come true – is a guess at the future that was included for this very same purpose. Are they really rejecting this possibility in the case of Daniel 7 and Daniel 2 (and Daniel 9 as we saw in chapter 7) simply because the predictions that these prophecies make about the future *did* come true? If so, there seems to me to be absolutely zero justification for this.

When I first discovered this fatal flaw in the mainstream views on these prophecies, I was jubilant. But I soon realised that the advocates of these views have never been properly challenged on this regard by evangelical scholars. Instead of simply agreeing that Daniel 11:40-45 never came true (and pointing out that the deliberate inclusion of this genuine prediction is indisputable grounds to seriously consider the possibility that Daniel 2, Daniel 7 and Daniel 9:24-27 were also included as genuine predictions) most evangelicals desperately try to postpone the fulfilment of Daniel 11:40-45 to *our* future! Yet it is obvious from the text that this was meant to be a prediction of Antiochus Epiphanes (or at least an immediate successor) because in Daniel 12:6 an angel asks another angel, *'How long will it be until the end of these wonders?'*, and the time-period in the second answer Daniel receives, which seems clearly meant to include the predicted conquest of Egypt described in Daniel 11:40-45, consists of only 'one thousand two hundred and ninety *days'* (page 326).

Of course, it has been argued that since the "sevens" (or 'weeks') of Daniel 9 are 'seven-*year* weeks' (rather than 'seven-*day* weeks'), the 'days' in Daniel 12 could mean 'years'. However, as I have always said in this book, if you can interpret a prophecy any way you like then any fulfilment is no longer surprising. You no longer have any reason to think it is anything but chance. The "sevens" in Daniel 9 were recognised as periods of seven years because such periods were evident in Jewish scripture, and because the prophecy wouldn't make any sense if the predicted events were squeezed into seventy seven-day weeks. There is no such justification for interpreting the '1290 days' and the '1335 days' in Daniel 12 as anything except days, and the same applies to the '2300 evenings and mornings' that we found in Daniel 8.

I am not saying that God couldn't fulfil such an unjustifiable interpretation of these prophecies if he wanted to. Of course he could! However, I suspect that because of the origin and content of these prophecies he wouldn't want to. In view of the fact that Daniel 11:40-45 has failed to come true, we have strong grounds to believe that the content of Daniel 8 and Daniel 11 *did not come directly from the mind of God or his true prophet Daniel.* For God to deliberately ensure the fulfilment of any interpretation of these prophecies would therefore be contrary to both Christian and Jewish theology because it would constitute divine endorsement of a prophecy that was neither wholly accurate nor remotely truthful about its origin. That is why I think we have no grounds to expect those time-periods to mean anything significant for our day.

It is important to remember though that this does not mean the inclusion of these prophecies was not God's work. I suspect it was. It's just that their purpose is not to give us accurate information about the future. I suspect that they were put there by God as a key to the meaning of the three prophecies of Christianity that the book of Daniel contains: Daniel 2:31-45, Daniel 7 and Daniel 9:24-27. Not only do they show beyond reasonable doubt that these prophecies *existed in the 160s BC* (as we saw in chapter 8), they clearly reveal how the Jews at that time *perceived their history –*

and thus how they would *interpret* Daniel 2, 7 and 9. Since their content strongly supports the *historically accurate* interpretation of these prophecies that we examined in chapters 2-6, their presence in the book of Daniel makes it quite irrational for modern scholars to speculate that those early readers might have interpreted a four-headed, four-winged leopard as the empire of Persia rather than the four-part-divided empire of Greece, or that they possibly believed Babylon had been conquered by an independent *Median* empire, or that they were somehow oblivious to the power of Rome. They are thus there to ensure that we can only reasonably interpret Daniel 7 and Daniel 9:24-27 the way they were *intended* to be interpreted. And as you saw in chapters 2-6, when you do this these prophecies turn out to contain stunningly accurate predictions of momentous world events associated with the fortunes of the holy people – the devout believers in Daniel's God – and these events do seem to endorse the Christian revelation.

As far as I can see, if current evangelical views on scripture do not allow God to include such pseudonymous works in the Bible as a means of providing a key by which its readers can easily appreciate the fulfilment of Daniel's genuine prophecies of Christ, then it is high time those evangelical views were changed. They are stopping ordinary Christians from appreciating the true extent of God's genius and provision. Adopting a more nuanced understanding of why God might have wanted different writings included in his Holy Book is clearly far more constructive than assuming they are always the inerrant words of God himself. It is with this in mind that I shall now take you through my equally enlightening experience of the rest of the book of Daniel.

NOVEL CONCLUSIONS FROM CHAPTER 9: Daniel 8 was included in the 160s BC to emphasise the predictive nature of Daniel 7. Rome, unnamed for political reasons, had by then ruled the Greek world for over twenty years and would easily be seen as the fourth empire in Daniel 7, her status as a Republic ensuring its eleven kings still lay ahead.

CHAPTER TEN

The Miracles and their Meaning

Lochgilphead Parish Church occupies a commanding position. From it you can see right down the town's main street to the war memorial on the front green, and from there out across Loch Gilp to where it opens into Loch Fyne. After a rare winter's snowfall, the mountains of Arran will suddenly materialize on the horizon like a vast gleaming iceberg blown in from the North Atlantic. It was at that church one Sunday morning that I remember a Sunday school teacher explaining to me how Jesus had walked upon water.

"Just beneath the surface of Lake Galilee," she hypothesized, "there were probably rocks poking up, as there are in Loch Gilp." She was referring to the ruined causeway that had once allowed a local landowner to bypass Lochgilphead on his way down the Kintyre peninsula after his carriage had tragically ended the life of a young child in the town. "Jesus," she argued, "must have just stepped carefully from submerged rock to submerged rock."

In other words, she was proposing that Christ performed this miracle using nothing more than his extensive local knowledge. It was a PR stunt – not dissimilar to Lady Di walking across a minefield! Although you might laugh, this teacher was in fact making a good point. How do we know that the miraculous signs we read about in the Bible were not humanly-orchestrated PR stunts or propaganda? How can we even know they happened?

One of my earliest memories of a Biblical miracle was the story of *Daniel in the Lion's Den* (Daniel 6). As a faith-strengthening tale with a powerful Judaeo-Christian moral, the account of Daniel's refusal to compromise when a law was passed that required him to refrain from prayer for a month on pain of death (page 39) is perhaps a very appropriate tale for a Christian church to tell its young people. But given the conclusions I have reached about the book of Daniel over the last few chapters, the question arises as to whether that story was real or merely a fictional account designed to inspire the Jews to hold onto their faith in the face of Antiochus' sacrilegious demands, and the near-certain death they faced if they didn't obey. After all, one of the earliest references to the book of Daniel (1 Maccabees 2:60) is a mention of *Daniel in the Lions Den* being used precisely for this purpose. But the same question arises about *all* the stories from Daniel 2 to Daniel 6. In each of these an identical "no compromise" moral is evident, and the prophet Daniel, or his equally-devout friends, brave a similar risk of death to demonstrate their faith in God before a powerful world leader.

One argument against the view that these stories were invented in the 160s BC is that they were written in a different language from Daniel 8-12, most of which, as we have seen, is very reasonably judged to date from that time. Apart from the first three-and-a-half verses of Daniel 2, Daniel 2-7 was all written in *Aramaic*. This is even the case in the ancient Dead Sea Scrolls copies of the book. Daniel 8-12 and Daniel 1, on the other hand, were written in *Hebrew*. Moreover, the style of the Aramaic used in Daniel 2-7 is thought by most experts to be much older than the second century BC. That is not conclusive evidence because a second century BC writer could in theory have copied an older style. However, he would have to have been very good at this in order to fool modern experts who have spent much of their careers analysing the writing styles of different eras in Jewish history.

More compelling evidence for the greater antiquity of Daniel 2-7 comes from the fact that some of these stories preserve historical details that never featured in later histories of the period. And some of these details have even been confirmed – to the surprise of many critical scholars – by the discoveries of modern archaeologists.

Perhaps the most famous of these discoveries relates to Daniel 5. In that story, the prophet Daniel is summoned by a king of Babylon called 'Belshazzar', and ordered to tell him the meaning of a disturbing vision he had just experienced while feasting from the holy vessels his predecessor Nebuchadnezzar had plundered from the Temple of Jerusalem shortly before he demolished it. Belshazzar had seen the fingers of a hand writing obscure words on the white plastered wall of his banqueting hall. Had he simply drunk too much wine from those holy vessels? He summoned his soothsayers and astrologers to find out. And when none of them could interpret the vision, the queen reminds the king about Daniel.

King Belshazzar promises Daniel that he will clothe him in purple and put a gold chain around his neck and make him 'the **third highest** ruler in the whole kingdom' if he can interpret this vision. After refusing those gifts, Daniel informs the king that the words mean his kingdom has been given to the Medes and Persians *due to his sin!* And Belshazzar, to his credit, keeps his promise. Purple robes are put on Daniel, a gold chain is placed around his neck, and he does get proclaimed *the third highest ruler in the kingdom.* Shortly afterwards, the Persian army led by a Mede called Darius breaks into the city and captures the palace. Belshazzar gets put to the sword, and Daniel's prophecy is fulfilled.

Now you might think it somewhat strange that Belshazzar would offer such a high reward for an interpretation of that particular vision. After all, Daniel could have said whatever he wanted since the king had no way to judge whether he'd interpreted the vision correctly or not. Even stranger is the fact that he follows through on his offer and grants that immense honour to Daniel for his extremely unfavourable reading. One would instead expect such a villainous king to say something like, "I think you're having me on, I've probably just had too much to drink!" and thrown Daniel into prison for worrying him with such a doom-laden prediction. When you first read this passage, the king's actions don't seem to make much sense. However, these actions do start to make sense when you consider them in their historical context (which is why I think there might indeed by some truth to this tale).

Firstly, by the time of the fall of Babylon the Babylonian army had already been soundly defeated by the Medo-Persian army of Cyrus the Great and his Persian *and Median* generals. With few soldiers left to defend her walls the city was probably awaiting the inevitable. Independent sources confirm that a feast was ongoing when the walls of the city were breached, but that was probably because her residents had decided that resistance to the Persians and Medes was futile, and would only cost more lives. They were therefore simply making the most of things while they still could.

With this in mind, Belshazzar's promise to Daniel was not really a reward at all. As both he and Daniel probably knew full well, it was very likely to mean the prophet's death. Although Cyrus the Great had spared the life of his own Median grandfather whose throne he had usurped ten years previously, and had done the same for the king of Lydia, the empire he had most recently conquered, and there may even have been reports that he had not yet executed Belshazzar's father Nabonidus (whom he also appears to have spared), he was far less likely to spare the lives of subordinate rulers. Being Nabonidus' son, Belshazzar was thus in great danger. Hence by making Daniel 'third highest ruler in the kingdom', he probably felt he was justifiably assigning to Daniel the very same fate that this impudent prophet had predicted for his royal self.

The really fascinating aspect of this story, though, is the fact that he makes Daniel '*third* highest ruler in the kingdom'. This very obviously indicates that, at the very least, the writer of this passage knew Belshazzar was not the only ruler. That in itself is not surprising because it was always well-known to historians that the king of Babylon whom Cyrus defeated (and whose life he most probably spared) was called *Nabonidus*, not Belshazzar. What is surprising is that this story preserves a memory of an inferior coregent son of Nabonidus called Belshazzar.

Until the British Museum acquired a clay tablet containing a cuneiform inscription that became known as the *Nabonidus Chronicle* from an antiques dealer in 1879, this king was unknown to historians except from the book of Daniel, and was widely believed to be an invention of the writer of that book. That clay tablet changed all that. It describes how Nabonidus spent ten years in self-imposed exile at an oasis many miles away from the city of Babylon, and left his son Belshazzar to rule the city in his absence.

It also indicates that Belshazzar never received his father's titles or his role at national feasts, which made him very much the second highest ruler in the kingdom. However, he would undoubtedly have been seen as king by the ordinary residents of Babylon who, for ten whole years, would have bowed down to him alone.

I find it quite strange that Daniel 5 tends to be rejected as a reliable historical source simply because it calls Belshazzar a king and a descendant of Nebuchadnezzar! The fact that this text informed us accurately of Belshazzar's existence long before the Nabonidus Chronicle came to light is simply ignored by those scholars. The Jews living in Babylon would definitely have perceived Belshazzar as their king, and they had no reason to question his probably false dynastic claim to be Nebuchadnezzar's grandson (the term translated 'father' in Daniel 5:11 actually meant 'male ancestor' and therefore 'grandfather' in this case – and it is worth pointing out that it is reported speech and therefore not actually a statement of what the writer himself believed). In view of this, the setting of Daniel 5 seems to me to be a perfectly reliable historical source for how an ordinary Jew living in Babylon would have perceived its fall to the Persians and Medes.

The one thing in Daniel 5 that does, on the face of it, conflict with what independent sources say about the fall of Babylon is the fact that it tells us the city was captured by a man called *Darius the Mede* (Daniel 5:31), who was subsequently 'made king over the realm of the Chaldeans' (Daniel 9:1). Critical scholars are quick to point out that all other sources say that Cyrus himself took the title 'King of Babylon' after its fall, and that the general who took the city was called *Gubaru* (or *Ugbaru*) – the governor of a land called 'Gutium'. Though they do locate this land within 'Media', they argue that Ugbaru isn't Darius because was never made *king*.

However, it seems to me that those scholars have argued them-selves into a hole here. We have already seen how they wrongly reject Daniel 5 because it calls the inferior coregent Belshazzar a king, when he was effectively no more than a governor of the kingdom of Babylon. I have – I think rightly – pointed out that the text is correctly recording how the Jews living in Babylon at the time would have *perceived* him. Yet those scholars are now saying that Darius the Mede can't be a real person because the text calls him 'king' and we know that the new king of Babylon was Cyrus.

Can you see the problem with this argument? The word 'king' in Daniel 5 is referring to the individual whom the Jews of Babylon considered to be ruling over them. Although there was a higher ruler of Babylon (as the writer clearly knew), it is Belshazzar who gets called 'king', and whose years from his inauguration as the second-in-command were used to date events. That is because he was the visible member of the coregency – the person whom they had to bow down to and obey on a regular basis. Consequently, when the Persians took the city, and Cyrus went off to oversee other parts of his vast empire for a couple of years (as he did) leaving a governor in charge of 'the realm of the Chaldeans', we should clearly expect the writer of Daniel 5 to refer to that governor as 'king'. Cyrus may even have given him the title 'King of Babylon' to ensure he had the authority necessary to fulfil his obligations (and there is some evidence that Cyrus did not immediately take that title upon his conquest of Babylon).

So, who was that governor? It appears he was none other than the governor of Gutium, the general Ugbaru who first captured the city. Since Gutium was a part of the realm generally known as 'Media' by the ancients, this governor was most probably a Mede just as Daniel 5 tells us. And it is also known from the Nabonidus

Chronicle that this governor *appointed subgovernors* to efficiently implement the taxation system Cyrus swiftly established over this relatively wealthy addition to his empire. That is exactly what Darius the Mede does in Daniel 6:1. Hence the only real problem with the account in Daniel 5 is the *name* of this subordinate king.

But names change from language to language, and people in authority often like to be called by a pseudonym, or a name that would be more acceptable to their subjects. Even in ancient times an individual could have several names, so maybe Darius was simply his first name. The idea that the name Ugbaru simply morphed into Darius over the years also seems plausible. A Greek text, for example, refers to this governor as Gobryas. So, perhaps Ugbaru became Gubaru which changed to Gobryas then to Goryas then Doryas and finally Darius. Alternatively, perhaps the ancient Persian pronunciation of Ugbaru sounded a bit like Darius to Jewish ears. Or maybe whatever it sounded like meant something obscene or laughable to some sect of the multi-ethnic population of Babylon causing them to erupt with mirth every time they heard the king announced. Or maybe it reminded them of an oppressor from their past or was the name of a god they worshipped. Either way it would have prompted that king to change his name to something more respectable to his subjects' ears. The argument that Darius the Mede was not Ugbaru the Mede because the name is different thus holds no weight whatsoever. It is like claiming that the house of *Saxe-Coburg and Gotha* no longer ruled Britain after the First World War because subsequent UK royals are Windsors, or that the first Roman Emperor was Augustus, not Octavian!

The Median ethnicity of this king Darius is regularly seized upon by critical scholars desperate to find support for their consensus on the four empires of Daniel 2 and Daniel 7 as a reason to believe that the writer of this story was making it up – or at least adapting it to suit his own purposes. They claim he was trying to make his readers interpret the second empire as *Media*, rather than as the historical Medo-*Persian* Empire that really conquered Babylon. In their view, he was trying to influence the interpretation of these prophecies much as the writer of Daniel 8 was doing in my theory, *but in the opposite direction.* (He was supposedly trying to make his readers interpret them *un*-historically rather than in the historically-accurate way that follows from Daniel 8).

That is a lot to read into the ethnicity of that provincial governor. It ignores the wealth of information that Medes did have high-ranking positions in the Persian administration and army. The last Median Emperor, Astyages, was Cyrus' grandfather according to the history books. So, when Cyrus seized the throne from him in 550 BC, it would have been like the UK's Prince William seizing the throne from Queen Elizabeth II. Although opposed by some, it was in fact welcomed by many Medes who did not see it as a conquest of their empire at all. Since the top general in Cyrus' army was a Mede called Harpagus, it is not surprising to find other Median generals leading Cyrus' army. But the strongest evidence against that popular mainstream view that the writer regards Darius as an independent king is found in the text of Daniel 5, 6 and 9.

Firstly, in Daniel 9:1, this Darius is 'made king over the realm of the Chaldeans'. The translation 'made king' presumably implies that he owed his kingship to somebody else (namely Cyrus). Secondly, in Daniel 6:8, 6:12 and 6:15, his decrees are described as being governed by 'the law of the Medes and Persians'. If he were the leader of an independent Media, why mention the Persians as though they were on equal terms with the Medes? This binational legal system clearly indicates that he belonged to a *Medo-Persian* empire, just like the one depicted by the two-horned ram in Daniel 8 whose horns represent the Median kings and the Persian kings. And thirdly, when he gets tricked into making a decree that condemns his favourite administrator to a night in the den of lions, he seems clearly afraid to cancel that decree. The very subjects who had tricked him into making that decree – and he is well aware of the fact that he's been tricked – inform him that he cannot cancel his own decree! And he accepts their judgement! That does not sound to me like the behaviour of a powerful emperor, or the attitude of folk to such an emperor. What had this Darius the Mede to be afraid of? The answer is very probably his overlord Cyrus.

Hence it seems to me that Darius the Mede offers not the least bit of support for the crumbling critical consensus on Daniel 2 and 7. He is very likely to constitute a real Jewish memory of the first governor that Cyrus placed over the kingdom of Babylon rather than someone the writer invented. The emphasis on his Median ethnicity is easily accounted for because a few decades later a Persian king also going by the name of Darius rose to rule over the Persian Empire. The writer or later editors of this passage were merely ensuring that their readers did not mistake this relatively weak provincial ruler for that mighty Persian emperor.

Working back from Daniel 6, we have now encountered both the struggling puppet king and conqueror of Babylon, Darius the Mede, and the inferior coregent king Belshazzar whom he slew. And we have found plenty of evidence that these passages were written much nearer to the time they describe than most critical scholars are prepared to admit. This, however, does not mean they weren't propaganda in the struggle against Antiochus IV Epiphanes. Even if they were written long before the second century BC, the writer of the book of Daniel in the 160s BC has clearly selected these particular stories for a purpose. And that purpose was to fire up the Jewish people to resist Antiochus IV.

Nevertheless, that does not mean God didn't want these stories included in the book of Daniel. Nor does it require God to have included them for the same purpose that the writer of Daniel 11 and Daniel 8 included them for. This writer may have been motivated to include them for a completely different purpose. But God could still have put these stories on his mind as a suitable means of fulfilling this purpose in order to ensure that they got included in the book of Daniel *for his own purposes*.

So, what might God have included them for? As we have seen, they do confirm the antiquity of the Aramaic parts of the book. The memories of Belshazzar and Darius the Mede contained in these passages would not be expected in a work that was all written in the second century BC. Another possibility is that as inspirational stories they would ensure the book's popularity in a way that characterless prophecies could not hope to achieve. Perhaps also, though, they may have been put there as genuine inspiration for the holy people who, if my interpretation of Daniel 7 is correct (and it is strongly supported by Christ in Mark 13:14-30 and Matthew 24:15-34), faced a far tougher challenge in the years to come than they did at the time of Antiochus Epiphanes. As you will see shortly, the stories found in Daniel 2, 3, and 4 are greatly supportive of this possibility.

One of the less well-known aspects of the book of Daniel is that it claims to be not exclusively the work of Jews. Daniel 4 claims to be a public testimony written by none other than the Great Babylonian king Nebuchadnezzar II – most famous for demolishing Jerusalem and the Jewish Temple in 587 BC and deporting a large proportion of the Jewish population to Babylon. Surprisingly the Jews seem to believe he came to faith in their God. Daniel 4 is the source of that tradition.

In it Nebuchadnezzar describes a dream he had of a gigantic tree, visible from all over the earth, with luscious foliage that offered shelter and food to all creatures. He sees 'a watcher and a holy one' (whatever they may be!) coming down from the sky. The latter in a loud voice commands that the tree be chopped down and its branches lopped off and stripped bare. But a stump is to be left in the earth and regularly watered by the dew of the sky to keep it alive. Its heart is to be changed from that of a man to that of an animal, and it is to live among the animals of the field for 'seven times' (Note for later this strange use of the word 'times').

Daniel, in fear for his life, tells the king that he wishes the interpretation of this dream were for his enemies, and that it means he would become so ill in mind that he would 'be driven from men' and would eat grass and live in the open among the animals of the field until 'seven times pass over him' and he acknowledges that God rules in the world of men, and gives its kingdoms to whomever he pleases. At this point his kingdom will be returned.

We are then duly informed that this is what happened. A year later, while walking in his famous gardens admiring the city he had built, he was struck down with mental illness so bad that he was driven from men and his hair grew thick like eagle's feathers and his nails became like a bird's claws. This went on, he tells us, until he praised and acknowledged God (which didn't happen, of course, until 'seven times had passed over him'). At that moment he was healed of the madness, his lords and counsellors gave him back his kingdom, and he was now a devout follower of Daniel's God.

What do we make of all this? A real event? A genuine royal proclamation? A piece of pro-Jewish religious propaganda? An attempt to justify the rebuilding of the Temple that Nebuchadnezzar had destroyed? And why would God want such a testimony included in the book of Daniel? Did he merely want to bring himself or his prophet the greater glory that the conversion of such a powerful king obviously brought with it? Or could God have wanted this testimony included because it explained the humbling of the winged lion in Daniel 7, and thereby made every reader of that astonishing prophecy of Christianity instantly aware that the first empire in the sequence of four is Nebuchadnezzar's Babylon?

Recall from chapter 3 (page 64) that the lion with eagles' wings standing for the first empire in that sequence has its wings torn off, is made to stand up on two feet, and is given the heart of a man. The allusion to Daniel 4 in these words is transparent (especially since the first empire is known to be Babylon from Daniel 2). A question I find interesting is whether that detail of the wings being torn off of the lion was always present in Daniel 7, or whether it was added after the addition of Daniel 4 in order to make it abundantly clear to all readers that the Lion with eagles' wings in Daniel 7 is definitely meant to be interpreted as Babylon.

As far as the fulfilment of Daniel 7 is concerned it doesn't matter. There is nothing to say that God cannot choose to improve his prophecy after it was first issued. Provided it got completed (as Daniel 7 obviously did) long before the time of the events it predicts, God is perfectly at liberty to alter it prior to that time in any way he thinks best without reducing the effectiveness of its fulfilment as a sign of his involvement. But if instead that detail *was* present in the original dream (and from the amazing fulfilment of Daniel 7 described in chapter 3 of this book we have no reason to doubt that this dream really did take place) then it suggests that a famous humbling of a Babylonian king was indeed a real event – and probably the very one that Daniel 4 documents.

Most scholars see this passage as fictional but inspired by a real occurrence. They think it was composed as a sort of explanation for the ten-year absence from Babylon of its last king Nabonidus. Yes, I know it says *Nebuchadnezzar*, but they think a later scribe substituted the name Nebuchadnezzar in place of Nabonidus because Nebuchadnezzar was more famous as the first destroyer of Jerusalem.

I am not convinced by this argument. It is true that Nabonidus spent ten years in a desert oasis called Tayma, far from the city, and he may well have spent much time there mingling with herdsmen and their flocks. But the reasons for this are unclear. It was a strategically important place from which trade routes could be controlled. So it may simply have been that. And Nabonidus had very good reasons to want to be far from the city of Babylon. He had spent much time promoting the cult of the Babylonian moon god (Sin), which was not the city's chief deity (a god called Marduk). This would not have endeared him to the powerful priesthood, so perhaps his stay in Tayma was to escape that ill-feeling and possible threat to his life.

Then again, maybe he did go there for health reasons. Is that a good enough reason to postulate scribal meddling in Daniel 4? My feeling is that if it had been Nabonidus, there ought to have been some mention in verse 36 of his son Belshazzar looking after the kingdom in his absence. The king in Daniel 4 merely refers to his 'lords and counsellors', with no mention of his son. Then again, such a mention could have simply been deleted by the scribe.

Whatever the truth of this, I think there is evidence that a scribe did tamper with this passage – at least in the 160s BC. That is because it tells us that the king's madness would last 'seven times'.

Judging from the growth of Nebuchadnezzar's hair and nails over that time-period, it seems obvious that the writer meant 'seven years'. So why didn't he just use the usual word for year? There was no risk that attempts to prevent the fulfilment of this period of madness would cause terrible human suffering, so there was no reason for God to make this time-period a puzzle.

The one person who did have something to gain from the inclusion of the word 'times' in this passage was the writer of Daniel 12:11. Writing around 165 BC, he clearly wanted his readers to interpret the 'time, times and half a time' in Daniel 12:7 as 'three and a half years' (his 1290 days until the end of Antiochus' oppression). Hence, I suspect that Daniel 4 did once say 'seven years', and that the writer of Daniel 12 has changed the Aramaic word for 'years' in this passage to the word translated 'times' in Daniel 7:25 (the only place 'a time, times and half a time' was written in Aramaic).

Why do I think that? Well the main reason is that, as I explained in chapter 4, the 'time, times and half a time' in Daniel 7 refers to a time of persecution that is meant to be the most terrible ever suffered by the holy people (see Mark 13:12-20, page 197). Judging from other times of hardship in Jewish scripture, three-and-a-half years of persecution would simply not warrant such a description. So I don't think 'times' originally meant 'years'.

Another reason to think Daniel 4 originally said 'years' rather than 'times' is the fact that the writer of Daniel 12 has his hero express total bewilderment on hearing the phrase 'a time, times and half a time'. This suggests to me that the writer himself, who presumably had a copy of Daniel 4 (the one he was putting into his completed book of Daniel), also didn't understand this phrase (which would be surprising if it had just meant 'three and a half years' as Daniel 4 now suggests). Since he had chosen to interpret it in a way that foretold an imminent end to his people's current sufferings, he had to ensure that the angelic messenger's interpretation in Daniel 12:11 (page 326) made sense to his readers. In other words, he had to make certain it could be justified from other parts of the book of Daniel. For me, that is a perfect motive for him to bring about the three tiny alterations to the original text of Daniel 4 that resulted in the word 'years' being swapped for the word 'times'.

Obviously, if the book of Daniel is a work of God, as the accuracy of Daniel 2, 7 and 9 suggests, then this alteration, if it occurred, has been *allowed* by God. God thus *wanted* the book of Daniel to suggest that the persecution predicted in Daniel 7 is only three-and-a-half years long. He wanted people to think it was what the Jews had suffered in the remaining years of Hadrian's life, or the "three-and-a-half years" from the destruction of the Temple by the army of Vespasian – the eleventh unlimited dictator to rule the Roman empire – in late August 70 AD until the fall of Masada in mid-April 74 which ended the *first* Jewish revolt (the extra month-and-a-half needed for this is justified by Daniel 12:12, page 326).

After those "three-and-a-half years" had passed, all who knew of this prophecy would think it had simply failed, and that the Jews (whether enslaved by Vespasian or exiled and disempowered by Hadrian) no longer posed a threat to the Roman empire. As Christ confirms in Mark 13:20, 'Unless the Lord had shortened the days, no flesh would have been saved; but for the sake of the chosen ones, whom he picked out, he shortened the days.' (page 108).

Had this shortening not been done, even if no one could work out the most probable endpoint of the 175 years that this time-period in Daniel 7 most likely stands for (see page 109), the existence of this prophecy would probably have destroyed the holy people. The very fact that it couldn't be argued to have failed would have led to not just serious but *sustained* oppression of the Jews and Christians by the Romans, and Christ's assessment that 'no flesh would have been saved' (where 'flesh' I suspect refers in this context not to 'humanity' or 'all animal life' but to the bodies of the holy people as opposed to their souls) would very likely have come true. This alteration was thus no failure of God's plan but an act of kindness.

As it was, the oppression during this 175-year period, though severe, was also sporadic, and it soon became focussed on the rapidly growing sect of gentile-friendly Judaism that really did pose a threat to the Roman Empire. It was very probably the way in which many Christians during those years of persecution bravely and peacefully accepted death rather than renounce their beliefs that swayed Roman hearts in favour of Christianity. And interestingly, the model they may well have based this unflinching faith upon is found in Daniel 3.

The third chapter of the book of Daniel is not about Daniel at all. It doesn't even mention him once. It is about three other Jewish youths of noble birth who were selected with Daniel to serve at king Nebuchadnezzar's court in Babylon. We know this because they are introduced as such in Daniel 1. However, if you are a sceptical person like me, it is worth noting that unlike Daniel 3 and almost all of Daniel 2-7, Daniel 1 was entirely written in Hebrew. Remember, the book of Daniel is bilingual in its earliest known copies. It changes from Hebrew into Aramaic midway through verse 4 of Daniel 2, and then back to Hebrew again at the beginning of Daniel 8. The whole of Daniel 8-12 is in Hebrew, and as we saw in chapters 7-9, we have several extremely good reasons to believe that this latter section of the book, minus a few verses of Daniel 9, was entirely composed in the mid-160s BC.

If you are not yet convinced of this, I strongly recommend reading this book's Appendix (pages 313-326) where I go through the long prophecy of Daniel 10-12 and point out all the historical details it alludes to, how it focusses strongly upon the actions of Antiochus Epiphanes, and how it makes a prediction about that king which almost certainly *failed to come true*. As I mentioned in chapter 6 (page 165), this by no means implies that its inclusion was not the work of the Holy Spirit. Although originating as pseudonymous propaganda, this section was absolutely perfect for the task God needed it for. It proves beyond reasonable doubt that Daniel 7 and the last few verses of Daniel 9 were definitely in existence in the second century BC; and it demonstrates clearly how the Jews of that time perceived their history, making it quite unreasonable to interpret the fourth kingdom in Daniel 7 and the ending of sacrifice in Daniel 9 as anything other than genuine predictions about the Roman empire. Nevertheless, it does make me a tiny bit suspicious of Daniel 1 – the only other Hebrew chapter in the book.

Without that chapter and a single verse at the end of Daniel 2, the story about the three youths in Daniel 3 would have nothing to do with the prophet Daniel. Then again, it is possible that Daniel 1 was merely translated into Hebrew from an earlier Aramaic introduction. After all, it provides the all-important historical setting, including Nebuchadnezzar's destruction of Jerusalem and how Daniel and those three youths found themselves at Nebuchad-nezzar's court (which must have happened somewhat earlier than the destruction of Jerusalem if the date in Daniel 2 is correct).

Moreover, through a simple story about Daniel and his friends refusing to eat food that the Jewish law forbade and insisting on being vegetarians despite the worries of the eunuch responsible for their care, it introduces the reader to their devout uncompromising faith and devotion to God. The writer of Daniel 10-12 would not want his own section read by readers who were unaware of exactly who Daniel was (and Daniel certainly wasn't well-known in the early second century BC as his absence from a comprehensive list of famous Jewish men composed around 180 BC by a Jewish sage called Jesus Ben Sira clearly shows – see the book of *Sirach* in the Apocrypha). Consequently, he had good reason to translate such a suitable introduction into Hebrew to make sure it wasn't missed. Perhaps he even left a tiny clue in there about his addition to Daniel's prophecies. The prophecy in Daniel 10-12 is set 'In the third year of Cyrus', while Daniel 1 finishes with the words 'Daniel continued even to the *first* year of king Cyrus' [my italics].

Anyway, getting back to Daniel 3, the story tells us that Nebuchadnezzar built an enormous gold statue (presumably representing Babylon's chief god Marduk) and set it up in a place called the plain of Dura in the Province of Babylon – and therefore probably not far from the city. All the dignitaries from across the realm were summoned to the dedication of that statue, and were required to bow down and worship it whenever the music played or be thrown into a fiery furnace within the hour. Daniel, by then a governor following his successful interpretation of Nebuchad-nezzar's statue dream, had presumably found some excuse not to attend since no-one accuses him of not worshipping the statue. However, his three friends Shadrach, Meshach and Abednego (the names given them by the Babylonians are far catchier than their Hebrew names) are duly accused and brought before the king.

The king offers them a second chance to comply. However, they decline the offer, assuring the king that their God can deliver them from his hand. In a rage, the king orders the furnace heated seven times as hot. The three are bound and thrown in fully clothed, and the heat kills the poor men tasked with carrying out this order. All of a sudden the king leaps up in astonishment and asks, *"Didn't we cast three men bound into the middle of the fire? Look, I see four men loose, walking in the middle of the fire, and they are unharmed. The appearance of the fourth is like a son of the gods!"* He then calls the three young men out and decrees that anyone who says anything against their God from now on will be cut to pieces.

The story of Daniel's three companions, their uncompromising refusal to bow down to the massive gold statue that king Nebuchadnezzar erected, and the presence of the angel protecting them from the heat of the furnace, would have been powerful inspiration for the Jews to say no to Antiochus' soldiers. It would also have given strength to the Christians suffering similar persecution centuries later at the hands of the Romans. But is there any indications that it might have been based upon real events?

Well, intriguingly, the historian Herodotus – whose reliability is admittedly seen as questionable by modern scholars – records a story about the fifth Persian Emperor Xerxes finding a huge gold statue in Babylon's Temple of Marduk, the city's chief deity. To the horror of the Babylonian priesthood, he melted it down to pay for his wars against the Greeks. Since the huge gold statue that Nebuchadnezzar raised in the province of Babylon almost a century earlier, according to Daniel 3, would be most likely an image of the city's chief deity (as he would not have wanted to anger his powerful priesthood), I would not be surprised if it had later ended up inside that great temple.

But remember, if it were merely an inspirational story, does that mean God isn't allowed to use it? Must God limit himself to using only factual accounts to accomplish his purposes? Is God really opposed to spreading his message via imperfect vessels that do not always tell things as they are? Clearly the answer is no. He uses imperfect vessels all the time. The writers of the Bible were imperfect vessels like us, often writing for impure motives. But out of their imperfect efforts God was fashioning a powerful tool to use to spread his word successfully to all peoples – even sceptics like me. The book of Daniel is perfect for that purpose, not because it was all definitely written at the time it claims, but because some of it almost certainly *wasn't*, and because the content of those parts betrays the existence and only justifiable meaning of its genuine prophecies – those that really were divinely inspired predictions of specific world events pertaining to the rise of Christianity: Daniel 7, Daniel 9:24-27, and of course Daniel 2:31-45, the dazzling statue dream of the great king Nebuchadnezzar of Babylon with which I began my journey into the book of Daniel.

In chapter 2 we found that when matched with established history, the meaning of that dream (pages 42-43) perfectly predicted the rise of Christianity in the time of the kings of the fourth distinct world-dominating empire from Babylon. As with Daniel 7, though, critical scholars say this is just a coincidence, and that the intended meaning of the dream was *not* the historical sequence of empires it portrays so accurately. Let us therefore take a closer look at what it says about these empires to see if this claim holds up.

Daniel's interpretation makes clear that the first of those empires – the gold head of the statue – was the Babylonian empire itself. Daniel calls it "You O king", but it is obvious he is identifying it as the Babylonian empire as a whole. The reason he identifies it as the king himself is almost certainly in order to make his interpretation as flattering as possible to that king. Only by doing that was he going to be able to predict the demise of that empire and yet escape with his life. In my opinion, the same reasoning fully accounts for why the second empire in this dream – the one represented by the silver chest and arms – is described as 'inferior'.

Why, critical scholars argue, would the Persian Empire, which was over three times the size of the Babylonian Empire, be described as *inferior* to it? They claim it is because the writer mistakenly thought there had been an extremely short-lived period of dominance by the nation of Media before the rise of Persia, and that it is in fact Media that the silver chest and arms represents. But this claim is not supported by any of the details found elsewhere in the book of Daniel. All of these, as we have seen throughout this book, indicate that its writer held the historically accurate view that Babylon was conquered by the *Medo-Persian* Empire of Cyrus. That is why the ram representing the empire to follow that of Babylon in Daniel 8 has both a *higher* horn standing for the Persians and a *lower* horn representing the Medes. That is why the bear in Daniel 7 is *raised up on one of its sides*. And that is also why the man who captures the city of Babylon in Daniel 5 rules it strictly according to 'the law of the Medes *and Persians*'.

Another problem with that very popular critical hypothesis is that it assumes the decisive factor in this dream's evaluation of those empires is either their size or their longevity. Yet, the superiority of Babylon over the next empire is represented by the difference between gold and silver. If that really were meant to symbolise greater size or longevity, how can the third empire be bronze (the bronze belly and thighs of the statue), and yet be described by Daniel as 'ruling the whole earth'? (See Daniel 2:39 on page 42).

If the preciousness of the metal stands for longevity or size and that third empire were Persia, as critical scholars claim, it should be represented by a metal far more precious than the metal (gold) representing Babylon. Persia dominated the world for almost three times as long as Nebuchadnezzar's Babylon (the empire of the *Chaldeans*, or what scholars often call the '*Neo*-Babylonians'), and her empire was at least three times larger. Moreover, one cannot claim that the writer of the book of Daniel was ignorant of this fact because Daniel 9:2 refers to Jeremiah's famous *seventy-year prophecy* which specifically refers to the length of time over which Babylon would 'be served by the surrounding nations' (Jeremiah 25:11). In other words, the duration of the world-dominance of Babylon – the first empire in the sequence – was almost certainly perceived to be only *seventy years*.

Some evangelical Christian interpreters appear to think that this is too brief for the whole of the gold head to be Babylon. They instead propose that Babylon was culturally linked to the empire of Assyria that Nebuchadnezzar's predecessor conquered, and that the gold head actually symbolises that centuries-old Mesopotamian culture. This may be what led St Jerome in the early fifth century AD to suggest that the wings of the winged lion – the first of the four beasts in Daniel 7 (and therefore the equivalent of the gold head in Daniel 2) – represent the Assyrian empire, which had reigned over Mesopotamia for hundreds of years prior to the rise of Chaldean Babylon. Whether this suggestion meant Jerome regarded Nebuchadnezzar's empire as a sort-of final flowering of the Assyrian Empire is in my view debatable. He may merely have been imagining those wings as the greatest of the Babylonian lion's *conquests* (since the Babylonians, in alliance with the Medes, did *conquer* the Assyrians).

Nevertheless, that ambiguous and speculative suggestion has been eagerly seized upon by interpreters desperate to overcome the problem of how the second empire can possibly be described as 'inferior' to Babylon if it constitutes the vast Persian empire that ruled most of the known world for two whole centuries. You can see its influence in the seventeenth century engraving of Daniel's four Beasts by Matthäus Merian on page 64.

To me, this suggestion makes no sense at all. There is nothing in Daniel 7 or Daniel 2 that justifies the assumption that the gold represents durability or cultural richness. And that assumption needlessly forces one to dispense with the vital lesson of Daniel 8 that distinct empires are the dominion of *distinct nations*. The Ptolemies, Seleucids, Antigonids and Attalids, for example, are counted as parts of a *single* empire in Daniel 8 because they were all *Macedonian*, and because they owed their respective spheres of influence to the conquests of Alexander the Great. The Medo-Persian empire is a change from the Babylonian one because it was founded by *the Medes and Persians*, who are a single empire because they were already united at the time they conquered Babylon. Hence the Babylonian empire has to be considered distinct from the Assyrian because it was founded by the *Chaldeans* – a different people. If one chooses to ignore this very obvious Daniel-8-inspired inference, one can hardly argue that Rome is the fourth empire from Daniel's time. Critics could simply say that she was culturally similar to Greece, and therefore not a distinct empire at all! Only the evidence in Daniel 8 that distinct empires are the conquests of distinct nations rules this out.

But with that straightforward *and fully justified* conclusion, the preciousness of the different metals simply cannot represent either size or longevity. As we saw in chapter 2, the third empire in the historically-accurate interpretation is Alexander's Macedonian Empire (Greece). At its height that nation ruled the whole of what was previously the Persian Empire together with Greece and territory in northern India. It was thus the largest of the first three, and it remained dominant for *twice as long* as the Babylonians.

So, if it isn't size or longevity, what does the preciousness of the metal symbolise? I think the only consistent answer is found in Daniel's praise of his king in Daniel 2:37-38. In his interpretation of the gold part of the statue, Daniel tells the king,

> **DAN 2:** [37] 'You, O king, are king of kings, to whom the God of heaven has given the kingdom, the power, the strength, and the glory. [38] Wherever the children of men dwell, he has given the animals of the field and the birds of the sky into your hand, and has made you rule over them all. You are the head of gold.'

If preciousness represents the power of the king, then the choice of metals makes perfect sense – though only when the vision is interpreted historically. Nebuchadnezzar and the Babylonian kings were the most powerful of all the predicted rulers of those empires. They could do whatever they liked. No one held them to account. That was not true of the Persian emperors who had to abide by a legal code called 'The Law of the Medes and Persians' as Daniel 6 makes clear. But even that was not as great a limit on power as afflicted the *Macedonian* kings (Alexander's successors). They had to content themselves with a fourth share of Alexander's empire due to its four-part divided nature (which is portrayed so powerfully by the four-winged, four-headed leopard in Daniel 7). And although most of the emperors of Rome ruled over the whole of their empire (making them more powerful than the Macedonian kings), they did so in theory at the behest of the Roman Senate (which they ignored at their peril). In this sense they did not have the absolute despotic power of Nebuchadnezzar, or even the ultimate law-making authority of Cyrus. The power of the Roman emperors is thus rightly indicated by iron.

But why did Daniel (or God) choose to rate those empire's according to the power of their kings? Is God a monarchist? Not it seems according to the Old Testament. God seems to have wanted the Israelites to be ruled by judges. He only reluctantly gives in to their demands for a king (see 1 Samuel 8:5-22). And unlike her judges, most of Israel's kings are not seen as heroes.

As far as I can see, the only reason for this choice of yardstick is the importance of preserving his prophet Daniel's *life*. It is not often appreciated that in his interpretation of this vision, Daniel was predicting the downfall of Nebuchadnezzar's empire. Had he said, 'After you will come a kingdom superior to yours', he would almost certainly have lost his head. By making Babylon the gold (the empire with the most powerful kings), Daniel was able to portray the conquest of his king's empire in a manner so flattering the king didn't notice the unfavourableness of this prediction.

Thus, the inferiority of the second kingdom in Daniel 2 is no reason to doubt that this vision portrays the historically accurate sequence of empires *Babylon-Persia-Greece-Rome*. Remember, the strongest reason to believe this is the symbolism of Daniel 7. The similarity between the features of the fourth kingdom in that vision and those of the fourth kingdom in Daniel 2 (especially the fact that the latter coincides with the rise of an eternal kingdom of God just as in Daniel 7) shows clearly that the same sequence of empires is being portrayed in both visions. And in Daniel 7, the third empire is symbolised by a *four-winged, four-headed leopard*, which everyone in the second century BC was sure to identify as 'Greece' (the empire of Alexander the Great). None of the other empires they knew of had split into four kingdoms governed by four ruling dynasties, and Alexander's had been split that way for the best part of a century. And just in case any reader wasn't aware of this fact, both Daniel 8 and Daniel 11 state it explicitly. Hence Daniel 7 shows unequivocally that the third empire in the sequence – the bronze belly and thighs of Daniel 2 – is the four-part-divided empire of Greece, making it inconceivable that the second empire was not meant to be Persia and the fourth Rome.

When I first realised this, it made me wonder why there is no four-part-divided symbolism in the bronze part of the statue. If that is the distinguishing feature of Greece, as Daniel 8 and Daniel 11 so clearly suggests, why is it absent from Daniel 2?

For me, the simplest answer to this one is that it probably *wasn't* absent from the dream. We have established beyond reasonable doubt that Greece is the bronze belly and thighs of the statue. Since the statue is of a man, it is probably quite reasonable to infer the existence of a fourth bronze part in that same anatomical region. Although that part will be relatively small compared to the other three, this would not be inconsistent with the historical reality. Alexander's home kingdom of Macedon and the two huge overseas Macedonian empires of the Seleucids and the Ptolemies emerged within twenty years of his death and are therefore perfectly represented by the statue's belly and two thighs. But the fourth part of that divided empire – the Attalid kingdom of Pergamon – didn't become independent until halfway through the third century BC, and it remained relatively small in size compared to the other three giants. Nevertheless, I can't resist pointing out that it did break free from the mighty Seleucid Empire – a fact that suggests this fourth Greek kingdom really did have balls!

As well as this four-part symbolism, there is another very strong piece of evidence in Daniel 2 that Greece is the third empire being depicted, and that is the fact that only the third empire is described as 'ruling the whole earth'. Admittedly the Persian Empire was of comparable size to the empire of Alexander. However, readers in the second century BC would be very unlikely to think of Persia as having 'ruled the whole earth'. That is because by their day the defeat of Persia by Greece at Marathon (490 BC) and then Salamis, Mycale and Plataea (480-479 BC) would have been widely known. The Persians were expelled for good from the Greek mainland – and this was long before Alexander, at the height of their power.

No matter how slight that set-back may have been in the eyes of modern historians, its frequent retelling all over the Greek world of the third century BC would have ensured that no-one in the second century BC saw Persia as a world-ruling kingdom. That status would only apply to Alexander who never lost any of the battles he fought. Hence the claim in Daniel 2 that the third empire would 'rule the whole earth' (Daniel 2:39, page 42) is strongly supportive of the obvious and straightforward historically-accurate view that it constitutes the Greek empire of Alexander the Great (as the leopard with four wings and four heads in Daniel 7 so clearly indicates to any scholar brave enough to interpret it the way everyone would have interpreted it in the second century BC).

If you are a sceptical person like me, you may by now be wondering why I am so interested in Daniel 2. Surely if what it predicts is all predicted by Daniel 7, it is much more likely to be derived from that more-detailed prophecy than to have been independently inspired. The interesting thing about Daniel 2, though, is that *not* everything it predicts features explicitly in Daniel 7. It does make some predictions that Daniel 7 doesn't mention. And if it were really derived from Daniel 7, one would expect it to have made some mention of three kings being subdued by an eleventh. That prediction is nowhere evident within it.

The predictions in Daniel 2 that are not found in Daniel 7 concern the timing of the everlasting kingdom of God. Daniel 2:34 tells us that the stone cut from a mountain strikes the statue on its feet of iron and clay (page 41). Since the statue represents just four human empires, and has legs of pure iron symbolising the fourth empire, those iron and clay feet can only stand for a *second phase* of that same fourth empire – a phase characterised by weakness resulting from the marrying of her people with those of the nations she conquered as the interpretation indicates. Yet the prophecy makes clear that it will still possess iron strength even in this latter phase.

Critical scholars who insist that this empire is Greece (Alexander's empire) – and thereby assume the writer got his history totally and inexplicably wrong – claim that this latter phase represents the four-part divided state of Alexander's empire from the end of the fourth century BC. They assume this even though no four-part symbolism is evident in that part of the statue. They then argue that the reference to intermarriage is an allusion to the dynastic marriages that were intended to stop the frequent wars between the Seleucid and Ptolemaic parts of that divided empire (see Appendix). But to me this claim makes no sense whatsoever. Both the Ptolemies and the Seleucids were extremely powerful and evenly-matched states. Yet critical scholars are claiming that the writer of this prophecy represented the Seleucids by iron and the Ptolemies, who won most of the early wars between them, by clay!

If that were really the case, how come he hasn't indicated the Attalid and Antigonid parts of the Greek empire, both of which do feature in Daniel 8, and are not totally ignored in Daniel 11 either?

As we saw in chapter 2, page 53, the fact that there are four distinct empires in this sequence means that when you match the prophecy with established history, the fourth one can only be identified as Rome. Moreover, the symbolic features of the four beasts in Daniel 7 and the two beasts in Daniel 8 indicate that this is exactly how the writer of the book of Daniel *intended* it to be identified. The fact that the third beast in Daniel 7 has four heads and four wings that readers were bound to interpret as the four Greek kingdoms, for example, means that whoever included this prophecy in the book of Daniel clearly intended its third empire to be recognised as Greece. And the fact that a single beast in Daniel 8 represents *the Medes and Persians* is highly indicative of that same intention. Since the fourth beast in Daniel 7 is described as 'different from all before it' and 'more powerful', the writer of the book of Daniel in the 160s BC can only have intended the empire it represents to be Rome (the Roman Republic of his day). It is therefore quite astonishing that the Roman empire *did indeed* change between two highly distinct phases of government as the legs and feet of the statue in Daniel 2 suggest. It was a republic from long before it rose to dominance, and then it changed to an autocracy under the emperors from Augustus onwards.

Now, it is possible that a writer in the second century BC who was deriving this prophecy from Daniel 7 could have worked this out. In his day, Rome was a republic, and she was already the ruling nation. Since Daniel 7 predicts that at least eleven kings would rise from this nation before the rise of God's everlasting kingdom, that nation's form of government had to change to an autocracy before then for that prophecy to be fulfilled. Nevertheless, it seems strange that he would distinguish the latter phase as *weaker than the former*, and *due to a mingling of peoples*.

As far as I can see, a mingling of peoples was indeed the most important factor that brought Rome's emperors to power. Rome's empire was so big that her soldiers hardly saw the home city. As a result, their pride and loyalty to the Republic was gradually replaced with an exclusive loyalty to their general, which allowed individuals to seize power by force, and led to the empire being weakened by civil wars that became much more frequent under the emperors than during the early days of the Republic.

However, a Jewish writer who was deriving Daniel 2 from Daniel 7 would be unlikely to present this latter stage as weaker than the former because that would suggest that this weakness was the reason for the eventual victory of the holy people (as indeed it may have been). To suggest this, would be to take the glory away from God, which is certainly not the done thing in Jewish literature. Moreover, since Daniel 7 describes how kings of that fourth empire would defeat and persecute the holy people, making out that this would take place during the *weaker phase* of that empire is not particularly honouring to his own people.

But perhaps the most unexpected thing in this passage is the fact that it is the stone that strikes the statue which grows into a mountain filling the whole world. It is not the mountain from which the stone was cut that fills the world.

As I pointed out in chapter 2, pages 45-47, that mountain filling the whole world is interpreted by Daniel as an everlasting *kingdom of God*. Some claim this is a heavenly entity rather than anything on earth. However, the whole point of a prophecy is to predict historical events. Interpreting this as some invisible spiritual event is just a waste of time because if you can interpret a prophecy any way you like, any fulfilment you find could just be chance and is therefore uninteresting. That mountain *has to be* a historical entity.

Now, the only historical entity one could describe as a 'kingdom of God' that might last forever is a *religion* – a *faith*. And if that second mountain is a religion, the first mountain *has to be interpreted as a religion too* – one from which the second religion was fashioned. Since the second mountain represents a heavenly kingdom (and hence religion) given to the 'holy people' at that later time in history, the first mountain must also represent a heavenly kingdom (and hence religion) of the holy people. And it would have to stand for an earlier religion from which that later religion was fashioned. In other words, it can only stand for the Jewish faith that Moses founded. Any Jewish writer deriving this passage from Daniel 7 in the second century BC would be expected to predict that the Jewish religion would grow to fill the world. One would *not* expect him to predict such a victory for a later heretical off-shoot of his beloved faith.

Hence, I am inclined to believe Daniel 2 is authentic. If so, it is very interesting that this plan of God's intervention in human history appears to have been first revealed to the greatest world-leader at the time: Nebuchadnezzar, the most powerful king of the Neo-Babylonian empire. He is after all the human being in the best position to make everyone aware of it.

But what was God's purpose in having this prophecy included, many years later, in the book of Daniel? After all, unlike Daniel 7, it doesn't predict anything so specific that its fulfilment ought to shock us into realising that it has to have come from God. So why did God include it?

My view is that God's purpose for Daniel 2 is two-fold. Firstly, its identification of the first empire as Babylon, and the third as 'ruling the whole earth' is intended to ensure that the sequence of empires in Daniel 7 is interpreted correctly. But secondly, Daniel 2 is there to show that the really important message of Daniel 7 is its prediction of the rise of the everlasting kingdom of God. It is not the Year of the Four Emperors. The prediction of three kings being subdued by the eleventh king of Rome's empire is only there so that its dramatic fulfilment awakens the rational mind to the realisation that this vision probably did come from God. It is omitted from Daniel 2 because Daniel 2 is telling king Nebuchadnezzar what God was specifically *wanting* to bring into being – *the everlasting world-wide kingdom* – and that did not include a Year of Four Emperors, which I think God ensured at the correct moment purely to convince us of his divine authorship of that 'everlasting kingdom' prophecy.

In other words, I think Daniel was given a second version of this prophecy half a century after decoding Nebuchadnezzar's statue dream, and in that second version God included the prediction of three kings being subdued by the eleventh king of the fourth empire (who would also defeat the holy people). He did this so that by ensuring the fulfilment of that *much more specific* prediction he could provide all later human beings with visible evidence that the religion which would take over the Roman Empire soon afterwards was indeed the work of a very real God. But it is that religious takeover that constitutes the *main message* of the prophecy. That is made very clear in Daniel 7 by the fact that when Daniel first asks for the meaning of the imagery, the angel merely tells him,

DAN 7: [17] "These great animals, which are four, are four kings [ruling kingdoms], who will arise out of the earth. [18] But the holy people of the Most High will receive the kingdom, and possess the kingdom forever, even forever and ever."

Daniel has to enquire again about the specific features of the fourth beast before God gives him the interpretation that was perfectly fulfilled by the Year of the Four Emperors and the length of time from Hadrian's expulsion of the Jews until the ending of the Great Persecution of Christians (a time, times and half a time: 175 years).

Sometime later he also gave Daniel the short and memorable prophecy in Daniel 9:24-27. He included within that prophecy the '483 times 360-day' time-period (sixty-nine "sevens") for the coming to Jerusalem of the king 'Christ' of that everlasting kingdom (who would get put to death shortly afterwards 'having nothing'). And he added a seven-year prediction for the death of the ruler who will end Jewish sacrifice so that, again, the fulfilment of that prediction could be easily seen from the history books, thereby confirming the divine authorship of this prophecy.

Finally, in the mid-160s BC, God ensured that the popular Jewish perception of the previous four centuries of history was included in the book of Daniel. He achieved this by seeking out a political writer who was trying to bolster Jewish morale in the struggle against Antiochus Epiphanes through making out that Daniel had predicted an imminent end to their current hardships. God inspired that writer to include within his book those three genuine Danielic prophecies as authentic-looking predictions of the really distant future. Since that writer did this in an effort to stop the sceptics denouncing his book as a forgery, he has made every effort to emphasise the predictive nature of these visions that diplomacy would allow. Although he hasn't named the fourth empire, he has included a vision (Daniel 8) that names the middle two. And whilst he has not identified Nehemiah's permission as the starting point of Daniel 9's time-period, he has come as close to doing so as he dared by including a prayer derived from Nehemiah's which he hoped would remind his readers of that most obvious 'decree to restore and rebuild Jerusalem' that their sacred books contained.

In my journey through the book of Daniel I have now come full circle. I began in chapter 2 with my astonishment at the accuracy of Daniel 2:31-45, and I leapt from there to the similar but incredibly specific version of this prophecy in Daniel 7. Having exposed the amazing fulfilment of its prediction that the eleventh king of the Roman empire would be different from the ten before him, subdue three of them, speak boastfully against the Jewish God, and successfully wage war upon the Jews, I sought out the most justifiable meaning of the time-period in this prophecy and discovered another amazing fit with history – one that is strongly supported by Christ's reference to Daniel in Mark 13:14-30.

I was then catapulted forward to Daniel 9, which Christ was quite clearly referring to with his 'abomination of desolation' statement. I there found, to my amazement, that the interpretation of the 'sixty-nine "sevens"' time-period that is most justified by the text of Daniel is the one that predicts the Triumphal Entry of Christ to within a month of the very day it is most likely to have happened (30th March 33 AD). I also discovered that the rest of this prophecy accurately predicted the Roman destruction of Jerusalem and its Temple and the continuation of sacrifice and offering there until Hadrian finally forbade the Jews from entering the city midway through the last seven years of his life. What astonished me most about this passage, though, was that the countdown from the founding of Aelia Capitolina (Hadrian's Jerusalem) in 131 until Hadrian's death in July 138 was given accurately as *seven years!*

I then observed that the prayer in Daniel 9 seems derived from Nehemiah 1 (and thus not written by Daniel). But I realised that this makes it such powerful evidence that Nehemiah's decree was the intended starting point of the sixty-nine "sevens" time-period that its inclusion was very probably God-inspired. This led me to look for God's purpose in other seemingly late additions to the book of Daniel. I first focussed on Daniel 10-12, which is set 'in the *third* year of Cyrus' whereas Daniel 1 tells us that Daniel lived on 'even until the *first* year of Cyrus' – a rather strange oversight on the part of the editor which makes me think he was trying to tell us something! In any case, the extremely detailed nature of that prophecy, and its inclusion of failed guesswork (Daniel 11:40-45), assured me that it wasn't the genuine article. Nevertheless, I realised that its structure, and in particular the point at which it ceased to be accurate, showed beyond reasonable doubt when the book of Daniel was most likely put together, and how its intended readers perceived their history. And this gave me strong grounds to believe that God inspired its inclusion for precisely this purpose.

Drawn back a few chapters by the very similar historical emphasis of Daniel 8, I soon had to admit that the same was most likely true of that beautifully dramatic portrayal of the history of Alexander's empire up to the period of Antiochus Epiphanes. In fact, I realised that the writer must have gone out of his way to create this otherwise unnecessary prophecy of Antiochus Epiphanes simply so that sceptical readers would not be able to successfully argue that Daniel 7 might have been a prediction of Antiochus too (which ironically is what mainstream scholars today *do* try to argue).

I then inquired about the potential purpose and authenticity of the rest of the book of Daniel. I noted how the stories contained in Daniel 5 and Daniel 6 preserved memories of ancient rulers that, especially in the case of king Belshazzar, have proved to be surprisingly accurate. I also noted how the settings of these stories, though frequently assumed by critical scholars to be fictitious, are not in fact inconsistent with established history as it might have been experienced by Jews living in Babylon in the sixth century BC. Whilst the inclusion of these heroic tales was almost certainly for the purpose of inspiring the Jews of the 160s BC to resist Antiochus' assault on their religion, I realised that God may also have wanted them included for the similar purpose of inspiring the holy people to remain faithful in the much more prolonged time of persecution that lay ahead. Hence in this last chapter I have bounced all the way down through the tales of Daniel 5 and 6, Daniel 4, and Daniel 1 and 3, and I have finally ended up back here at Daniel 2!

I want to finish this journey, though, by reminding you about what I regard to be the most astounding part of the book of Daniel because it has been so terribly and unjustifiably misinterpreted by mainstream and evangelical scholars alike.

Daniel 7, the last chapter in the Aramaic section of the book, presents a sequence of four monsters representing distinct ruling nations. The first is a lion with eagle's wings that gets its wings torn off, is made to walk like a man, and is given a man's heart. The second is a bear raised up on one side with three ribs in its mouth between its teeth. It gets told to rise and eat its fill of flesh. The third is a four-winged, four-headed leopard that receives the power to rule. And the fourth is a totally distinct and far more powerful unidentified monster with large iron teeth and bronze claws that breaks its victims up with its iron teeth and tramples the residue underfoot. It has ten horns on its head, and as Daniel watches, a little horn grows up among them and uproots three of those ten horns.

It then grows thicker, gains a mouth speaking boastfully and a pair of eyes, and is seen to be waging war against the holy people and defeating them. Heavenly thrones and a Gandalf-like represent-ation of God then appear in the dream. A river of fire flows out from under God's throne, and a heavenly judgement takes place in which the fourth beast is slain and consumed by the heavenly fire while the other beasts live on for a time in a powerless state. Immediately afterwards, one like a son of man arrives on a cloud and is led up to and enthroned next to God. Daniel then gets told by one of the angels in attendance that the ten horns are ten kings of that fourth distinct and most powerful empire, and that its eleventh king would be different from the ten, and would subdue three of them. He would also fight against the holy people and defeat them, and he would think to change their times and law. The holy people would then be given into his hand for a time, times and half a time, after which they would receive the kingdom and possess it forever.

We saw in chapters 2, 3 and 4 that established history is *perfectly represented* by this prophecy. Even its prediction that the eleventh king of the fourth distinct empire from Babylon would be different from his predecessors, subdue three of them, speak boastfully against God and defeat the holy people was precisely fulfilled by history. And it was fulfilled by *major world events* (page 53 & 82).

Noticing that the thickness and embedded eyes of the eleventh horn weren't interpreted in the text, we then realised that with just one word-change, these would perfectly represent the remaining pagan emperors prior to Constantine I. In particular, the eyes were a perfect symbol for Hadrian, the successor of the eleventh king most famous for attempting to change Jewish times and laws, and into whose hand the holy people really would be given for a time, times and half a time. Since the rise of Christianity most obviously fulfilled the 'everlasting kingdom' prediction, the ending of that time-period had to be the Edict of Toleration that officially ended the persecution of Christians. We were therefore amazed to find that the meaning of 'a time, times and half a time' most justified by Jewish scripture (175 years) reached precisely from that edict all the way back to the moment the holy people were most clearly given into Hadrian's hand. And our doubts were further dispelled by the fact that this interpretation is strongly supported by what Christ had to say about that time of persecution in Mark 13:14-30.

But even if you quibble about this reinterpretation of the time-period, the very fact that the eleventh king of the Roman empire almost certainly subdued three of its ten previous kings, famously defeated the Jews, and was by his father's lowly status illegitimate in the eyes of Rome's ruling elite, is by itself utterly astonishing. Since the Year of the Four Emperors was perhaps the most famous political event of the first century, even if this prophecy had merely pictured the uprooting of those three horns by the eleventh horn on the head of the beast representing the Roman empire, *that alone* would have been enough to make it an astoundingly accurate portrayal of future history. The addition of the prediction that this king would be different from the others, exceedingly blasphemous, and a conqueror of the Jews makes it even more impressive.

Critical scholars, whilst rightly acknowledging that the horns have to stand for kings, have perhaps deliberately steered away from this accurate interpretation through a strange insistence that a king who attacks the Jews has to be Antiochus Epiphanes unless otherwise stated. As I pointed out in chapter 7, there is absolutely no need for another prediction of Antiochus in this book. It already has two perfectly good ones. What the writer really needed was authentic-looking prophecies that predicted events that were still to happen. If his book didn't include such prophecies the sceptics would almost certainly denounce it as a forgery and its purpose would have failed. That is why insisting that any king who attacks the Jews has to be Antiochus Epiphanes makes no sense whatsoever. It could easily be a prediction of a *future* king who attacks the Jews. That is definitely what the early readers of this prophecy would have thought, and they would therefore have sought to understand the timing of the predicted events from the given information in order to *find out* whether or not that was the case.

Since they would not be trying to make it predict Antiochus Epiphanes, they would not be squeezing any unhistorical Median conquest of Babylon into the sequence of empires as mainstream scholars do today. Instead they would interpret it in exactly the way Daniel 8 – which was probably created for this very purpose – suggests. And in Daniel 8, the Greek Empire is portrayed as a goat with a single horn that breaks off and grows into four ginormous horns representing the four successor kingdoms of that empire. The intended readers were never going to interpret the four wings and four heads on the leopard in Daniel 7 as anything other than those four successor kingdoms and their associated ruling dynasties.

The well-informed among them might even see the connection of the goat and leopard being symbols of Dionysus and thus of the religion of that empire. But even if they failed to notice this, they could hardly have missed the fact that the bear's higher and lower sides are analogous to the higher and lower horns of the ram in Daniel 8. That ram is clearly indicated to represent a continuous Medo-Persian Empire – not separate states of Media then Persia – so the bear ought to be interpreted in exactly the same way.

I find it quite alarming that critical scholars almost universally attach no significance to the fact that the bear in Daniel 7 has a higher and lower part *just like the ram in Daniel 8*. The three ribs between its teeth have not yet been explained in this book, but we have already encountered their most obvious meaning. Recall from our discussion of the Persian king Cyrus' conquest of Babylon (page 240) that this Persian king surprisingly spared the lives of three emperors he toppled. Those were his Median grandfather king Astyages, Croesus king of Lydia, and thirdly, the head of the Babylonian Empire Nabonidus (Belshazzar's father). Since the ribs are the remains of what the bear ate, it is very likely that they were intended to represent that honourable preservation of these three kings – an act of mercy that was very unusual at the time (though probably not by the second century BC as the writer of Daniel 8 doesn't bother to include any analogy to them on his ram).

The corresponding symbolism in Daniel 8 thus guides any reader unfamiliar with the relevant history to the historically accurate interpretation of Daniel 7 – the interpretation that ensures that in the second century BC this prophecy would have been understood to predict events that lay a long time in the distant future. And as we have just reminded ourselves, those very specific, momentous and time-limited predictions really did come to pass!

Even the requirement demanded by history that the event of the holy people gaining 'the kingdom' (almost certainly the territory of the fourth beast) be a *religious* takeover rather than a Jewish conquest is perfectly defensible from the prophecy. It is supported by the at-first puzzling claim that the other three beasts live on after the fourth is destroyed. As we saw in chapter 3, that claim can only be reconciled with history if the beasts really stand for the *religions* of the conquering nations (just as the Dionysian goat and leopard for Greece most obviously indicates). So, the killing and burning of the fourth beast by the fire that came from the heavenly throne can only symbolise the destruction of Rome's *religion*, which was brought about in the fourth century AD by Christianity.

Despite this amazing evidence in support of Christianity, you will be hard-pressed to find any other evangelical commentary on Daniel that recognises these facts. Almost every one of them interprets the horns on the fourth monster as *kingdoms* rather than kings. They defend this view by observing that the four successor kingdoms of the Greek Empire are represented by four horns on the goat in Daniel 8, and by pointing out that the word translated 'kings' in Daniel 7 appears to be used ambiguously to denote ruling kingdoms *as well as* ruling individuals.

Before I get into the main reason why this interpretation is not justifiable, it is worth pointing out that there are other horns on the goat in Daniel 8 that do represent individual kings. Its first horn is Alexander the Great and its last horn is Antiochus Epiphanes. Moreover, the two horns on the ram in the same chapter represent *consecutive lines* of kings, since one grows after the other (the Persian kings succeeded the Median ones). As far as I can see, the writer just chose horns to represent the Greek successor kingdoms because using heads and wings would make it far too obvious that he was directing attention to Daniel 7. But as you can see, it is heads and wings in Daniel 7 – not horns – that stand for successor kingdoms. That is what the four horns on the goat really tells us.

But the strongest argument against the very popular evangelical hypothesis that the horns in Daniel 7 stand for kingdoms is that it makes the prophecy *easy to fulfil* due to the relatively flexible idea of what constitutes a kingdom, and the far greater lifetime of a kingdom compared to a king. You'll notice also that the interpreters who promote this view are very selective over who they consider to be the holy people. They generally restrict this term to the followers of their particular church. Some even go so far as to associate other denominations with unfavourable elements of this vision's symbolism. Protestant commentators like Isaac Newton, for example, have argued that the Vatican State is the little horn! As I have said throughout this book, if you can interpret a prophecy any way you like you can easily find a fulfilment in history – even one that supports whatever ideology you prefer – and you therefore have no reason to be surprised by that fulfilment. Such a fulfilment would tell you nothing interesting. It could just be chance. It is only when the *most justifiable* interpretation of the prophecy is fulfilled by history that you have reason enough to sit up and pay attention – and only when it predicts rare events in a narrow enough window of time.

As we have seen, Daniel 7 tells us that the horns are kings. And since we have no indication elsewhere *in that prophecy* that they might instead stand for successor kingdoms we should reject that alternative possibility outright. We should stick with the most obvious interpretation unless the text of the prophecy suggests otherwise. If the eleventh king to rule over the Roman empire did not subdue three emperors before him and wage war upon the holy people (which must mean any devout followers of the Jewish God since it must include Daniel) then we should conclude that this very improbable aspect of the vision has failed to come true (as one would expect). The amazing thing is that this most justifiable interpretation *really did come true* – and it is only with the clearest and most obvious definition of king that this can be recognised.

It is true that by the same policy one ought really to assume that it was the same king (Vespasian) who thought to change times and law and who had the holy people handed over to him for a time, times and half a time. And, assuming the 'three-and-a-half years' interpretation of 'a time, times and half a time', perhaps he did. But as I pointed out in chapter 4, we then encounter the eyes and mouth and imposing nature of that eleventh horn, and a later observation of it fighting and defeating the holy people. One also realises that a duration of three-and-a-half years is not a defensible meaning for the 'time, times and half a time' as a period of hardship in Jewish history.

It is that latter aspect of the text which, in my opinion, forces one to the view that the imposing phase of the eleventh horn stands for a sequence of emperors. It must do because the only totally defensible candidate for the meaning of 'time' in that time-phrase is the 'fifty-year period' specified by Leviticus 25:8-10, and that would make the time-period 175 years long – much longer than any single king's reign. Hence only if the eleventh horn stands for more than one king can its destruction be the victory of the holy people *after those 175 years* as the passage quite clearly implies.

Recognising this, it becomes perfectly legitimate to look for the official end of the persecution of Christians (Galerius Edict of Toleration), and count back 175 years as we did in chapter 4. The amazing thing is that we then reach Hadrian's expulsion of the Jews and his raising of the abomination of desolation, and Hadrian is perfectly represented by a pair of eyes! That century-and-three-quarters was the only time in history when the holy people (devout followers of the Jewish God) had no state protection whatsoever and were unable to defend themselves against their persecutors. And it appears very much to be what Christ was referring to in Mark 13:14-30 and Matthew 24:15-34 (long before it came about).

I think this is a truly remarkable find – not least because it is well-supported by Christ himself who said the time-period would begin 'before this generation passes away'. I don't think it is interpreting the prophecy in anything but the most justifiable way because 'three and a half years' is not a very justifiable interpretation of 'a time, times and half a time', and the most justifiable interpretation of that time phrase – the interpretation most strongly indicated by the "sevens" in Daniel 9 – forces one to the view on the eleventh horn's symbolism that I have presented here. And remember, it was only a year or so after that time-period that Constantine I defeated his rival Maxentius to become sole emperor in the West having seen a strange sign in the sky and had a dream that told him it was the sign of Jesus (presumably the one predicted in Matthew 24:30, page 113) and that with it he would conquer.

So there we have it. The sign of the son of man did indeed appear in the sky from one end to the other shortly after that time period, just as Jesus predicted. Emperor Constantine I saw it, together with his whole army, and was persuaded to paint it onto the shields of his soldiers. As a result, from then on anyone who set eyes on these troops saw this sign, whether they were within the Roman empire observing the arrival of officials or out-with it engaging those troops in battle or spying on their movements. As news spread of those changes in the west, eventually all eyes would indeed come to see that sign of the Son of Man, and many nations would indeed bow down and worship him.

Although the sign has changed, the conversion of the world to Christianity is still happening today through the efforts of many individuals. However, the rate of conversion has slowed. In the West, at least, people are beginning to doubt the claim that Jesus the Son of Man was from God. And part of the problem is the stubbornness with which modern evangelicals stick rigidly to outdated and indefensible views on scripture that in their minds limit what God is allowed to include in the Bible.

As far as I can see, there are no grounds for limiting God in this way. God is perfectly entitled to construct his sacred scriptures from whatever texts he deems appropriate. When you open your mind to this fact, you really do discover what a truly powerful tool for evangelism God has fashioned in the book of Daniel.

If I have convinced you of this in this book, I strongly encourage you to tell others about it. It will, I think, give you solid grounds for your faith that can never be taken away. But don't keep it to yourself. There are many who would love to share in that sureness of faith that this real fulfilment of prophecy provides, and until the academic world has overcome the biases that prevent its experts from acknowledging this fulfilment of prophecy, those needy people are only going to hear about it from people like you and me who have the knowledge and the guts to disregard these conventions and speak what we can honestly defend as the most justifiable position. So play your part in the spread of the gospel to the ends of the earth that Jesus Christ predicted in Matthew 24:14. It is now time to wake up the world again to the reality of that God of Jesus Christ by showing them the true power he has displayed in the fulfilment of those most justifiable interpretations of Daniel 2:31-45, Daniel 7 and Daniel 9:24-27.

EPILOGUE

A First-century Daniel and the Message of Christ

The earliest surviving commentary on Daniel that is of any length is found in the book *Antiquities of the Jews* by the first-century Romano-Jewish historian Josephus. Written around 94 AD, it provides a detailed summary of the content of Daniel 1-6 and Daniel 8 by a man who was very much an admirer of this prophet. In fact, his own life somewhat mirrored that of Daniel's to a rather surprising extent.

As an aristocratic resident of Judea, Josephus had been called upon to organise the defence of Galilee against Vespasian when the first Jewish revolt against Rome began in 66 AD. Captured at the fall of the city of Jotapata, he appears to have been spared by Vespasian because of his talents as an interpreter who might be able to persuade the Jewish people that loyalty to Rome was far wiser than rebellion. Just as Daniel had been taught Babylonian customs, Josephus had been Romanised from his youth. He was therefore the ideal translator for Vespasian's purposes. But the similarity of his story to that of Daniel goes much further than this. Just as Daniel had been selected by king Nebuchadnezzar for his abilities, Josephus attracted the attention of Vespasian's son, the future emperor Titus. And amazingly if it is true (and we have only Josephus' word on this), his subsequent rise to a position of huge intellectual power in Rome was through delivering a prophecy that eventually proved to be accurate. Again, that is exactly how Daniel rose to a position of authority in Nebuchadnezzar's empire.

Vespasian, the eleventh unlimited dictator to rule over the Roman empire, was still a general in the service of the emperor Nero when he captured Josephus in 67 AD. As a rebel commander, Josephus was about to be sent off to the emperor in Rome, where he faced certain death. Probably in desperation, he asked to speak to Vespasian and said the only thing likely to stop his extradition. He predicted that Vespasian would become emperor, and that 'those who come to the throne after Nero will not last'. Obviously, it was then dangerous for Vespasian to send him to that paranoid ruler of Rome, which was why he remained a captive with the army in Judea. But when in a year or so, Vespasian emerged as the victor of the Year of the Four Emperors, he remembered Josephus' prophecy, brought him out of captivity and made him a free man, heaping honours and patronage upon him just as Nebuchadnezzar did to Daniel when he realised God had accurately revealed to Daniel the contents of his statue dream (see chapter 2).

These similarities with the story of Daniel are quite striking. And remember, Josephus witnessed, or at least lived through, a destruction of Jerusalem and her Temple in 70 AD, just as Daniel did in 587 BC. But the thing I find so amazing about all this is that Josephus – a highly educated Jewish historian – was thereby in a position to witness and report at first hand the rise of the eleventh king to rule over the Roman empire. He was personally acquainted with the very person who fulfilled the specific prediction of the eleventh king who subdues three before him in Daniel 7! And what he says in *Antiquities* (c. 94 AD) – or at least what he does *not* say – strongly suggests to me that he knew this.

The first point to note is that Josephus interprets the silver chest and arms of the statue in Daniel 2 as the Medo-Persian Empire, just as we have done in this book. He even goes as far as to suggest that the two silver arms symbolise the Persian king Cyrus together with Darius the Mede of Daniel 5-6, whom he identifies as a son of the Median king Astyages whom Cyrus deposed (a view probably drawn from the Greek writer Xenophon which is not nearly as defensible as the view that Darius the Mede was simply the Median general Gubaru who took the city for Cyrus and was subsequently called its king by Cyrus to help him command the people's loyalty). The important point I wish to get across here is that Josephus makes absolutely no suggestion that this silver chest and arms could possibly have stood for Media alone, as most critical scholars today claim. He explicitly identifies it as the Medo-Persian Empire under Cyrus. It was well-known in his day that this was the nation that conquered Babylon.

My second point is that in his account of Daniel's interpretation of the bronze belly and thighs of the statue, he adds that the third kingdom, which that part of the statue represents, will 'come from the west'. He therefore definitely identified it as Alexander and the Macedonians. And he claims that the fourth kingdom, which is 'like unto iron', will 'put an end to the government of the former'. He clearly believed that this fourth kingdom was Rome as we shall see shortly.

Intriguingly, he also shifts the words 'have dominion over the whole earth' from the third kingdom to the fourth kingdom. This, however, need not indicate that his version of the book of Daniel was different in this respect from the one that has come down to us. That is because it is quite possible that this was a deliberate and easily excusable (and hardly noticeable) mistake designed with his Roman readers in mind to assign greater power and glory to that fourth empire. He knew that if any of them bothered to match up the dream with recorded history they would easily work out that it predicted the power and dominion of their own empire, and he would not have wanted them thinking Daniel had predicted the extent of Roman power to be less than that of Alexander.

It is probably for the very same reason that he has completely omitted to mention the feet of the statue being made of mixed iron and clay. He did not want to advertise anything negative about the Roman Empire in this work because he and his readers were very much a part of that empire. Moreover, he owed his scholarly position to its current ruling dynasty who would undoubtedly want to approve this work that they had effectively paid for.

The important point here is that Josephus was thus absolutely certain that the fourth kingdom in Daniel 2 (and by implication Daniel 7 as well) was Rome. This is made all the more obvious by the fact that he sees the fulfilment of 'the stone striking and shattering the statue and becoming a mountain that filled the whole world' as being an event that was *yet to come*. He sees this as something that still lay in *his future* – the future of the Roman Empire as it was at the time of writing, around 94 AD.

It seems to me he took a bit of a risk mentioning that stone at all. The Romans who did their homework were bound to work out what its most obvious meaning was, as Josephus readily acknowledges later on (see below). I guess to not mention it having retold the prophecy thus far would be too big an omission to claim as an oversight. And he may have felt its ambiguity made it safe enough. At least Daniel 2 did not predict a war between the holy people and a king of that fourth kingdom, as Daniel 7 does. It merely predicted an eternal kingdom that those holy people would receive – though if his readers did connect the dots, they would see that this eternal kingdom (or even just the stone the dream mentions) seems to be somehow responsible for the *demise* of that fourth kingdom.

Perhaps to mitigate that risk a little he chooses not to mention that the stone strikes the statue on its iron (and clay) part – the part representing that fourth kingdom, and thus the Roman empire. And he very tactfully declines to speculate on the meaning of the stone. In fact, he makes the following remarkable excuse,

> 'Daniel did also declare the meaning of the stone to the king but I do not think proper to relate it, since I have only undertaken to describe things past or things present, but not things that are future; yet if anyone be so very desirous of knowing truth, as not to waive such points of curiosity, and cannot curb his inclination for understanding the uncertainties of futurity, and whether they will happen or not, let him be diligent in reading the book of Daniel, which he will find among the sacred writings.'

(Josephus' *Antiquities of the Jews*, translated by William Whiston, book X, ch.10, par.4)

I think Josephus simply couldn't help himself here. He is clearly a great fan of the prophet Daniel and was not going to miss this opportunity to plug his favourite book. It is interesting, though, that he does not do the same with either Daniel 7 or Daniel 9.

Neither of these amazing prophecies are discussed in *Antiquities* or in any of Josephus' surviving works. Nevertheless, we can be reasonably sure that both of them were present within his copy of the book of Daniel because he makes two allusions that are almost certainly to these very passages. In *Antiquities 10:11:7*, after an enthusiastic retelling of Daniel 8, he informs his readers,

> 'In the very same manner Daniel also wrote concerning the Roman government, and that our country should be made desolate by them'

The fact that this statement comes immediately after his detailed discussion of Daniel 8 (the prophecy in which the Medo-Persian Empire is represented by a ram and the Greek Empire by a goat) means that the first part of it can only be alluding to Daniel 7. Only in Daniel 7 are the empires represented by beasts like in Daniel 8, which is what 'the very same manner' in this context would seem to imply. And we know from his detailed interpretation of Daniel 2 that Josephus would definitely see Daniel 7 as a prediction of the Roman empire. But the words 'made desolate' also suggest Daniel 9:24-27, which refers to an 'abomination of desolation' and the destruction of Jerusalem and her Temple. If Josephus was so eager to demonstrate the predictive powers of Daniel's prophecies, why did he not discuss these prophecies in detail as he did Daniel 2 and Daniel 8?

It can hardly be because he thought they'd failed. A total destruction of Jerusalem and her Temple had taken place just two decades before, exactly as Daniel 9 explicitly predicted. He'd been there. He'd seen at first hand the desolation that the Roman armies had brought to his country. The most likely reason is in fact quite the opposite.

In his earlier book *The Jewish War* (c.75 AD), he tells us that he himself prophesied that Vespasian would become emperor with the words **'Are Nero's successors till they come to thee still alive?'** (book III, chapter 8, paragraph 9, William Whiston translation). Given that Vespasian would have insisted on approving this work, this was either the truth or else a falsehood that Vespasian himself would have had to have commissioned. Josephus wasn't going to invent such a claim himself and risk the wrath of his reigning emperor and patron. So is Josephus a prophet?

I think there may be a much simpler explanation for this accuracy. It is tempting to conclude that he just made this prediction up in a desperate bid to save his life, and in this case the prediction just happened by chance to come true. However, if he really did allude to *other emperors following Nero and not being able to hold onto power*, there may be more to it than that. That is because he was very familiar with the book of Daniel. He knew for a fact that the fourth beast in Daniel 7 – the one with the ten horns and the eleventh that uproots three – was Rome. Although he would probably have had as much trouble as the ancient historians in deciding who the first king of the Roman empire actually was, it is quite possible that he, like us, realised that an unlimited reign length was the only really defensible criterion that distinguishes a king from just any leader of a nation. He would then have recognised Sulla as the first king of the Roman empire and Julius Caesar as the second followed by Augustus and his successors. When he was captured by Vespasian during the reign of Nero – the *seventh* of those kings – he may well have been eagerly waiting to see what would happen after Nero's death. In his brief moments of respite from his wartime activities, he may even have been running a few potential scenarios for the meaning of that subduing of three kings through in his head, and he might have guessed that the most plausible one for a visible and dramatic fulfilment would be three emperors whose reigns were extremely short.

Josephus instead attributes his knowledge to divine inspiration (as opposed to contemplation and guesswork). However, intriguingly he does invoke his knowledge of 'the sacred books' as one of his *sources* of that inspiration, and he also tells us that he was *'able to give shrewd conjectures about the interpretation of such dreams as have been ambiguously delivered by God'*.

What he says on this matter is recorded in *The Jewish War* (book III, chapter 8, paragraph 3) which I have reproduced below. Having discovered Josephus' underground hiding place after the fall of Jotapata, Vespasian sends a Roman tribune called Nicanor who had once been a close friend of Josephus to try to persuade him to give himself up in exchange for his life. In describing his reaction on hearing this request, Josephus tells us the following:

> 'As Nicanor lay hard at Josephus to comply, and he understood how the multitude of the enemies threatened him, **he called to mind the dreams which he had dreamed in the night time, whereby God had signified to him beforehand both the future calamities of the Jews, and the events that concerned the Roman emperors.** Now Josephus was able to give shrewd conjectures about the interpretation of such dreams as have been ambiguously delivered by God. **Moreover, he was not unacquainted with the prophecies contained in the sacred books**, as being a priest himself, and of the posterity of priests: and just then was he in an ecstasy; and setting before him the tremendous images of the dreams he had

lately had, he put up a secret prayer to God, and said, "Since it pleaseth thee, who hast created the Jewish nation, to depress the same, and since all their good fortune is gone over to the Romans, and since thou hast made choice of this soul of mine to foretell what is to come to pass hereafter, I willingly give them my hands, and am content to live. And I protest openly that I do not go over to the Romans as a deserter of the Jews, but as a minister from thee."'

(Josephus' *The Jewish War*, translated by William Whiston, book III, ch.8, par.3)

But how could he have known that Vespasian would follow the three successors of Nero (rather than being one of them for example)? Well, let's remember that the prophecy also says that this eleventh horn would *'wage war against the holy people and defeat them'*. Since Josephus was bound to see the Jews as the holy people, this was of course precisely what Vespasian was doing at that very moment. Josephus may well have realised that if this prophecy came from God, it was highly unlikely that any of the first ten kings of world-dominant Rome would wage war against and defeat the holy people. God would simply not allow such a thing. He wouldn't allow it because even if the eleventh king did the same thing later on, the fact that a previous king of that same empire had done it already would render this aspect of the fulfilment of this prophecy much less surprising. Therefore, in my opinion it is quite possible that Daniel 7 allowed Josephus to guess correctly that Vespasian would be that eleventh king.

But how does this explain why he makes no explicit mention of Daniel 7 or Daniel 9 in his account of the book of Daniel? To understand that, we need to remind ourselves that Josephus wrote his books in Rome under the patronage of the Flavian

Dynasty emperors, Vespasian, Titus and Domitian. He even took the emperor's name Flavius to honour his distinguished patrons, and throughout his books he only has extremely good things to say about them. Were he to describe Daniel 7 or Daniel 9 he may have felt that he would be breaking that commitment.

The eleventh horn in Daniel 7 is described as a 'little horn' and is also extremely boastful (see page 66). Moreover, a straightforward reading of the text suggests that he meets his end as a result of God's judgement in favour of the 'holy people' whom he defeated. So, perhaps the reason Josephus didn't mention Daniel 7 was to avoid saying anything negative about his patrons.

Of course, if that was the case – and I can see no other plausible reason for this omission – it means he must definitely have thought that the eleventh horn was Vespasian (or at least been concerned his readers would think this). As I have said, I cannot think of any other good reason why he skipped this passage in his detailed retelling of Daniel 1-8. Hence, the fact that he has done so is to my mind clear evidence that he really did realise just how accurately this prophecy had been fulfilled by the Year of the Four Emperors.

But why didn't he discuss Daniel 9? Although we now know that Daniel 9 was fulfilled by a later ruler – the one who put an end to sacrifice and offering – Josephus couldn't have known this was going to happen. However, he did witness the fulfilment of the destruction of Jerusalem and its Temple that Daniel 9 predicts. He might therefore have assumed that this was another prediction of Vespasian – who he clearly felt was the emperor by whom his country had been 'made desolate'. And if so, his reluctance to describe this passage becomes perfectly understandable. In his understanding, Daniel 9 would have been saying that the desolation of Judea was *'an abomination'* – not the best choice of words for the greatest achievement of the first two Flavian Dynasty emperors (an achievement immortalised by Titus in a huge commemorative arch in the centre of Rome that can be seen to this day). And like Daniel 7, Daniel 9 also suggests that the death of the king it speaks of is a judgement from God (see page 121).

To my mind the most significant observation about Josephus' discussion of the book of Daniel is the fact that nowhere does he even hint that there might be some small chance that Daniel 7 and Daniel 9 were once thought to be about the Greek Seleucid king Antiochus Epiphanes who attacked Jerusalem in 168 BC (as most critical scholars today claim to believe). The reason this is highly significant is because Josephus had *extremely good reasons* to make such a suggestion. It was the perfect get-out clause. It would have provided him with a very good way of answering the embarrassing questions that might be fired at him by Roman intellectuals who chose to read the book of Daniel and discovered that it predicted what appeared to be the conquest of the Roman Empire by followers of his God – or worse still, what appeared to be a very unflattering portrayal of Vespasian. By suggesting that some people think that these prophecies were predictions of Antiochus Epiphanes, he would have given himself an easy way out of such embarrassing situations.

The fact that he has *not* suggested this, when he had such a powerful incentive to do so, is surely a big sign that such a view is not remotely tenable. It wasn't tenable in Josephus' day; and it is no more tenable today. Only that explains why Josephus didn't make such a suggestion. To suggest it would have cost Josephus all credibility in the eyes of his fellow Jews who were well aware that the four-headed four-winged leopard in Daniel 7 had to be

Alexander's Macedonian Empire along with its four successor kingdoms, and the highly distinct and most powerful monster that follows it could therefore only be Rome.

The evidence in *Antiquities* is thus strongly against the mainstream view of critical scholars on Daniel 2, Daniel 7 and Daniel 9:24-27. Josephus had nothing to gain from supporting the view that Daniel 2, 7 and 9 predicted the Roman empire. In fact, he could have easily found himself with some very embarrassing questions to answer if his rival Roman intellectuals had bothered to take an interest in these prophecies. It would have been far safer for him to at least suggest that there was a chance they were about Antiochus Epiphanes as modern scholars do today. Doing that would have given him a get-out clause if that tricky situation arose. The fact that he does nothing of the sort shows that such a view was simply not defensible (as I have hopefully shown in this book).

Josephus was very familiar with the history of the Seleucid kingdom and Antiochus Epiphanes, and he knew all about the Medes and Persians, yet he makes no attempt to even hint that Daniel might have been seeing a representation of Media in the form of his lopsided bear. This is especially good grounds to dismiss that currently popular mainstream hypothesis because Josephus had so much to gain from suggesting that such an interpretation was possible, and despite this he doesn't even give it a moment's thought. He instead goes out of his way to show that the second empire is that of the Medes and Persians, even though this means that the fourth can only be Rome. This was extremely risky. By identifying the fourth empire as Rome, he was bound to make any readers who were familiar with the book of Daniel wonder whether the uprooting of the three horns on the fourth beast in Daniel 7 was The Year of the Four Emperors, and therefore whether the little horn that fights the holy people and speaks against God was Vespasian.

Although Vespasian was long dead by 94 AD, when *Antiquities* was written, his son Domitian was still in power. Consequently, such a revelation could still have been very embarrassing for Josephus. That is almost certainly the reason he does not discuss Daniel 7. But even Daniel 2 could have got him into trouble if anyone had bothered to work out what the stone striking the statue on its feet of iron and clay and shattering them really meant. As we saw in chapter 2, its only justifiable meaning in this context is that a religion (an everlasting kingdom of God) formed out of Judaism (the mountain from which the stone was magically cut) would take over the whole Roman Empire. It would then spread out into the rest of the world and render the religions that had held together all the former empires completely powerless – like chaff blown away by the wind.

The only religion that did this was Christianity. It was founded in the time of the early Roman Emperors by a Christ (Anointed One) who almost certainly arrived at Jerusalem in the very month and year that the most justifiable meaning of the *Sixty-nine "sevens"* time-period in Daniel 9 predicts for the arrival of its Most Holy Anointed One (Christ). And this Christ got put to death empty-handed just as Daniel 9 also predicts. Yet the religion he fashioned out of the Jewish faith, and taught to his Jewish disciples, spread slowly but steadily throughout the whole Roman Empire.

As it did so, various calamities hit Judaism that are also predicted in Daniel 9. Shortly after the accession of Vespasian depicted in Daniel 7, Jerusalem and her Temple got destroyed by the Romans resulting in a period of simmering resentment amongst Jews that led to other attempted insurrections which the Romans crushed mercilessly. In 131 AD Hadrian founded his promised new Jerusalem, but his plans to dedicate it to a Roman god triggered another massive revolt in Judea. The huge Roman invasion that followed, and the eventual crushing of the revolt, resulted in the Jews being expelled in large numbers from Judea and refused entry to Jerusalem (now renamed *Aelia Capitolina*) on pain of death.

All Jewish sacrifice and offering was thus ended, the population of Judea massacred, and a large statue of Hadrian raised on the site of the Temple. That was in the spring of 136 AD (though Jewish sacrifice and offering was probably ended a year or so before when the Romans gained the upper hand). Hadrian died on 10th July 138, exactly seven years after founding his new Jerusalem, just as Daniel 9 amazingly predicted. But the persecutions of the "holy people" continued, gradually focussing on the sect known as 'Christians'. And for *a hundred and seventy-five years* from 136 AD neither Jews nor Christians had any power to resist their oppressors. They endured sporadic periods of intense hardship culminating in the Great Persecution of Christians that was officially ended by the emperor Galerius in the spring of 311.

If the word 'time' in Daniel 7 is considered to refer to the fifty-year length of the Jubilee period in Leviticus 25:3-10 (the passage that also yields the seven-year weeks of Daniel 9), this was exactly 'a time, times and half a time' (175 years) from the expulsion of the Jews from Judea in 136 AD. During the next year (312) the Christian emperor Constantine I saw 'the sign of the Son of Man' in the sky, and following a dream, instructed his soldiers to paint that sign onto their shields so that every eye would see it. He soon became the sole emperor in the West; and over the next twenty years extended his control over the whole Roman world.

Within decades Christianity completely replaced the Roman religion, as is most clearly predicted in Daniel 7 by the killing and burning of the monster representing that religion by the fire that came from the throne of God. The religions represented by the beasts associated with the previous empires survived for a time in regions of the world that were beyond the reach of the Roman Empire. But gradually Christianity spread there too. The stone that struck the statue on the part representing the Roman Empire really has become a mountain filling the whole world.

Josephus was regarded by many Jews as a traitor. He had opposed their revolt against Rome from the start, or so he claimed, but had done his duty by organising the resistance in Galilee. When that had failed he'd offered his services to the Romans, not to bring down his own people (which he felt was inevitable), but to save them from destruction by persuading them not to resist. Ultimately, he may well simply have wanted to save his own skin and avoid a lifetime of slavery (and who can blame him for that). But whatever his motives, God blessed him and honoured him with a high position at the court of the conquering emperor, just as he seems to have done for Daniel over half a millennium before. The parallels are indeed so striking I suspect this wasn't chance.

I believe God honoured him because of his willingness to speak out about the book of Daniel regardless of the dangers he faced in doing so, and despite the criticism from his fellow Jews. As far as I can see, the lesson of the book of Daniel is that God is not so much concerned with the nations of the world. They are perishable – they are merely a means to an end. He is concerned that people recognise the gospel of Jesus Christ as being from him, and thereby have the opportunity to choose the salvation that Jesus Christ claims to be offering.

Of course, the main thing that holds sceptical people back from embracing this Gospel is that they cannot understand why a loving and compassionate God would not make that salvation available to everyone – or at least to everyone who has lived a relatively good life. They can understand why God might exclude those who were deliberately cruel and unkind to their neighbours. People like that might ruin the society he may wish to create. However, the idea that only those who choose to follow Jesus get raised again would exclude a lot of very decent folk who have worked hard for family and friends and tried their best to serve others in whatever professional capacity their life has led them to. If the alternative afterlife is as bad as the gospels make out, it seems extremely cruel of God not to automatically guarantee salvation to those relatively decent law-abiding citizens. Yet it is the fact that salvation is not automatically guaranteed to relatively good people that seems to be why the Gospel is so important. How can a God who refuses to save people from a fate worse than death be the perfectly loving saviour the New Testament claims he is?

I wrestled with this question for a long time before any hint of a solution came to me. When it did, it came not from my research into scripture but from an entirely different direction. In chapter 1 of this book I mentioned my interest in consciousness, and in what physical entities in my brain constitute my different types of experience – what brain-based entity constitutes a colour or a sound or a smell or a feeling of touch or pain or temperature. I knew that to explain the amazing organisation of these things that the brain effortlessly produces – to account for the way it arranges those mysterious entities into meaningful representations of our sensory inputs and the world beyond – those entities, whatever they are, must do stuff that contributes to our brain's activity.

Only that would allow a scientific account of their organisation – a story that will explain their organisation in a manner similar to how science accounts for similarly-organised structures in nature. For entities to evolve design-like arrangements, they must do something that favoured the survival of the genes that coded for those design-like arrangements. Even those of us who do not attribute such design-like structures to Darwinian evolution would probably still agree that if the organised entities did nothing at all they would, with time and random changes, soon cease to be so organised. But if experiences must therefore act upon the brain, what are the laws that govern those interactions?

The simplest view I came across was put forward in 1928 by a British astrophysicist called Arthur Eddington (see Eddington's *The Nature of the Physical World*, available online). He basically said that the laws in question are the laws of physics we already know about. He pointed out that the things we call 'particles' that the laws of physics describe are not the tiny billiard balls that the word 'particles' often conjures up. In fact, science doesn't tell us what particles *are*. It only tells us about what they *do*. What we describe as a 'particle' is actually just the *effect* of some deeper *non*-particle-like entity. We know those deeper entities are non-particle-like because the patterns formed by those effects can only be explained if the entities causing them are widely spread-out (or what physicists refer to as 'non-localised' or 'wavelike').

Eddington's largely unappreciated spark of genius was to recognise that we have every reason to expect those underlying non-localised entities to consist of experiences and the minds that experience them. After all, we know that some part of our brain's activity consists of experiences. Physicists don't know what the rest of it consists of at the level of tiny particles because they don't know what those particles really are. So, the principle of preferring the simplest of a set of competing hypotheses (commonly known as *Occam's razor*) strongly suggests we should expect those particles to be the effects of the same sort of entities that our mind and experiences constitute. After all, why postulate the existence of a totally knew sort of substance to explain what particles are, when we already know of a perfectly suitable candidate in the form of our different types of experience (each of which must be able to *affect* our brain activity – and thus act upon matter – to account for the way it has become adapted to encode particular information)?

Eddington was adamant that he did not mean matter was made up of *intelligent* minds like ours. In his view, the minds that make it up are merely having experiences and responding to them in some simple way. They are not thinking about those experiences or planning what to do about them. Nor are they comparing them with past experiences like we do. They just respond in a non-thought-involving way, and that response changes the experiences of neighbouring minds in ways that make the effects of those neighbouring minds abide by the laws of physics.

What Eddington perhaps didn't realise, though, is that we – our intelligent minds – might ultimately be no different in nature from those non-intelligent minds that Eddington expects to be making up the rest of the brain and everything else. Our seeming intelligence could be just a result of the way the brain is constantly organising the inputs to our mind. When our brain gives us the visual sensation of an object, it may also be supplying fainter sensations of similar objects stored in its memory banks, together with appropriate feelings that capture the significance of that object compared to others we may be looking at. If our brain were to stop controlling our experiences in such a highly organised fashion, there's a very good chance that we would instantly cease to be intelligent consciousnesses, and become instead merely another of the nonintelligent minds making up the rest of matter.

For me, it was this observation that suggested a reason why the God behind the gospel of Jesus might not be able to automatically grant eternal salvation to every human being. If we are ultimately no different an entity from all the other minds whose interactions make up matter (according to Eddington and other philosophers), a perfectly just God would on grounds of fairness feel obliged to give one of those other minds the chance of experiencing life as an intelligent thinking being who can remember its past and look forward to the future and enjoy some understanding of its present circumstances. We have no reason to expect such a God to give us another go after the death of our bodies because if he did he would be denying that opportunity to some mind that has never yet experienced such an amazingly meaningful life. Instead, we should anticipate an eternity of participation in the structure of matter – experiencing and responding to experiences with *no* understanding of our circumstances or expectation of what the future will bring. Compared to our current rich and meaningful lives, the thought of such an existence terrifies me (though I suspect that once returned to that natural role, one will not be able to bemoan one's circumstances, or even remember that things were ever any different).

Fortunately, though, we need never find out. According to Jesus Christ, we need only believe and trust in him and God will raise us again after death and put us in the same rich and meaningful role within the brain of a new organism. Christ even suggests that God will recreate some of the memories we had before death. But how can God do that without being unfair to those other minds?

The simple answer is that he can't. The reason God can offer us this promise of salvation, in this view, is that there is a moral constraint that trumps fairness. If God is committed to being perfectly righteous, as the Christian God appears to be, he must first and foremost act in ways that reduce unnecessary suffering if it is in the best interests of the affected minds. Being a God who loves his creations and wants to raise them again in the future, he has come up with a plan that allows him to do that without being unjustifiably unfair to other minds. The Gospel – the *Good News* – is God's chosen means of alleviating the suffering that gets caused in human minds by the fear of death, and the terrifying prospect of a frighteningly impoverished afterlife. By promising us he will raise us again, God removes that second source of suffering in an instant. And it goes without saying that a righteous God is committed to keeping his promises, no matter how unfair those promises may be to other minds.

The one thing that would stop God keeping this promise is if, after accepting that salvation, a person makes no effort to be loving and kind to his neighbours, and instead chooses to be cruel and unkind. Such a person, when raised with the same memories, is likely to cause further suffering in God's future society. Consequently, God is obliged by his moral imperative (to reduce suffering) *not* to save such a person despite his acceptance of Christ's offer.

The fact that suffering would not be reduced if God were to raise people who were not themselves committed to reducing suffering is what, for me, explains the moral requirements of Christ's teaching. *Repentance* is a commitment to stopping oneself causing needless distress, and attempting to remove any distress that one has caused in the past. So Christ calls us to repent. *Loving one's neighbour as oneself* entails acting in a way that positively reduces suffering in the world. Even the requirement that we *love God with all our heart, all our soul, all our mind, and all our strength* can be explained in this view. Christ asks us to do this first and foremost, not because God somehow *needs* all this love from us to make him feel happy or appease his wrath or something, but because it shows those around us the importance of the Gospel message. Remember, God is committed to reducing suffering, but only when it is in the best interests of the suffering minds. Simply loving one's neighbour without drawing any attention to the Gospel message may not be in their best interests. Turning to Christ is by far the best thing that can happen to them because it ensures their salvation – it gains them eternal meaningful life – so it is important that we advertise our own commitment to Christ in all that we do.

And finally, this view also explains why God cannot automatically save nice people. If he did this, he would be saving people who weren't suffering from the fear of death or the terrifying prospect of an impoverished afterlife, and that would be breaking his commitment to being fair to the minds that have not yet experienced the richness of an intelligent life. God must offer a choice because the willingness to seek his salvation is what separates those who desperately want to live again from those who don't really care. The promise of eternal life is only for the former, because it can only be offered as a means of reducing suffering, and the latter are simply not suffering in any way that this Gospel message is going to alleviate.

Intriguingly, from those theological inferences it seems to me that God's desire to reduce suffering may result in some resurrections of nice people who don't turn to Christ. I imagine it would be hard for people to be totally happy in the next life knowing that their loved ones didn't make it. Consequently, I suspect that God will also raise the loved ones of those he saves as a means of alleviating that potential source of sorrow. I take this to be supported by the famous "Sheep and Goats" parable of Matthew 25:31-46. If they won't lose their reward because they were kind to those who are God's children, that suggests to me they will also be saved. So, don't despair if a friend has passed away not knowing Christ. Remain faithful yourself, and work hard for Christ, and ask for the salvation of that friend. Provided they were a relatively decent person, you may well still meet him or her in the life to come.

I don't know whether the ideas I have put forward here are correct. I have provided them because they seem to me to be the only justifiable answer to the question of why the Gospel message is so urgent. They at least offer a defensible answer to the troubling question of why a God who loves us all would not automatically resurrect us to save us from the impoverished afterlife that the Gospel suggests awaits those who do not accept and follow Christ.

What is important, though, is that we do recognise this urgency in the Gospel message. Whatever the reason for it, Christ does appear to have taught that we need to turn to him if we want to escape that impoverished afterlife and gain eternal life. Judging from the astonishing accuracy of the prophecies in Daniel 2, 7 and 9:24-27, we need to take that message very seriously indeed. Each of those prophecies clearly endorses the message of Christ. The first two by predicting Christianity and describing it as 'God's everlasting kingdom', and the third by accurately predicting the moment of Christ's Triumphal Entry and describing him as 'most holy'. The fact that all three made accurate predictions, which in the case of Daniel 7 and Daniel 9 are so specific that their fulfilment cannot reasonably be put down to chance, and the fact that the predicted events could not have been deliberately engineered by humans, strongly indicates the involvement of a superhuman intelligence. Since their context in the book of Daniel identifies that intelligence as Daniel's God, we have every reason to conclude that this God has endorsed the message of Jesus Christ, and we therefore have very strong grounds to believe that Christ's message is true.

The good news is that this salvation is open to every single one of us. Whatever we have done in the past, God is prepared to grant us eternal life provided we commit ourselves to making amends for our errors and any lack of love of our fellow citizens that we may have previously exhibited, and provided we are willing to follow Christ's teaching from now on. To be certain of that salvation all we need to do is repent (make amends) for any suffering we have caused, and love our neighbour as ourselves. We need to go out of our way to be nice to people. And we must remember to do everything with thanks and praise to the God of Jesus Christ because it is through doing this that the people we help will be steered towards the real eternal benefit of Christ's salvation.

Finally, I'd like to warn anyone in this world who thinks it is justifiable to sacrifice the lives or health of unsuspecting citizens for the sake of some supposedly greater national or personal gain, or who feel it is okay to deceive the people to accomplish such ends. God does not care about whether nations or wealthy families stand or fall. This is very clear from Daniel 2 and Daniel 7. He cares about individuals and how nice they are to one another. He cares about the poor people languishing in jail for crimes they did not commit. He cares about the people starving or falling sick due to the suppression of knowledge that would feed and cleanse the environment by people whose only concern is in maintaining some nation's military or financial advantage over other nations (and thereby protecting their own family's wealth or status).

If that applies to you (and it will certainly not apply to most of the readers of this book), I can assure you that if you want to receive the eternal life that Christ is offering – if you want to escape the eternal participation in the structure of matter that otherwise awaits you – you will need to make amends for any such acts you have committed. You will need to break the oaths of secrecy that are used to cover over such crimes and do whatever it takes to expose or put an end to the lies and murderous schemes you have been a party to – even if that costs you your life. The eternal life you will gain in such circumstances is *far far* more valuable than the few more miserable years you may have left on this earth, and you will certainly not qualify for it if you don't make any effort to make amends for the suffering you have caused other human beings.

Remember, the accuracy of Daniel 2, 7 and 9:24-27 is powerful evidence that Christ's offer of eternal life is real. If you don't take it up you will become merely a tiny bit of the matter out of which everything is made – forever experiencing the meaningless flow of experience by which the random behaviour of those tiny bits of matter is made to follow the laws of physics. If you do not want that eternity of formless and meaningless experience then you need to take action to expose the crimes you have been a party to in an effort to free those wrongfully convicted and prevent others suffering in similar ways in the future. Only when you take those risks in the name of Jesus Christ as an act of repentance for the suffering you have caused, will you be blessed and assured of salvation.

As Christ himself said, 'It is easier for a camel to go through the eye of a needle than for a rich man to enter the kingdom of God'. The rich and powerful of this world (and I mean the super-rich who use their wealth to steer national policy, not people with a few million in the bank) usually have very much more to make amends for, and far more to lose as a result, than those who earn an honest living. I very much hope that the objective evidence of God's endorsement of the Gospel that I have presented in this book will persuade even those rich and powerful people who control our world that they really are heading for an eternity of poverty, meaninglessness and helplessness; and that they would instead gain an eternal intelligent life if they were only willing to use their riches to bring joy to the poor, expose evil, and alleviate suffering.

Of course, most of us have caused far less suffering, and have therefore far less to repent for. However, we can still show our commitment to Christ's teaching by going out of our way to do good to our neighbour. Worshipping God regularly is also important because doing that goes some way to fulfilling Christ's primary command. Moreover, many Christians claim that persistent prayer often resulted in a sense that the Holy Spirit that Christ spoke about was guiding their lives – and this is certainly consistent with what Christ taught about the Holy Spirit in John's gospel.

Remember, though, the Gospel message is not merely a command to reduce suffering by helping people, repenting, and loving one's neighbour. The most important part of it is one's acceptance of Christ as being from God. One's commitment to those philanthropic and charitable acts has to be from a desire to follow Christ's teaching because it is this – and this alone – that is going to guarantee you salvation. That is why it is going to be so important for the sceptical amongst us to consider the astonishing fulfilment of specific prophecy that is evident in Daniel 2, Daniel 7 and Daniel 9:24-27. That fulfilment of prophecy is what tells us that Jesus was from God, and it is quite clear from Jesus' teaching that believing this claim is the most important requirement if you want to have another intelligent life. This was what guaranteed the salvation of the thief crucified next to Jesus in Luke 23:40-43. He acknowledged Christ's divinity, and asked Jesus to remember him. And Christ said to him, "Today you will be with me in Paradise".

As we saw in chapter 3, the prediction of an everlasting Kingdom of God that would take over the Roman Empire is accompanied in Daniel 7 by a perfectly accurate and totally genuine prediction of *the Year of the Four Emperors* – a passage that specifically told us the eleventh unlimited dictator of the Roman empire would subdue three before him, be different from all ten, speak against the Jewish God, and make war on the Jews and defeat them. Even these very specific and unlikely details were dramatically fulfilled by history. The fact that this fulfilment of a genuine ancient prophecy endorsing Christianity as God's everlasting kingdom *could not have been engineered by human beings* tells us that Christianity *was God's plan*. And remember, the same message is conveyed by the fact that by far the most justifiable meaning of the time-period for the coming of a 'most holy exalted leader' called 'Christ' in Daniel 9:25 points precisely to the most likely year and month for Jesus Christ's Triumphal Entry (as I demonstrated in chapter 6).

As we saw in chapter 5, that same prediction in Daniel 9 is followed by a very specific prophecy of major world events: The destruction of Jerusalem and its Temple, the ending of Jewish sacrifice and offering, and the Jerusalem visit and unpleasant death of the Roman ruler responsible for the latter. Amazingly, this ruler's death is predicted to happen *exactly seven years* (of 360 days) after the foundation ceremony of the new Jerusalem he promised to build. Yet, despite the specificity of this prophecy, all these things came to pass *exactly as Daniel 9:24-27 said they would*. I find that utterly astonishing. For me it is ample grounds to believe in the God of Jesus Christ, and trust Christ's teachings.

After completing the first draft of this book, I made an amazing discovery about Daniel 9:24-27 that strengthened my confidence in the divine authorship of these prophecies even further. Recall how in chapter 5 (page 130), I identified the founding of Aelia Capitolina as the moment 'the ruler who will come' began to confirm his 'promise to many', and I presented lots of evidence that this took place in 131 AD, making Hadrian's death on 10th July 138 a perfect fulfilment of that prophecy's final "seven" *to the nearest whole year.* Inspired by the perfect fulfilment of the 'Christ' prediction in Daniel 9:25 (when each "seven" is interpreted as *'7 times 360 days'*), I then predicted that the founding of Aelia Capitolina will turn out to have occurred in mid-August 131. Having since then learned that the *Mishnah* asserts it took place on *the 9th of Av,* I went looking at the lunar data to see what days that could have been in the year 131 AD. The two possibilities seem to be 21st July or 20th August! If it was the second (the result of an early intercalation to delay the festival season), the seven times 360 days overshoots Hadrian's death *by just four days!* In fact, since preparing the site for such an important ceremony probably took two or three days, and since 19th August was a sabbath (a Saturday), the confirming of Hadrian's promise may well have begun on *16th* August, making the prophecy accurate *to the day!*

Admittedly, scholars are wary of the claim that Aelia Capitolina was founded on *the 9th of Av,* the anniversary of the destruction of *both* Jewish Temples. I am not. I think it is likely this date was *deliberately chosen* to remind the Jews of their conquered status.

Of course, there is always the minuscule possibility that the fulfilment of those prophecies occurred by chance. However, due to the specificity and time-limited nature of the predictions those prophecies make, and to the fact that it is by far their most *justifiable* interpretation that has come true, that possibility is so unlikely that it ought to be ruled out. We ought to be *highly sceptical* of such a claim. The evidence strongly points to deliberate fulfilment; and since no human being would have had the power or the motivation to bring about all the events required, we can only reasonably attribute that fulfilment to the involvement of a *non*human intelligence. The text of the prophecy portrays that nonhuman intelligence as Daniel's *God*, and so did Jesus of Nazareth who fulfilled the 'Christ' prediction in Daniel 9:24-27. Hence, I think that is the only reasonable conclusion we can reach.

That is the power of Daniel. That short book constitutes hard objective evidence that the Christian gospel really is from God. I think that is its purpose. It provides the sceptic with sufficient reason to take the claims of Jesus Christ seriously. It opens the door to eternal life for the doubting Thomases of this world so that even they have the opportunity to accept Jesus as their Lord and thereby escape the eternity of impoverished, meaningless and memoryless experience that Christ says awaits the nonbeliever.

Remember, although science cannot currently tell us what our experiences are, it does give us very strong reasons to believe that any experience we may have after death is not going to be of the rich, meaningful and intelligent sort we currently enjoy. To have this type of experience again we – our consciousnesses (minds) – almost certainly need to be correctly linked up to the brain of some kind of organism so that each distinct type of sensory input that brain receives gets encoded in an appropriate sort of experience: Colours for vision, sounds for hearing, pains for damage, etcetera. I would bet that this is very unlikely to happen by chance. For a meaningful and exciting afterlife, we need a God who knows where we end up after death to put us back into such a brain.

Fortunately, the one revelation about God that we have strong objective reasons to trust says that this is precisely what God promises to do. However, he is only able to grant that promise to us as a means of alleviating the suffering that comes from fear of our future fate, and that of our loved ones, and he can only grant it to those committed to not causing suffering in the afterlife. Nevertheless, he gives us a way to ensure we fit that category. We must accept Jesus as being from God and do our best to obey his commands. It is as simple as that. And the accuracy of Daniel 2:31-45, Daniel 7 and Daniel 9:24-27 provides more than enough objective evidence that this message is indeed from God.

I hope the miracles I have shared in this book go some way to convincing you to look into that evidence for yourself. Even if you are already a believer, I think that appreciating this evidence does wonders for your confidence in the faith you now have. And if you are not yet a Christian, I hope it will encourage you to pray persistently to the God of the universe who I believe really does hear our prayers, and ask that God to give you a sign of his reality and interest in you, just like the one he gave me (see 'The Miracle on the River Kwai' in the *Introduction* to this book – page 9).

When you have accepted the reality of that God, I hope what you have read in this book will remind you to ask for the eternal life Christ is offering us. The odds of us ever finding ourselves steering an intelligent organism again by nature's random shuffling of whatever components of matter minds happen to constitute, must be almost zero. Only God can find our mind after the death of our body and ensure that it gets selected for the necessary role in a future intelligent organism by the blind forces at work in that organism's development. However, we must ask God to do this while we still can. We need to express our desire for that eternal life so that God knows we are unhappy about the alternative. And we must do all we can to follow in the ways and teachings of Jesus Christ to ensure we will no longer be a cause of suffering, and to ensure that others hear of this opportunity for eternal salvation. Most of all, we must repent for all the suffering we have caused other people by attempting where possible to make up for that evil through helping those we have hurt, or by going out of our way to help other people in need whom we would not otherwise be inclined to help. That at least seems to me to be the message of Christ's *Good Samaritan* example (Luke 10:25-37).

When we do that, I believe those impossible odds will no longer matter. Like that five-year-old with whom I began this book, you too will say, "Please God, let it be me! I ask this prayer in Jesus name. Amen", and your vastly greater request will also be instantly granted. Though you won't know it then, a new imperishable body (according to St Paul) will be created for you in a utopian world with your memories implanted, and after death God will transfer you there in the blink of an eye where you will forever be filled with life and joy and happiness in God's presence.

> *Behold, I tell you a mystery. We will not all sleep, but we will all be changed, in a moment, in the twinkling of an eye, at the last trumpet. For the trumpet will sound and the dead will be raised incorruptible, and we will be changed. For this perishable body must become imperishable, and this mortal must put on immortality. But when this perishable body will have become imperishable, and this mortal will have put on immortality, then what is written will happen: "Death is swallowed up in victory."*
>
> *(1 Corinthians 15:51-54)*

APPENDIX

Annotated Text of Daniel 10-12 with Timeline

Since the final prophecy in the book of Daniel is too long and detailed to reproduce in full within the main text of this book, I have included this appendix for that purpose. I have also divided up the text of the prophecy into five chunks to make it easier to digest, and I have inserted historical notes where needed. Although such notes amount to my own interpretation of what the prophecy refers to (or was fulfilled by), the match with history in this case is so good that those identifications are generally quite obvious. In fact, so few interpreters disagree with them that I have deliberately chosen not to preface those notes with the traditional 'some scholars think that…', which I think is somewhat misleading in those circumstances.

It is worth remembering, though, that all mainstream critical scholars consider the majority of this prophecy to be an account of history written from hindsight. And I agree with them on this. Unlike in the case of Daniel 2, 7 and 9:24-27, there is no evidence for the existence of this prophecy prior to the latest event that it accurately portrays, and a part of it (Daniel 11:40-45) predicts a military campaign that doesn't appear to have taken place at all. Evangelical scholars have traditionally opted for reinterpreting that part of the prophecy in a way that will allow it to still be fulfilled in our future. I am not in favour of this approach. The fact that the most justifiable interpretation of part of this prophecy hasn't come true suggests to me that I should not be assuming that this prophecy came out of the mouth of one of God's heavenly messengers in the sixth century BC. So I am inclined to agree with critical scholars about the origin of this prophecy. Nevertheless, I strongly disagree with the claim that this means some part of the book of Daniel was not the work of the Christian God.

I do think the presence of Daniel 10-12 in the book of Daniel is God's work. However, I think its purpose was never to accurately predict the future. I think it has been inserted into the book of Daniel after the events it accurately predicts as a record of how the Jews at that time perceived their history. I think God has thus included it in that book as a key to the interpretation of the genuine prophecies of Christ and Christianity that are found in Daniel 2, 7 and 9, and to establish a date from which we can be certain that these genuine prophecies were in existence – a date that is long before the events that fulfilled them took place. Only by inserting such a key could God make the fulfilment of Daniel 2:31-45, Daniel 7 and Daniel 9:24-27 *objective evidence* of his endorsement of the Christian gospel.

That is my view, anyway. If you are interested in that possibility, and, like me, see no reason why God wouldn't want to provide the readers of Daniel with such a key, then you will probably find this view greatly confirmed by the rest of the content of this prophecy. As you will see, its rambling sequence of allusions to the campaigns, decisive battles and generally indecisive marriage alliances between the Seleucid kingdom (to the north of Israel) and the Ptolemaic kingdom (to the south), seems far too detailed to have constituted a genuine prediction. That is not because God isn't *capable* of fulfilling such a prophecy. It is because it just seems strange that God would set himself such a string of pointless world events to bring about in the correct order. It also seems hard to imagine Daniel being able to accurately recall a prophecy of this nature after he woke up ready to write it down. And I can't think why, for example, Antiochus III would have taken on Rome if he'd known what was written in this text (which if it had existed in his day would already be famous for accuracy).

For me, the most convincing evidence of its nonpredictive nature is the fact that the existence of such a prophecy would almost certainly have become extremely famous well before many of its predictions came about, and yet there is not the slightest indication in suitably ancient writings of such a famously accurate prophecy. In a list of famous Jewish men compiled by the Jewish sage Jesus Ben Sira around 180 BC (the book of *Sirach* in the Apocrypha) the prophet Daniel doesn't even make an appearance, whereas all the other prophets are listed. That seems to me to be inexplicable if Daniel 11 was written prior to Ben Sira's time. However, it is perfectly understandable if Daniel's prophecies only consisted of Daniel 2:31-45, Daniel 7 and Daniel 9:24-27. The events predicted by these prophecies still lay in Ben Sira's future. Consequently, Ben Sira would have been very hesitant about including Daniel in his list for fear that these prophecies would not come true, showing Daniel to be a false prophet.

Due to the fairly lengthy nature of Daniel 10-12, I have divided its content up as follows, indicating the period in history to which each section relates and what I regard as its general theme:

Daniel 10:1-11:2 – Gabriel and The Prince of Persia

Cyrus' third year in Babylon to Xerxes' invasion of Greece

(536-480 BC)

DAN 10: [1] In the third year of Cyrus king of Persia a thing was revealed to Daniel, who was known as Belteshazzar; and the thing was true, even a great warfare. He understood the thing, and had understanding of the vision.

[2] In those days I, Daniel, was mourning three whole weeks. [3] I ate no pleasant bread. No meat or wine came into my mouth. I didn't anoint myself at all, until three whole weeks were fulfilled.

[4] In the twenty-fourth day of the first month, as I was by the side of the great river, which is Hiddekel [Tigris], [5] I raised my eyes, and looked, and behold, there was a man clothed in linen, whose thighs were adorned with pure gold of Uphaz. [6] His body was like the beryl, and his face as the appearance of lightning, and his eyes as flaming torches. His arms and his feet were like burnished bronze. The voice of his words was like the voice of a multitude.

[7] I, Daniel, alone saw the vision; for the men who were with me didn't see the vision; but a great quaking fell on them, and they fled to hide themselves. [8] So I was left alone, and saw this great vision. No strength remained in me; for my face grew deathly pale, and I retained no strength. [9] Yet I heard the voice of his words. When I heard the voice of his words, then I fell into a deep sleep on my face, with my face toward the ground.

[10] Behold, a hand touched me, which set me on my knees and on the palms of my hands. [11] He said to me, Daniel, you greatly beloved man, understand the words that I speak to you, and stand upright; for I have been sent to you now. When he had spoken this word to me, I stood trembling.

¹² Then he said to me, "Don't be afraid, Daniel; for from the first day that you set your heart to understand, and to humble yourself before your God, your words were heard. I have come for your words' sake. ¹³ But the prince of the kingdom of Persia withstood me twenty-one days; but, behold, Michael, one of the chief princes, came to help me because I remained there with the kings of Persia. ¹⁴ Now I have come to make you understand what will happen to your people in the latter days; for the vision is yet for many days."

¹⁵ When he had spoken these words to me, I set my face toward the ground, and was mute. ¹⁶ Behold, one in the likeness of the sons of men touched my lips. Then I opened my mouth, and spoke and said to him who stood before me, "My lord, by reason of the vision my sorrows have overtaken me, and I retain no strength. ¹⁷ For how can the servant of you my lord talk with you my lord? For as for me, immediately there remained no strength in me. There was no breath left in me."

¹⁸ Then one like the appearance of a man touched me again, and he strengthened me. ¹⁹ He said, "Greatly beloved man, don't be afraid. Peace be to you. Be strong. Yes, be strong."

When he spoke to me, I was strengthened, and said, "Let my lord speak; for you have strengthened me."

²⁰ Then he said, "Do you know why I have come to you? Now I will return to fight with the prince of Persia. When I go out, behold, the prince of Greece will come. ²¹ But I will tell you that which is inscribed in the writing of truth. There is no one who holds with me against these, but Michael your prince.

DAN 11: ¹ As for me, in the first year of Darius the Mede, I stood up to confirm and strengthen him [probably Michael]. ² Now I will show *you* the truth. Behold, three more kings will stand up in Persia [Cambyses II, Bardiya then Darius I]; and the fourth [Xerxes I] will be

far richer than all of them [He inherited a vast empire with a very efficient taxation system due to his father Darius' successful reforms and military campaigns]. When he has grown strong through his riches, he will stir up all against the realm of Greece [This almost certainly refers to Xerxes' invasion of Greece in 480 BC which ended in his defeat at the battles of Salamis, Mycale and Plataea. The prophecy then jumps forward 150 years to the rise of Alexander the Great].

Daniel 11:3-17 – The Rise and Splitting of Greece
Alexander the Great to Antiochus III's peace with Ptolemy V
(335-193 BC)

³ A mighty king will stand up [Alexander the Great], who will rule with great dominion, and do according to his will. ⁴ When he stands up, his kingdom will be broken, and will be divided toward the four winds of the sky, but not to his posterity, nor according to his dominion with which he ruled; for his kingdom will be plucked up, even for others besides these [Here we have four weaker Greek kingdoms emerging from Alexander's empire: Ptolemaic Egypt, Seleucid Syria and Asia, Antigonid Macedon, and somewhat later Attalid Pergamon (which took the place of an earlier "fourth" Macedonian kingdom established by Alexander's general Lysimachus in Thrace and later conquered by the Seleucids)].

⁵ The king of the south [Ptolemy I] will be strong. One of his princes [Seleucus I] will become stronger than him, and have dominion. His dominion will be a great dominion [the Seleucid Empire]. ⁶ At the end of years [the end of the Second Syrian War] they will join themselves together; and the daughter [Berenice] of the king of the south [Ptolemy II] will come to the king of the north [Antiochus II] to make an agreement; but she will not retain the strength of her arm.

He will also not stand, nor will his arm; but she will be given up, with those who brought her, and he who became the father of her, and he who strengthened her in those times [Antiochus II, Berenice, and her infant son Antiochus – 'he who strengthened her' – all died at the hands of the exiled queen Laodice and her supporters in order for her to put her own son Seleucus II on the Seleucid throne. She'd been exiled so that Antiochus II could marry Berenice and was thus taking her revenge. Ptolemy II 'the father of her' dies around the same time].

⁷ But out of a shoot from her roots one will stand up in his place [Berenice's brother Ptolemy III], who will come to the army, and will enter into the fortress of the king of the north [Seleucus II], and will deal against them, and will prevail. [Ptolemy III launched a very successful punitive campaign against Seleucus II known as the Third Syrian War]. ⁸ He will also carry their gods, with their molten images, and with their goodly vessels of silver and of gold, captive into Egypt. He will refrain some years from the king of the north. ⁹ He [Seleucus II] will come into the realm of the king of the south, but he will return into his own land [Seleucus II had to abandon his response to Ptolemy III's punitive expedition in order to secure his remaining territory after a serious revolt split the Seleucid Empire]. ¹⁰ His sons [Seleucus III and Antiochus III] will wage war, and will assemble a multitude of great forces, which will come on, and overflow, and pass through. They will return and wage war, even to his fortress [Beginning of Fourth Syrian War].

¹¹ The king of the south [Ptolemy IV] will be moved with anger, and will come out and fight with him, even with the king of the north [now Antiochus III]. He [Antiochus III] will send out a great multitude, and the multitude will be given into his [Ptolemy IV's] hand [Battle of Raphia, 217 BC – the end of the Fourth Syrian War]. ¹² The multitude will be lifted up, and his heart will be exalted. He will cast down tens of thousands, but he won't prevail. ¹³ The king of the north [Antiochus III again] will return, and will send out a multitude greater than the former. He will come on at the end of the times [around 200

BC! – the Fifth Syrian War], even of years, with a great army and with much substance.

¹⁴ In those times many will stand up against the king of the south [now Ptolemy V]. Also the children of the violent among your people will lift themselves up to establish the vision [What vision? Could the writer be referring to this vision to suggest that it existed thirty-five years before? Or could this refer to a premature attempt to fulfil Daniel 7 or Daniel 2?]; but they will fall. ¹⁵ So the king of the north [Antiochus III still] will come and cast up a mound, and take a well-fortified city [Probably his capture of Gaza in 201 BC]. The forces of the south [Ptolemy V] won't stand [Battle of Panium, 200 BC], neither will his chosen people, neither will there be any strength to stand. ¹⁶ But he who comes against him [Antiochus III] will do according to his own will, and no one will stand before him. He will stand in the glorious land [Judea/Israel passed from Ptolemaic control to Seleucid control after the battle of Panium in 200 BC], and destruction will be in his hand. ¹⁷ He [Antiochus III] will set his face to come with the strength of his whole kingdom, bringing with him equitable conditions. He [Ptolemy V] will perform them. He [Antiochus III] will give him the daughter of women [his daughter Cleopatra I], to corrupt her [make her act deceitfully for his gain]; but she will not stand, and won't be for him.

Daniel 11:18-27 – Seleucid Defeat and Taxation (by Rome) Antiochus III's war on Rome till Antiochus IV's war on Egypt (192-170 BC)

¹⁸ After this he [Antiochus III] will turn his face to the islands, and will take many; but a prince [Roman general] will cause the reproach

offered by him to cease. Yes, moreover, he will cause his reproach to turn on him [This refers to Rome's crushing victory over Antiochus III at the Battle of Magnesia in 189 BC, and the humiliating treaty of Apamea that followed. The latter secured Rome a constant flow of tribute, and the Seleucid heir as a hostage – even Antiochus IV Epiphanes spent time as a hostage of the Roman Senate before he took the Seleucid throne (and he wouldn't have been able to ascend that throne were it not for the fact that the rightful heir Demetrius remained in Rome as a hostage)]. [19] Then he will turn his face toward the fortresses of his own land; but he will stumble and fall, and won't be found.

[20] Then one [Seleucus IV] who will cause a tax collector [his general Heliodorus, who famously attempted to plunder the Jerusalem Temple to obtain the funds owed to Rome] to pass through the kingdom to maintain its glory will stand up in his place; but within few days he shall be destroyed, not in anger, and not in battle [Seleucus IV was apparently assassinated by his 'tax collector' Heliodorus in an attempted coup].

[21] In his place a contemptible person will stand up [Antiochus IV Epiphanes], to whom they had not given the honor of the kingdom; but he will come in time of security, and will obtain the kingdom by flatteries. [22] The overwhelming forces will be overwhelmed from before him, and will be broken. Yes, also the prince of the covenant. [23] After the treaty made with him he [Antiochus IV] will work deceitfully; for he will come up, and will become strong, with a small people [probably the men of Pergamon]. [24] In time of security he will come even on the fattest places of the province. He will do that which his fathers have not done, nor his fathers' fathers. He will scatter among them prey, plunder, and substance. Yes, he will devise his plans against the strongholds, even for a time.

[25] He will stir up his power and his courage against the king of the south with a great army [Antiochus IV's first invasion of Egypt, 170 BC – the Sixth Syrian War]; and the king of the south [Ptolemy VI (or at least his guardians as he was just a child)] will wage war in battle with an

exceedingly great and mighty army; but he won't stand; for they will devise plans against him. ²⁶ Yes, those who eat of his dainties will destroy him, and his army will be swept away. Many will fall down slain. ²⁷ As for both these kings, their hearts will be to do mischief, and they will speak lies at one table [After defeating and capturing Ptolemy VI, Antiochus attempted to make him his puppet king, rather than rule Egypt directly and risk alarming Rome, but within a year Ptolemy had rebelled]; but it won't prosper, for the end will still be at the appointed time.

Daniel 11:28-45 – Antiochus' Persecution of the Jews
The persecution and the unknown conquest of Egypt
(169-164 BC)

²⁸ Then he [Antiochus IV Epiphanes] will return into his land with great wealth. His heart will be against the holy covenant. He will take action, and return to his own land [This probably refers to Antiochus IV's plundering of the Jerusalem temple. His real persecution of the Jews was after his second invasion of Egypt a year later as we shall see next].

²⁹ He [Antiochus IV Epiphanes] will return at the appointed time, and come into the south [Egypt]; but it won't be in the latter time as it was in the former. ³⁰ For ships of Kittim [Roman navy carrying the Senate's ambassador Gaius Popillius Laenas] will come against him. Therefore he will be grieved, and will return, and have indignation against the holy covenant [the Jewish faith], and will take action. He will even return, and have regard to those who forsake the holy covenant.

³¹ Forces will stand on his part, and they will profane the sanctuary, even the fortress, and will take away the continual burnt offering [Antiochus IV Epiphanes enforced Greek sacrifice in place of Jewish sacrifice at the Jerusalem Temple – He did not 'cause sacrifice to cease' there, but merely

appropriated it for his god]. Then they will set up the abomination that makes desolate [An idol or altar to Zeus was set up in the Temple – A phrase almost certainly taken from Daniel 9 appears to have been used to describe this event]. ³² He will corrupt those who do wickedly against the covenant by flatteries; but the people who know their God will be strong, and take action.

³³ Those who are wise among the people will instruct many; yet they will fall by the sword and by flame, by captivity and by plunder, many days. ³⁴ Now when they fall, they will be helped with a little help; but many will join themselves to them with flatteries. ³⁵ Some of those who are wise will fall, to refine them, and to purify, and to make them white, even to the time of the end; because it is yet for the time appointed.

³⁶ The king will do according to his will. He will exalt himself, and magnify himself above every god ['Epiphanes' means 'God manifest'], and will speak marvelous things against the God of gods. He will prosper until the indignation is accomplished; for that which is determined will be done. ³⁷ He won't regard the gods of his fathers, or the desire of women, or regard any god; for he will magnify himself above all. ³⁸ But in his place he will honor the god of fortresses. He will honor a god whom his fathers didn't know [maybe the *Roman* god Jupiter Capitolinus to whom he built a temple in Antioch] with gold, silver, and with precious stones and pleasant things. ³⁹ He will deal with the strongest fortresses by the help of a foreign god. He will increase with glory whoever acknowledges him. He will cause them to rule over many, and will divide the land for a price.

⁴⁰ At the time of the end [Mainstream scholars suspect that the rest of this passage is the writer making a guess about the immediate future since Epiphanes did not invade Egypt a third time – It had to be quite detailed to convince the sceptics! I find it quite surprising that they don't ever suggest the same might apply to Daniel 2, 7 and 9.] the king of the south will contend with him; and the king of the

north will come against him like a whirlwind, with chariots, with horsemen, and with many ships. He will enter into the countries, and will overflow and pass through [Note the flood metaphor of Daniel 9:27 being used to mean full-scale war]. [41] He will enter also into the glorious land, and many countries will be overthrown; but these will be delivered out of his hand: Edom, Moab, and the chief of the children of Ammon. [42] He will also stretch out his hand on the countries. The land of Egypt won't escape. [43] But he will have power over the treasures of gold and of silver, and over all the precious things of Egypt. The Libyans and the Ethiopians will be at his steps. [44] But news out of the east and out of the north will trouble him; and he will go out with great fury to destroy and utterly to sweep away many. [45] He will plant the tents of his palace between the sea and the glorious holy mountain; yet he will come to his end, and no one will help him.

Daniel 12 – Rewards for those who Stand Firm
The 1290 days of Trouble from the End of Sacrifice in 167 BC

DAN 12: [1] At that time Michael will stand up, the great prince who stands for the children of your people; and there will be a time of trouble, such as never was since there was a nation even to that same time. At that time your people will be delivered, everyone who is found written in the book. [2] Many of those who sleep in the dust of the earth will awake, some to everlasting life, and some to shame and everlasting contempt. [3] Those who are wise will shine as the brightness of the expanse. Those who turn many to righteousness will shine as the stars forever and ever. [4] But you, Daniel, shut up the words, and seal the book, even to the time of

the end. [Note here how the writer provides a reason for why nobody had heard of this prophecy before. A similar command occurs in Daniel 8:26. But intriguingly, there is no such command in Daniel 2, 7 or 9]. Many will run back and forth, and knowledge will be increased."

⁵ Then I, Daniel, looked, and behold, two others stood, one on the river bank on this side, and the other on the river bank on that side. ⁶ One said to the man clothed in linen, who was above the waters of the river, "How long will it be to the end of these wonders?"

⁷ I heard the man clothed in linen, who was above the waters of the river, when he held up his right hand and his left hand to heaven, and swore by him who lives forever that "it will be for a time, times, and a half; and when they have finished breaking in pieces the power of the holy people, all these things will be finished."

⁸ I heard, but I didn't understand. Then I said, "My lord, what will be the outcome of these things?"

⁹ He said, "Go your way, Daniel; for the words are shut up and sealed until the time of the end. ¹⁰ Many will purify themselves, and make themselves white, and be refined; but the wicked will do wickedly; and none of the wicked will understand; but those who are wise will understand.

¹¹ From the time that the continual burnt offering is taken away, and the abomination that makes desolate set up, there will be one thousand two hundred and ninety days. ¹² Blessed is he who waits, and comes to the one thousand three hundred and thirty-five days.

¹³ But go your way until the end; for you will rest, and will stand in your inheritance at the end of the days."

Timeline – The historical fulfilment of Daniel 2, 7, 9 & 11*

70-YEAR DOMINANCE OF CHALDEAN **BABYLON**

THE **FIRST EMPIRE** IN THE SEQUENCE OF FOUR (DAN.2)

"The first was like a lion, and had eagle's wings. I watched until its wings were plucked, and it was lifted up from the earth, and made to stand on two feet as a man. A man's heart was given to it." (DANIEL 7:4)

DATE   RELEVANT HISTORICAL EVENT (& Daniel Ref.) (* means 'alluded to in Daniel 11')

609 BC: Fall of Assyria (Harran). Babylon rises to dominance in alliance with Media.

605 BC: Nebuchadnezzar II becomes king of Babylon. Babylon defeats Egypt.

605 BC: Daniel and other noble Jewish youths taken to Babylon as political hostages.

603 BC: Daniel interprets Nebuchadnezzar's statue dream of four empires (Dan. 2).

According to Dan. 3, Nebuchadnezzar sets up a huge gold idol for worship.

601 BC: Nebuchadnezzar invades Egypt and is repulsed. Jerusalem rebels.

597 BC: King Jeconiah of Judah deported to Babylon. Zedekiah made king of Judah.

589 BC: King Zedekiah rebels against Babylon. Nebuchadnezzar besieges Jerusalem.

587 BC: Nebuchadnezzar destroys Jerusalem and her Temple. Many Jews deported.

Dream of luscious tree cut down, whose stump is given the heart of a beast.

According to Dan. 4, Nebuchadnezzar becomes mentally ill for seven years.

Nebuchadnezzar humbles himself and recovers. His throne is restored to him.

568 BC: Nebuchadnezzar invades Egypt and is again repulsed.

562 BC: Nebuchadnezzar dies. His son Amel-Marduk becomes king.

560 BC: Amel-Marduk assassinated by brother-in-law Neriglissar who becomes king.

556 BC: Neriglissar dies leaving the kingdom to his son Labashi-Marduk.

556 BC: Labashi-Marduk is deposed and Nabonidus becomes king.

553 BC: Nabonidus makes his son Belshazzar coregent in Babylon and leaves the city.

553 BC: Daniel dreams of four monsters representing four empires (Dan. 7).

The second is a bear **raised up on one side** with <u>**three ribs between its teeth.**</u>

551 BC: Setting of Daniel 8 (Daniel's 'ram and goat' vision of Persia & Greece).

550 BC: **Cyrus of Persia** seizes Median throne (but **spares Median king <u>Astyages</u>**).

546 BC: Cyrus conquers Lydia but **spares** the life of its **king <u>Croesus</u>**.

539 BC: Cyrus' Medo-Persian forces defeat Babylon's army (**sparing <u>Nabonidus</u>**).

539 BC: Belshazzar sees the writing on the wall (Dan. 5) and his life ends as predicted.

539 BC: Gubaru (probably Darius the Mede) captures Babylon and gets made its king.

208-YEAR DOMINANCE OF **MEDO-PERSIA**

THE **SECOND EMPIRE** FROM TIME OF DANIEL'S DREAM

"Behold, there was another animal, a second, like a bear. It was raised up on one side, and three ribs were in its mouth between its teeth. They said this to it: 'Arise! Devour much flesh!'" (DANIEL 7:5)

539 BC: Setting of the 'Seventy 'Sevens'' Prophecy (Dan. 9).

538 BC: Setting of Daniel in the Lions' Den (Dan. 6).

538 BC: Gubaru (Darius the Mede) dies. Cyrus takes the title 'King of Babylon'.

538 BC: Cyrus lets the Jews return to rebuild their Temple at Jerusalem.

536 BC: Setting of Daniel 10-12 (Daniel's "prophecy" of the Syrian wars).

530 BC: Death of Cyrus. His son Cambyses II becomes king of Persia.

525 BC: Persia under Cambyses II conquers Egypt. Pharaoh Psamtik III commits suicide.

522 BC: Cambyses dies of an infected wound. Cyrus' son Bardiya becomes king.

522 BC: Darius seizes the throne, slaying the man claiming to be Bardiya as an imposter.

521 BC: Darius reconfirms the Edict of Cyrus permitting rebuilding of Jewish Temple.

516 BC: Second Temple of Jerusalem completed.

509 BC: Founding of the Roman Republic.

490 BC: Greeks repel invading Persian force at Battle of Marathon.

486 BC: Darius dies and Xerxes I becomes king of Persia.* (Dan. 11:2)

484 BC: Xerxes melts down huge gold statue he finds in Babylonian temple.

480 BC: Xerxes sacks Athens* (Dan. 11:2). Greeks defeat Persian fleet at Salamis.

479 BC: Persian expulsion from Greece following defeats at Plataea and Mycale.

465 BC: Xerxes is murdered. Artaxerxes I becomes king of Persia.

457 BC: Artaxerxes I of Persia permits Ezra to restore Mosaic Law at Jerusalem.

444 BC: **Artaxerxes I permits Nehemiah to rebuild Jerusalem (Dan. 9:25).**

424 BC: Artaxerxes I dies and is succeeded by his son Darius II.

404 BC: Death of Darius II. His son Artaxerxes II becomes king.

358 BC: Death of Artaxerxes II. His son Artaxerxes III becomes king.

338 BC: Death of Artaxerxes III. His son Artaxerxes IV becomes king.

336 BC: Artaxerxes IV dies and the throne passes to Darius III.

336 BC: Philip II of Macedon dies and Alexander III (the Great) becomes king.

335 BC: Alexander the Great becomes king of all Greece (Dan. 11:3).

333 BC: Alexander the Great defeats Darius III at Battle of Issus.

332 BC: Alexander welcomed into Egypt as liberator.

331 BC: Alexander defeats Darius III at Gaugamela and conquers the Persian Empire.*

141-YEAR DOMINANCE OF **GREECE**
(ALEXANDER'S MACEDONIAN EMPIRE)

THE **THIRD EMPIRE** FROM TIME OF DANIEL'S DREAM

"After this I looked, and behold, another, like a leopard, which had on its back four wings of a bird. The animal also had four heads; and dominion was given to it." (DANIEL 7:6)

327 BC: Alexander the Great invades and conquers part of India.

323 BC: Alexander the Great dies* unexpectedly in Babylon leaving an unborn son.

323 BC: His general Ptolemy* seizes his body and carries it off to Egypt. (Dan. 11:5)

321 BC: Seleucus (a commander in Ptolemy's army)* made governor of Babylon. (11:5)

317 BC: Alexander's mother Olympias has his half-brother Philip Arrhidaeus executed.

316 BC: Olympias gets captured and executed by Cassander (governor of Macedonia).

315 BC: Alexander's general Antigonus takes Babylon. Seleucus flees to Ptolemy.

312 BC: Seleucus (with Ptolemy's help) retakes Babylon from Antigonus.

311 BC: Antigonus unsuccessfully attempts to make peace with the other generals.

310 BC: Alexander IV (Alexander the Great's son) gets murdered along with his mother.

309 BC: Alexander the Great's illegitimate son Heracles also murdered.* (Dan. 11:4)

306 BC: Antigonus and his son Demetrius declare themselves kings.

305 BC: Cassander declares himself **king of Macedon**. Lysimachus **king of Thrace**.

304 BC: Ptolemy I declares himself **king of Egypt**, and Seleucus I **king of Asia**.

301 BC: Battle of Ipsus: Antigonus defeated and killed by Seleucus and Lysimachus.

301 BC: Greek Empire **splits in four***: Egypt, Asia, Thrace (later Pergamon), Macedon.

297 BC: Cassander dies. His sons quarrel over the succession.

294 BC: Demetrius (son of Antigonus I) takes over Cassander's **kingdom of Macedon.**

287 BC: Lysimachus expels Demetrius from Macedon.

283 BC: Demetrius dies a prisoner of Seleucus I.

282 BC: Ptolemy I dies. Succeeded by Ptolemy II (second king of **Ptolemaic Egypt**).

282 BC: Ptolemy I's other son Ptolemy Ceraunus flees to Lysimachus.

281 BC: Battle of Corupedium: Seleucus I conquers Thrace. Lysimachus is killed.

281 BC: Seleucus I killed by Ptolemy Ceraunus who takes throne of Macedon.

281 BC: Seleucus I is succeeded by Antiochus I (the second **Seleucid** king of Asia).

279 BC: Ptolemy Ceraunus killed by invading Gauls.

277 BC: Antigonus II re-establishes **Antigonid** dynasty of kings at **Macedon**.

274 BC: Antiochus I invades the Ptolemaic lands, triggering First Syrian War.

271 BC: End of war: Ptolemy II reconquers all lands and makes territorial gains.

261 BC: Eumenes I establishes **Attalid** independence at **Pergamon**.

Alexander's Empire is again **split in four*** and remains so until 168 BC.

261 BC: Seleucid king Antiochus I dies and is succeeded by his son Antiochus II.

261 BC: Antiochus II begins Second Syrian War with Ptolemy II (making some gains).

252 BC: Marriage of Antiochus II to Berenice ends Second Syrian War.* (Dan. 11:6).

246 BC: Laodice has Berenice and Antiochus II murdered to make son Seleucus II king.*

246 BC: Ptolemy II dies in Egypt and is succeeded by Ptolemy III (Berenice's brother).*

246 BC: Ptolemy III mounts successful punitive war against Seleucus II.* (Dan. 11:7-8)

239 BC: Split in Seleucid Empire ends Third Syrian War* and allows rise of Pergamon.

229 BC: Seleucus II's brother Antiochus Hierax defeated by Attalus I of Pergamon.

227 BC: Antiochus Hierax dies a fugitive in Thrace. Pergamon gains his territories.

225 BC: Seleucus II falls from horse and dies. His son Seleucus III becomes king.

223 BC: Seleucus III gets assassinated. His brother Antiochus III becomes king*.

221 BC: Antiochus III makes a failed attempt to invade Ptolemaic lands.* (Dan. 11:10)

219 BC: Antiochus III invades Ptolemaic land sparking Fourth Syrian War* (Dan. 11:10)

218 BC: Hannibal crosses the Alps to invade Italy (beginning Second Punic War).

217 BC: Battle of Raphia: Ptolemy IV defeats Antiochus III.* (Dan. 11:11)

202 BC: Battle of Zama: Rome defeats Carthage. Hannibal flees to Antiochus III.

201 BC: Judea goes over to Antiochus III. Antiochus captures Gaza.* (Dan. 11:14-15)

200 BC: Battle of Panium: Antiochus III defeats the forces of Ptolemy V.* (Dan. 11:16)

193 BC: Marriage of Ptolemy V to Cleopatra I ends Fifth Syrian War.* (Dan. 11:17)

192 BC: Antiochus III takes over Greek islands angering Rome.* (Dan. 11:18)

191 BC: Battle of Thermopylae: Antiochus III defeated in Greece by Rome.

189 BC: Battle of Magnesia: Rome decisively defeats Antiochus III.* (Dan. 11:18)

500-YEAR DOMINANCE OF PAGAN **ROMAN** EMPIRE

THE **FOURTH** DISTINCT EMPIRE FROM DANIEL'S DREAM

"After this I saw in the night visions, and, behold, there was a fourth animal, awesome and powerful, and exceedingly strong. It had great iron teeth. It devoured and broke in pieces, and stamped the residue with its feet. It was different from all the animals that were before it. It had ten horns. I considered the horns, and behold, there came up among them another horn, a little one, before which three of the first horns were plucked up by the roots: and behold, in this horn were eyes like the eyes of a man, and a mouth speaking great things... I looked, and the same horn made war with the holy people, and prevailed against them, until the ancient of days came, and judgment was given to the holy people of the Most High, and the time came when the holy people possessed the kingdom." (DANIEL 7:7-8 & 21)

"The fourth animal will be a fourth kingdom on earth, which will be different from all the kingdoms, and will devour the whole earth, and will tread it down, and break it in pieces. As for the ten horns, ten kings will arise out of this kingdom. Another will arise after them; and he will be different from the former, and he will put down three kings. He will speak words against the Most High, and will wear out the holy people of the Most High. He will plan to change the times and the law; and they will be given into his hand until a time and times and half a time." (DANIEL 7:23-25)

188 BC: Peace of Apamea: **Roman Republic** secures vast tribute from Seleucid Empire.

187 BC: Antiochus III killed raiding a temple. Seleucus IV becomes king.* (Dan. 11:19)

178 BC: Seleucus IV's tax collector Heliodorus raids the Jewish Temple.* (Dan. 11:20)

175 BC: Seleucus IV assassinated: Antiochus IV Epiphanes seizes throne.* (Dan. 11:21)

171 BC: Greek king Perseus of Macedon rebels against Rome.

169 BC: Antiochus IV conquers Egypt, but reinvades the next year.* (Dan. 11:25)

168 BC: Rome defeats Perseus, and the following year breaks up his kingdom.

168 BC: Rome orders Antiochus out of Egypt. He attacks the Jews.* (Dan. 11:30)

167 BC: Antiochus defiles the Temple. Judas Maccabeus rises in revolt.* (Dan.11:31-32)

165 BC: **Book of Daniel completed. Daniel 2, 7 and 9 included to predict the future.**

"He will corrupt those who do wickedly against the covenant by flatteries; but the people who know their God will be strong, and take action." (DANIEL 11:32 – PROBABLY SELF-FULFILLED)

164 BC: Judas liberates Jerusalem and rededicates the Jewish Temple.* (Dan. 12:12)

164 BC: Antiochus Epiphanes dies in Persia. Demetrius I becomes Seleucid king.

161 BC: Judas Maccabeus sends embassy to Rome.

160 BC: Judas dies fighting the Seleucids. His brothers continue the struggle.

153 BC: Judas' brother Jonathan made High Priest of the Jews.

143 BC: Jonathan captured and killed by Seleucids. His brother Simon takes over.

133 BC: Attalus III of Pergamon dies and in his will leaves his kingdom to Rome.

104 BC: Aristobulus I (grandson of Simon Maccabeus) declares himself king of Judea.

85 BC: Sulla defeats Mithridates VI, king of Pontus, and recovers Greece for Rome.

82 BC: **Sulla** is made **'Dictator'** in Rome with **no time limit imposed**.

81 BC: Sulla resigns from his dictatorship, restoring the republic.

78 BC: Sulla dies at his country villa near Puteoli.

71 BC: Slave revolt of Spartacus crushed by Roman general Crassus.

65 BC: Pompey defeats Mithridates VI conquering his kingdom of Pontus.

63 BC: Roman general Pompey captures Jerusalem and chooses its king.

59 BC: First Triumvirate between senators Julius Caesar, Pompey and Crassus.

56 BC: Julius Caesar conquers Gaul (France). Triumvirs granted five more years.

55 BC: Caesar unsuccessfully invades Britain.

54 BC: Caesar invades Britain again but returns to quell revolts in Gaul.

53 BC: Crassus killed in the East. Pompey refuses to renew alliance with Caesar.

52 BC: Caesar defeats Vercingetorix and consolidates his hold on Gaul.

49 BC: Caesar marches on Rome after being recalled by the Senate.

48 BC: Caesar defeats Pompey at Battle of Pharsalus in Greece.

48 BC: Pompey killed in Egypt. Caesar aids and befriends queen Cleopatra VII.

44 BC: **Caesar** accepts office of **Dictator for Life,** and later gets assassinated.

42 BC: Triumvirs Octavian and Antony defeat Caesar's assassins at Philippi.

41 BC: Antigonus (a Maccabean prince) made king of the Jews by Parthians.

40 BC: Herod the Great appointed 'King of the Jews' by the Senate in Rome.

37 BC: Herod defeats Antigonus and is proclaimed king in Jerusalem.

36 BC: Triumvir Lepidus is stripped of his offices, leaving just Octavian and Antony.

31 BC: Battle of Actium: Antony, defeated by Octavian, commits suicide.

27 BC: Octavian titled 'Augustus' and 'Princeps' by Senate. End of *Republic* phase.

23 BC: Augustus Caesar (Octavian) granted tribunician power for life.

19 BC: **Augustus** granted **consular power for life**. True end of *Republic* (Dan. 2:41).

4 BC: Birth of Jesus of Nazareth. Death of Herod the Great.

6 AD: Judea becomes a province of the Roman Empire.

13 AD: **Tiberius'** powers **made equal to those of Augustus** who dies in AD 14.

26 AD: Pontius Pilate appointed Prefect of Judea (probably by Sejanus).

29 AD: Ministry of John the Baptist begins. Jesus gets baptised.

31 AD: Sejanus denounced in the Senate and executed for treason.

33 AD: Jesus of Nazareth's Triumphal Entry (around 29th March). (Dan. 9:25)

33 AD: Jesus of Nazareth crucified at Jerusalem (3rd April). (Dan 9:26)

> *"From the going out of the word to restore and rebuild Jerusalem to the Christ, the prince, will be seven "sevens" and sixty-two "sevens". It will be built again, with street and trench, even in troubled times. After the sixty-two "sevens" the Christ will be put to death, and will have nothing." (DANIEL 9:25-26)*

36 AD: Pontius Pilate is removed from office for mistreating the Samaritans.

38 AD: Tiberius dies. His heir **Caligula** becomes **emperor** in his place.

41 AD: Caligula is killed by Praetorian Guard who then make **Claudius emperor**.

43 AD: Claudius begins successful conquest of southern Britain.

54 AD: Claudius dies suddenly (probably poisoned). **Nero** is made **emperor**.

64 AD: Christians made scapegoats for a fire in Rome and suffer persecution.

66 AD: **First Jewish revolt against Rome**. Nero sends Vespasian to put it down.

67 AD: Vespasian reconquers Galilee, defeating the Jews. Josephus gets captured.

68 AD: Eight copies of Daniel are hidden with other scrolls in caves at Qumran.

68 AD: Vespasian approaches Jerusalem. Rabbi spared who later reinterprets the Law.

68 AD: Galba rebels. Nero commits suicide. **Galba** becomes **emperor**.

69 AD: 'The Year of the Four Emperors'. Galba-Otho-Vitellius-Vespasian. (Dan. 7:24)

    Jan: Galba killed. **Otho** made **emperor**. Vespasian's brother Sabinus made Prefect.

    Apr: Otho persuaded to fight Vitellius. Commits suicide. **Vitellius** made **emperor.**

    Jul: Eastern legions pledge to Vespasian. He claims to be the Christ. (Dan. 7:25)

    Dec: Vitellius killed. Sabinus (still Prefect) dies in Rome. **Vespasian** made **emperor.**

"Ten kings will arise out of this kingdom. Another will arise after them; and he will be different from the former, and he will put down three kings. He will speak words against the Most High, and will wear out the holy people of the Most High. He will plan to change the times and the law; and they will be given into his hand until a time and times and half a time." (DANIEL 7:24-25)

70 AD: Jerusalem and her Temple are utterly destroyed by the Romans. (Dan. 9:26)

74 AD: Remaining rebels commit suicide at Masada. Josephus writes *The Jewish War.*

94 AD: **Josephus writes about the book of Daniel** in *Antiquities of the Jews.*

105 AD: Tacitus writes about the Year of the Four Emperors in his *Histories.*

115 AD: Tension between Jews and Romans erupts into widespread violence. (Dan. 9:26)

117 AD: Roman General Quietus finally puts down this Jewish 'Kitos' revolt.

130 AD: **Emperor Hadrian visits Jerusalem and promises to rebuild it. (Dan. 9:27)**

130 AD: Hadrian outlaws circumcision according to *Historia Augusta.*

131 AD: **Aelia Capitolina founded** on 9th of Av on top of Jerusalem's ruins. (9:27)

132 AD: Second Jewish revolt against Rome begins led by Simon Bar Kokhba. (9:26)

135 AD: Hadrian puts an end to Jewish sacrifice and offering (St Jerome). (Dan. 9:27)

135 AD: Jewish revolt crushed. Statue set up on ploughed-over Temple Mount. (9:27)

136 AD: Jews expelled (Dan. 7:25). Judea renamed Palestine. Aelia Capitolina continues.

138 AD: **Hadrian dies** of disease on 10th July, **seven years after founding Aelia**. (9:27)

"The people of the ruler who will come will destroy the city and the sanctuary. His end will be with a flood, and war will be even to the end. Desolations are determined. He will confirm a covenant with many for one "seven". In the middle of the "seven" he will cause the sacrifice and the offering to cease. On an overspreading he will set up the abomination of desolation, even until the full end, that which is determined, is poured out on him." (DANIEL 9:26-27)

177 AD: Severe persecution of Christians in Lugdunum (Lyons).

202 AD: Emperor Septimius Severus forbids conversion to Judaism or Christianity.

229 AD: Cassius Dio writes about the Jewish revolt of Bar Kokhba.

235 AD: Emperor Maximinus orders that the leaders of the churches be put to death.

250 AD: Emperor Decius forces everyone but Jews to sacrifice or be executed.

253 AD: Emperor Valerian initiates similarly severe persecution of Christians.

260 AD: Emperor Gallienus ends Valerian persecution.

270 AD: Porphyry writes first critical account of Daniel in *Against the Christians.*

303 AD: Emperor Diocletian begins the Great Persecution of Christians.

311 AD: Galerius' Edict of Toleration officially ends the Great Persecution. (Dan. 7:26)

312 AD: Constantine I defeats Maxentius to become sole ruler of the West. (Dan. 7:27)

> He and his whole army saw a Christian sign appear in the sky, and he was later told in a dream that "with this sign you will conquer".

"Immediately after the oppression of those days, the sun will be darkened, the moon will not give its light, the stars will fall from the sky, and the powers of the heavens will be shaken; and then the sign of the Son of Man will appear in the sky. Then all the tribes of the earth will mourn, and they will see the Son of Man coming on the clouds of the sky with power and great glory. He will send out his angels with a great sound of a trumpet, and they will gather together his chosen ones from the four winds, from one end of the sky to the other." (MATTHEW 24:29-31)

"I looked in the night visions, and behold, there came with the clouds of the sky one like a son of man, and he came even to the ancient of days, and they brought him near before him. Dominion was given him, and glory, and a kingdom, that all the peoples, nations, and languages should serve him. His dominion is an everlasting dominion, which will not pass away, and his kingdom that which will not be destroyed." (DANIEL 7:13-14)

"The kingdom and the dominion, and the greatness of the kingdoms under the whole sky, will be given to the people of the holy people of the Most High. His kingdom is an everlasting kingdom, and all dominions will serve and obey him." (DANIEL 7:26-27)

"In the days of those kings the God of heaven will set up a kingdom which will never be destroyed, nor will its sovereignty be left to another people; but it will break in pieces and consume all these kingdoms, and it will stand forever. Because you saw that a stone was cut out of the mountain without hands, and that it broke in pieces the iron, the bronze, the clay, the silver, and the gold; the great God has made known to the king what will happen hereafter. The dream is certain, and its interpretation sure." (DANIEL 2:44-45)

ACKNOWLEDGEMENTS

The ideas presented in this book have been developed and modified over more than twenty years, and I owe a considerable debt of gratitude to the large number of unsuspecting churchgoers who have patiently endured a bit of Daniel-bashing over coffee after many a church service or homegroup meeting. Those whose patience deserves particular mention are Andrew Wilmshurst, Brian Duckfield, Graham Powell, Sam Taylor, Dave Swift and Bobby Pendreigh. I'd also like to thank the creators of websites and Wikipedia articles on the book of Daniel and related subjects because, whilst my views differ quite radically from what's currently on the Web, I have gained much food for thought from long browsing sessions, and my research has on many occasion been sent in productive directions by some obscure piece of information shared on a blog or website article. Most of all, though, I'd like to thank Ruth and Jim for their constant support and encouragement, Alison for her helpful advice, and Fiona, Amie and Joseph for constantly reminding me of the miracles that this book is about.

OTHER BOOKS BY C. S. MORRISON

THE BLIND MINDMAKER
Explaining Consciousness
without Magic or Misrepresentation

Published in 2016 by *CreateSpace Independent Publishing Platform*
ISBN: 978-1541283954. 296-page paperback available on Amazon.com

"There is something very refreshing about this book.
It is free of the tired jargon of philosophy of mind.
It sticks to a scientific agenda in a way that a lot of scientists
would do well to emulate."

Jonathan C. W. Edwards
(*Journal of Consciousness Studies, 24, No.7-8, 2017, p.237*)

UNEXPECTEDLY FORETOLD OCCURRENCES
Scientific Evidence that there is a God who Loves You
(and why scholars don't discuss it)

Published in 2016 by *CreateSpace Independent Publishing Platform.*
ISBN: 978-1537728049. 164-page paperback available on Amazon.com

A RHYME, RHYMES AND HALF A RHYME
A Collection of Poems celebrating the Book of Daniel

Published in 2017 by *CreateSpace Independent Publishing Platform.*
ISBN: 978-1973750642. 122-page paperback available on Amazon.com

www.ingramcontent.com/pod-product-compliance
Lightning Source LLC
Chambersburg PA
CBHW070553100426
42744CB00006B/263